THE MYTHOLOGY OF CRIME AND CRIMINAL JUSTICE

Victor E. Kappeler
Eastern Kentucky University

Mark Blumberg
Central Missouri State University

Gary W. Potter
Eastern Kentucky University

WAVELAND
PRESS, INC.

Prospect Heights, Illinois

For information about this book, write or call:

Waveland Press, Inc.
P.O. Box 400
Prospect Heights, Illinois 60070
(708) 634-0081

Chapter Opener Photo Credits

Chapter 2, Jan Weissman. Chapter 3, Jeni Ogilvie. Chapter 4, The Bettmann Archive. Chapter 5, The Bettmann Archive. Chapter 6, © Armando F. Mola. Chapter 7, © Armando F. Mola. Chapter 8, The Bettmann Archive. Chapter 9, The Bettmann Archive. Chapter 10, The Bettmann Archive. Chapter 11, The Bettmann Archive.

Acknowledgments

Our book made its way into print through the vision of many people who either directly contributed to the work or contributed to the authors' development. Not the least of these people are Carol and Neil Rowe of Waveland Press, Inc. They either took a risk or just became tired of reading traditional criminal justice textbooks. We openly acknowledge their vision and contribution to our work and the field of criminal justice. We also note the special contributions of Dr. Philip Jenkins for allowing us to include two of his excellent articles (chapters 3 and 4). What is less evident is the extent to which his writings shaped the intellectual filter through which this work was sifted. We acknowledge that much of this book has its origin in his writings and contributions to crime and justice. Special thanks are also owed to Dr. Harriet Fowler and John Mobley for their contributions to our work which came in the form of advice and friendship. From both of these scholars, we have learned a great deal and owe them a debt of gratitude. We also thank Peggy Blumberg for her thorough reading of the galleys.

One of the demands of "scholarly" writing is to credit the source of information and ideas. We have attempted to meet this demand but have always found this a difficult task since the origins of ideas is often the product of past conversations, education, and misplaced readings that tend to fold into one another. In order to meet this demand, at least in part, we acknowledge the contributions of the following persons to our development: Dennis Longmire, Frank Williams, Victor G. Strecher, Peter B. Kraska, Larry K. Gaines, Stephen Mastrofski, William Chambliss, Donald Wallace, James J. Fyfe, Lawrence W. Sherman, Douglas Heckathorn, Robert Antonio, Roger C. Barnes, Geoffrey Alpert, and the late Donald J. Newman.

The authors contributed chapters which discuss areas of particular interest to them. Vic Kappeler was primarily responsible for chapters 1, 2, and 12. He co-authored chapter 7 with Mark Blumberg. Mark contributed chapters 9, 10, and 11. Gary Potter wrote chapters 5, 6, and 8. Writing this book was a collaborative effort — three authors plus the contributions acknowledged above aided by all the influences whose origins cannot be clearly delineated.

About the Authors

Mark Blumberg is Professor of Criminal Justice at Central Missouri State University in Warrensburg, Missouri. He received his undergraduate and master's degrees in Sociology from the University of Kansas, Lawrence. Dr. Blumberg received an additional master's and doctoral degree in Criminal Justice from the State University of New York, Albany. He has written extensively on both police use of deadly force and on the impact of AIDS on various criminal justice issues. Dr. Blumberg has authored numerous book chapters and journal articles. His work has appeared in *Crime and Delinquency*, the *Criminal Law Bulletin*, *Justice Professional*, the *Prison Journal*, *Journal of Criminal Justice*, the *American Journal of Police* as well as in other publications. He is the author of an edited book entitled, *AIDS: The Impact on the Criminal Justice System*. At present, Dr. Blumberg is involved in field research that is examining the efficacy of various strategies for dealing with illicit drug markets.

Victor E. Kappeler is Associate Professor of Police Studies at Eastern Kentucky University in Richmond, Kentucky. He received undergraduate degrees in Police Administration and Juvenile Corrections as well as a master's degree in Criminal Justice from Eastern Kentucky University. Dr. Kappeler received his doctoral degree in Criminal Justice from Sam Houston State University in Huntsville, Texas. Dr. Kappeler has written articles on issues related to police deviance and civil liability which have been published in the *American Journal of Police*, the *Journal of Police Science and Administration*, *The American Journal of Criminal Justice*, *Criminal Law Bulletin*, the *Journal of Criminal Justice*, and *Police Chief*, among others. He is co-author of a forthcoming book *An Introduction to American Policing*, with Larry K. Gaines and Joseph B. Vaughn and is founding editor of *Police Liability Review* and *Police Forum*.

Gary W. Potter is Associate Professor of Police Studies at Eastern Kentucky University in Richmond, Kentucky. Dr. Potter received his doctorate in Community Systems Planning and Development from Pennsylvania State University. He has co-authored *Drugs in Society*, with Michael Lyman, and *The City and the Syndicate*, with Philip Jenkins. He is also the author of *The Porn Merchants*. Dr. Potter has written articles on issues related to organized crime which have been published in *The American Journal of Police*, *Corruption and Reform*, *The American Journal of Criminal Justice*, *Deviant Behavior*, *Criminal Justice History*, *Police Forum*, *Criminal Justice Policy Review*, *Policy Studies Review* and the *Journal of Criminal Justice*, among others.

Contents

11 Debunking the Death Penalty   213
Myths of Crime Control and Capital Punishment

12 Merging Myths and Misconceptions of Crime and Justice   235

Preface

In some respects,"The Mythology of Crime and Criminal Justice" may seem an unlikely book. In a humorous vein, it is somewhat unlikely that graduates from the Pennsylvania State University, State University at New York, and Sam Houston State University would collaborate on anything more than professional conferences or occasional forays for field research purposes. It is said that these institutions of higher education approach issues of crime and justice from very divergent perspectives and produce very different scholars of justice. Perhaps this too is a myth of criminal justice. Admittedly, we do have very diverse backgrounds and interests; thus, perhaps it was unlikely that we would collectively produce a book that addresses "myths" in criminal justice given the broad range of possible topics. That is, however, one of the wonders of academia and one of the strengths of the social sciences. Divergent people, ideas, and approaches to understanding contribute to an environment where varying perspectives, interests, and backgrounds can blend to create unique works.

On a more serious note, the most unlikely part of this collaboration is that a publisher would agree to expend the resources and energies required to produce and market this work. It is not that each author has not published books in the past or made scholarly contributions to the literature (or so we would like to think). Rather, this book does not fit neatly into any specific academic category. The book is not pure sociology, criminology, or criminal justice. It is certainly not a work that would fall under any single recognized ideological or theoretical framework. It is neither a radical nor a traditional approach to criminology, conflict or functionalist sociology, or a traditional systems or empirical approach to criminal justice.

What we have tried to create is a work that focuses on very popular issues of criminal justice — issues that have captured the attention of the public as well as the scholarly community. Our hope is that the work challenges many popular notions of crime, criminals, and crime control. Unlike many other texts available, this book offers students of crime and justice an alternative to traditional criminal justice texts. Each chapter of this book questions our most basic assumptions of crime and justice and traces the development of a crime problem from its creation to society's integration of a myth into popular thinking and eventually social policy.

At the risk of characterizing the work as everything to everybody, we feel that it has broad application in criminal justice education. The materials that make up this work were specifically written or selected because of their challenging perspective, clarity of argument, and ease of understanding. Although the book was written for the undergraduate student, much could be gained by using our work in the graduate classroom. Such a collection can be used as an alternative to standard introductory treatments of criminal justice or as a supplement to criminology or issues-orientated classes. Even though we feel the work has broad application in criminal justice education, it was not intended to be the last word in myths of crime or justice. Rather, we hope that the text will serve as a very good starting point for understanding the realities of criminal justice and as an alternative to reinforcing crime myths in the classroom.

Victor E. Kappeler
Eastern Kentucky University

Mark Blumberg
Central Missouri State University

Gary W. Potter
Eastern Kentucky University

chapter 1

The Social Construction of Crime Myths

People study social problems for a variety of reasons. The most obvious is to find solutions to society's concerns. Sometimes the solution must be sought not only in the content of the issue itself but in why a particular problem becomes more prominent than another. Many scholars in many disciplines look at the origins, diffusion, and consequences of social issues which capture the public's attention. Two very different perspectives can be used to explain the existence of a social problem. One perspective would be taken by people who have been characterized as "claims-makers," "moral entrepreneurs," "political activists," "social pathologists," and "issue energizers" (Schoenfeld, Meier and Griffin, 1979). These individuals have vested interests in the problem they bring to the public's attention. From their perspective, the social problem they are uncovering is real and has grave consequences. These individuals usually advocate formal social policy to address the new problem. To these individuals their social problem is real in its existence, unique in its characteristics, and grave in its social consequences.

The other perspective is taken by people who study social problems and how those problems are constructed. These people often see social problems as being constructed from collective definitions rather than from individual views and perceptions. Since social problems are collective constructions based on many individual perceptions and presentations of information, they can never truly exist in their collective and socially distorted form. These people often speak of social problems in terms of their origins and attribute the conception and definition of the problems to the mass media (Fishman, 1976), urban legend (Best and Horiuchi, 1985), group hysteria (Medalia and Larsen, 1958), ideology (Ryan, 1976), political power (Quinney, 1970), or some other often latent social force that directs public attention and shapes the definition and characteristics of emerging social problems.

We have chosen the term "myth" to describe some of the collective definitions society applies to certain crime problems. The word myth seems most appropriate to the social definition of many different kinds of criminal behavior brought to the public's attention. One common meaning of myth is a traditional story of unknown authorship, with a historical basis, serving usually to explain some event. The events of myth are based upon "exaggeration" or heightening of "ordinary" events in life. Other uses of the term carry with it the connotation of nonscientific, spoken or written fiction used as if it were a true account of some event.

The phrase "crime myth" does not stray too far from these accepted definitions. Crime myths are usually created in nonscientific forums through the telling of crime-related fictions or sensational stories. These crime fictions often take on new meanings as they are told and retold and at some point evolve into accepted truth for many people.

The fiction in crime myth comes not only from fabrication of events but from the transformation and distortion of events into social and political problems. Many of our contemporary issues of crime and justice are the product of some real event or social concern. Most crime mythology is the product of breakdowns in logic, contradiction, and distortion. As crime-related issues are debated and redebated, shaped and reshaped in public forums, they become distorted into myth.

This book focuses on the processes by which these events become distorted and are given unprecedented social consideration. Single authors of short crime-related fictions are given scant attention. Instead, we attempt to illustrate the range of social processes by which popular thought concerning a crime issue transforms the original concern into a crime problem taking on the characteristics of myth. This distortion of the reality of crime and criminal justice issues into myths emerges from a "collective," sometimes "unconscious," enterprise (Mannheim, 1936). Our inquiry concentrates on current issues in crime and justice that have reached or are near their myth potential plus the costs of myth production to society.

The Function of Crime Myths

The study of myths in crime is not a novel or merely academic undertaking; crime myths are real in the minds of their believers and have definite social consequences. Crime myths have numerous effects on our perceptions; we may not even be conscious that they are at work. Myths tend to organize our views of crime, criminals, and the proper operation of the criminal justice system. They provide us with a conceptual framework from which to identify certain social issues as crime-related, develop our personal opinions on issues of justice, and apply ready-made solutions to social problems. The organization of views through crime myths contributes to the cataloging of crime issues into artificial distinctions between criminals, victims, crime fighters, and viable social responses to crime.

Myths also support and maintain established views of crime, criminals, and the criminal justice system, causing a tendency to rely on established views of crime and justice. Myths reinforce the current designation of conduct as criminal, supporting existing practices of crime control and providing the background assumptions for future designation of conduct as criminal. In a sense, society becomes intellectually blinded by the mythology of crime and justice. The established conceptual framework may not enable us to define issues accurately, to explore new solutions, or to find alternatives to existing socially constructed labels and crime control practices.

Myths tend to provide the necessary information for the construction of a "social reality of crime (Quinney, 1970)." Crime myths become a convenient mortar to fill gaps in knowledge and to provide answers to questions social science either cannot answer or has failed to address. Where science and empirical evidence have failed to provide answers to the public's crime concerns, mythology has stepped in to fill the knowledge void. Collectively, crime myths create our social reality of crime and justice. Finally, crime myths provide an outlet for emotionalism and channel emotion into action. They not only allow for interpretation of general social emotions and sentiment but direct those emotions to designated targets. Crime myths allow for social action based on emotionalism while providing justification for established views of behavior, social practice, and institutional responses to crime.

Criminal Mythmakers

The social construction of myths of crime and criminal justice seems to follow a series of recurrent patterns. These patterns allow for an unprecedented amount of social attention to be focused upon a few isolated criminal events or issues. This attention is promoted by intense, but often brief, mass media coverage of a select problem. Intense social concern with an issue is achieved by a variety of means. The mass media, government, law enforcement officials, interpersonal communications, and the interests of reform groups all play a major role in focusing the public's attention on select social problems. There is, if you will, a myth-producing enterprise in our society. One of the largest and most powerful mythmakers in this enterprise is the mass media.

Modern mass communication has virtually replaced traditional vehicles of communicating myth. Mass communication is a formalized and institutionalized system of conveying messages. It consists of sending messages by way of technology to large groups of people. The traditional process of communication and myth distribution, once based solely on word of mouth and later extended by the written word, has been replaced by rapid electronic-based communication. This modern mass communication system has enabled myths to spread in unprecedented numbers and with frightening speed. Over 40 years ago, Edwin H. Sutherland (1950) noted that, "Fear is produced more readily in the modern community than it was earlier in our history because of increased publicity. . ." (143). What were once stories restricted in dissemination to small interactive social groups are now instantly projected to millions of people internationally by the mass media. This increased ability to project myth has been coupled with an ever-decreasing circle of people who control the means and mediums of myth production. This restricted number of mythmakers has given the modern media and government almost a monopoly of the myth industry. Today, the media and government select our crime problems for us and focus our attention on social issues. The role of the individual and small social groups no longer predominates in the dissemination of modern crime mythology.

Media as Mythmaker

The media chooses and presents unique crime problems for public consumption. The selection of crime problems is often limited to the most bizarre or gruesome act a journalist or investigator can uncover. Incident and problem selection are driven by the competitive nature of modern media. By culling unique and fascinating issues for public exhibition, the media ensures the marketability and success (viewers and advertising dollars) of a given media production. Once an incident has been selected, it is then presented as evidence of a common, more general, and representative crime problem. The practice of using sensational stories to attract readers and increase profit is sometimes referred to as "yellow" journalism. Television news has not escaped the economic lure of sensationalism. Local stations learned "late in the 1960s, that news could make money—lots of money. By the end of the 1970s, news was frequently producing 60 percent of a station's profits . . . and a heavily entertainment-oriented form of programming began to evolve" (Hallin, 1990:2).

Prompted by the nature of the media industry, television and newspaper reporters focus on "hot topics" of entertainment value. In the early states of myth development, a media frenzy develops which allows for expanded coverage of isolated and unique events. Typically, the appearance of an uncritical newspaper or magazine article exploring a unique social problem starts the chain of events. The journalist has uncovered a "new" social evil. Other journalists, not wanting to be left out, jump on the bandwagon. The accounts which follow may eventually blossom into highly publicized quasi-documentaries or even movies that graphically portray the problem. Social problems reach their media-built myth potential when sensationalism reaches its height and when they are reported by tabloid-television investigators. In this fashion, isolated incidents become social issues and, through politicalization, eventually crime problems.

Media frenzies often start in single newsrooms and later spread across information mediums, giving the false impression of order and magnitude to criminal events. As Mark Fishman (1976) points out in his discussion of "crime waves":

> Journalists do not create themes merely to show an audience the appearance of order. . . . In particular, editors selecting and organizing the day's stories need themes. Each day news editors face a glut of "raw materials" out of which they must fashion relatively few stories. . . . The chances that an event or incident

will be reported increase once it has been associated with a
current theme in the news (535).

Once a theme has been set by a single newsroom, selection of
newsworthy stories are based on the existing news theme. Themes
then spread across communication mediums giving the impression
of a crime epidemic.

While the media plays an important role in the identification and
construction of crime myth, it is not the sole participant in the
enterprise. Journalistic freedom of topic selection is often guided
by events and influences external to the media. While the media
may be guilty of not reporting an incident in the proper perspective,
the media is not solely to blame for sensational reporting.
Unfortunately, repugnant crimes do occur. Some events which are
blown out of proportion still warrant public attention. Each myth
area considered in this book also contains legitimate cause for public
concern. We will return to the media's role in constructing crime
myths later.

Government as Mythmaker

There are other methods beyond the naturally occurring bizarre
and unusual crimes captured by the media that begin the myth
construction process. These sometimes contrived or directed
government events help alert the media to a new "hot topic." In
some cases, the directed information helps refocus a media frenzy.
Harold Pepinsky and Paul Jesilow (1985) opened their book *Myths
that Cause Crime* with a powerful statement: "The sooner we
recognize that criminal justice is a state protected racket, the
better" (10). In the context of crime myth, as used here, this means
that the government has a vested interest in maintaining the
existing social definition of crime and extending this definition to
groups and behaviors that are perceived to be a threat to the existing
social order. Similarly, the government has an interest in seeing
that the existing criminal justice system's response to crime is not
significantly altered in purpose or function. While some "system
tinkering," (Kraska, 1985) is permissible, major change in the
system's response to crime is never implemented. We build more
prisons, mete out longer prison terms, reinstate the death penalty,
and move more offenders through the criminal justice system at
faster speeds, but all these changes are intellectually bonded by a
punishment/control philosophy.

The government secures its interest in identifying crime and
criminals and maintaining the established criminal justice system

by promoting crime myths. Since the government can control, direct, and mold messages, it is one of the most powerful myth-makers in the crime production enterprise. The government can suppress information for national security reasons; it can punish "obscenity"; it can reward the media for presenting official versions of crime myths. Compelling messages and rewarding the mass media for myth presentation is frequently done under the guise of "public service announcements" and press briefings.

The government functions not only as a controller and director of the mass media — it is a form of media. The government controls extensive print publication resources, commissions and funds research, operates radio stations, and exposes the television viewing audience to government-sponsored messages. Additionally, the government tunes the media in to certain crime myths by directing their attention and holding controlled press briefings. "Reporters' dependence on authorities makes them — and by extension media consumers — particularly vulnerable to deliberate attempts to mislead by governments and agencies" (Hynds, 1990:6).

The "war on drugs" is an excellent illustration of the government's role as a media starter in the myth construction enterprise. In 1990, President Bush's Administration arranged for the Drug Enforcement Administration (DEA) to conduct a high-profile drug arrest. Since public focus on the "drug war" was waning due to concern over other social problems, the administration needed an "event" to refocus public and political attention on the "drug war." Following a DEA drug bust just outside the White House, the president made a national television address concerning the drug issue. It was later learned that the DEA had to go to considerable means to persuade the drug dealer to meet the agents at their desired location — just outside the White House. Thus, as we will discuss later, the event had all the necessary characteristics for creating a crime myth.

The current administration is not unique in its willingness to create crime myths. The Bureau of Narcotics campaign against marijuana (1937) under the leadership of Harry Anslinger is another classic example of the media's dissemination of government-sponsored crime myths. The Bureau of Narcotics, wanting to expand its bureaucratic domain by adding marijuana to the list of controlled substances it was responsible for monitoring, put together a series of mythological and outrageous stories about atrocities allegedly committed by people under the influence of marijuana. These stories included the murder of a Florida family and their pet dog by a wayward son who had taken one toke of marijuana. Newspapers printed this story and others like it. Thus, the myth of the "dope fiend" was born out of the minds of law enforcement officials. The media involvement with the Bureau of Narcotics disinformation campaign continued with editorial calls for the suppression of the dangerous drug. In fact, such hysteria resulted that the Bureau's own legal counsel recommended discontinuation of the propaganda campaign. During the height of the media frenzy and while the Marijuana Tax Act of 1937 was being debated in Washington, news stories covering the testimony of leading medical experts about the relative safety of the drug and objections by the scientific community to the criminalization of marijuana were lost in the coverage of the government-created crime wave (see Galliher and Walker, 1977). Suffice it to say that whether self-initiated or governmentally generated, the media and government focus public attention on unique social problems; crime myths thus begin to take shape.

Creating Crime Myths

An occasional media or government attraction to some unique crime or problem may be beneficial in some cases. As Philip Jenkins and Daniel Katkin (1988) argue in their examination of child sexual abuse, intense media focus may produce some good even when it is based on exaggeration and distortion. Public attention and media focus on the unusual problem cannot by itself create a crime myth. In order for a myth to develop to a point where it becomes more than a social concern for a majority of citizens, it must be properly packaged and marketed. A requirement for myth production often repeated throughout this work is that for a crime problem to reach its myth potential, it must be reported to occur in "epidemic" proportion. A quantum leap must occur from uncovering an incident to depicting it as pervasive. Only by exaggerating the magnitude of the problem can public attention be sustained for prolonged periods, can fear be instilled, can calls for institutional control be made, and can public support be mustered to institute formal sanctions.

Exaggeration of the magnitude of a problem and the manufacturing of a crime myth are accomplished by several means. First, the media can suddenly focus upon crimes that it had previously ignored (Fishman, 1976). The media can collect and selectively choose crimes to present to the public. The organization of these presentations can create the image of a crime problem when they are taken out of their geographical, temporal, or social contexts. Crime myths are also created when the media fails to pursue stories beyond their initial reporting. Crimes reported to constitute a pattern may later be found unrelated or even conceptually distinct. There is, however, no requirement that the media correct their mistakes or recall their myths. Joel Best and Gerald Horiuchi's (1985) study of Halloween sadists' attacks against children found that the media greatly exaggerated its occurrence.

> There simply was no basis for Newsweek's (1975) claim that "several children had died." The newspapers attributed only two deaths to Halloween sadists, and neither case fit the image of a maniacal killer randomly attacking children. In 1970, five-year-old Kevin Toston died after eating heroin supposedly hidden in his Halloween candy. While this story received considerable publicity, newspapers gave less coverage to the follow-up report that Kevin had found the heroin in his uncle's home, not his treats. . . . In 1974, eight-year-old Timothy O'Bryan died after eating Halloween candy contaminated with cyanide. Investigators concluded that his father had contaminated the treat. . . . Thus, both boys' deaths were caused by family members, rather than by anonymous sadists (490).

The fear generated from exaggerating Halloween sadism not only affected the general public, but also organizations and individuals who are expected to have valid information regarding the reality of crime. Beginning in 1983, the International Association of Chiefs of Police (IACP) and the confectionery industry established, through sponsorship, a "Halloween Candy Hotline." The hotline was devised to give police departments technical assistance with suspected candy tampering cases. According to a news item by the IACP, the hotline received sixty-eight calls in 1990, but the article failed to note if any of these calls were actual tamperings (Editorial Staff, 1991:70). Although the Halloween hotline does serve as an example of a positive effect of exaggerating crime, it raises questions as to whether the nation's leading police executives are able to discern between actual crime problems and myths of crime.

How often does the media distort or exaggerate the crime problem in our society? Harry Marsh (1991) reviewed the research devoted to the study of the content of newspapers. His examination of literature from 1983 through 1988 found the following patterns:

- The vast majority of newspaper crime coverage pertains to violent or sensational crimes.

- The high percentages of violent crimes reported in the newspapers are not representative of the percentages reflected in official crime data.

- The over-emphasis of violent crimes and failure to address personal risk and prevention techniques often lead to exaggerated fears of victimization in certain segments of society.

- Newspaper coverage tends to support police views and values about crime and criminals . . . (67-68).

Misuse of statistics creates crime myths. Vested interests can manipulate "facts" when parties have control of information and access to channels of dissemination. As we shall see in later chapters, debates on organized crime are particularly susceptible to misuse and control of information. Statistics presented for public consumption are often clouded by broad definitions of crime that tend to group distinct behaviors, offenders, and victims into single categories giving the impression of an epidemic. In a study of the social reaction to sex crimes, Sutherland (1950) wrote, "Fear is seldom or never related to statistical trends in sex crimes. . . . Ordinarily, from two to four spectacular sex crimes in a few weeks are sufficient to evoke the phrase 'sex crime wave' " (144). Statistics and information often mislead the public when they are stripped from their original context and inferences are made between research studies. Causal links are often inferred or claimed between the crime myth under construction and some other more pervasive social concern. For example, in recent years the use of drugs has been linked to other crimes, high school drop-outs, decreased employee productivity (Kraska and Kappeler, 1988), the corruption of the police and contracting AIDs, as well as a multitude of other social maladies. The incidence of drug use in society may or may not have been perceived as a major social threat, but when coupled with other spin-off social problems, the perception of epidemic is ensured. In later chapters we will explore the myth-built links between drug use and other social problems.

Characterizations of Crime Myths

In order for the momentum of a crime myth to be prolonged and public support for institutionalized controls to be generated, myths must be accompanied by certain characterizations. Momentum is achieved if the crime problem has traits that either instill fear or threaten the vast majority of society in some appreciable way. Not unlike Greek mythology, modern crime myths must follow certain themes for success. There must be "virtuous" heroes, "innocent" victims, and "evil" villains who pose a clear and certain threat to the audience. Only then can a crime myth reach its potential. Characterizations common among myths in crime and criminal justice include the identification and targeting of a distinct deviant population; the presence of an "innocent," "virtuous," or "helpless" victim population; and the existence of a substantial threat to established norms, values, or traditional lifestyles.

Crime myths are often built around unpopular groups in society. This targeting helps to ensure sustained support for a myth. Unpopular groups in society are particularly vulnerable as possible targets of mythical fears. Groups most vulnerable to myth targeting are those that are easily distinguishable from the dominant social group. Distinctions are often as crude as race, color, or national origin, but need not be limited to visual appearance. Minorities and immigrants have had their share of myth targeting. Differences in religious beliefs, political views, or even sexual preferences are attractive targets for mythmakers. This characterization in the construction of crime myth has been used by hate groups, pro-slavery advocates, supporters of prohibition, and advocates of the death penalty. The distinction has been used to develop crime control policy, enact criminal laws, and even bring nations to war.

The importance of this characterization of "difference" cannot be overstated. Scholars have observed the importance of casting groups as different for targeting purposes. In his insightful book, *Blaming the Victim*, William Ryan (1976) states:

> This is a critical and essential step in the process, for difference is in itself hampering and maladaptive. The Different Ones are seen as less competent, less skilled, less knowing — in short less human. The ancient Greeks deduced from a single character-istic, a different language, that the barbarians — that is, the "babblers" who spoke a strange tongue — were wild, uncivilized, dangerous, rapacious, uneducated, lawless, and, indeed scarcely more than animals. [Such characterization] not infrequently justifies mistreatment, enslavement, or even extermination of the Different Ones (10).

Fear of minorities, foreigners, and differences in cultural or religious values has led to the creation of some shocking myths of organized crime. The birth of the Mafia myth in America is based on the created fear of cultural differences. The murder of New Orleans police chief David Hennessey in 1890 provides an excellent example. New Orleans was one of the cities that experienced a large influx of Italian immigrants during the end of the 19th century. Chief Hennessey was gunned down on a New Orleans street one night. As he was dying, the chief was said to have uttered the words

"Dagos, Dagos." Officers later rounded up a large number of petty criminals of Italian descent and presented them before a grand jury that indicted them for the chief's murder. Since evidence of their involvement was lacking, the jury acquitted them of the charges. Acquittal did not deter the citizens of New Orleans who marched to the jail, seized the defendants (and others who were not even on trial) and killed eleven of them. This lynching and subsequent trials and acquittals of "different ones" is said to be the genesis of the American Mafia myth (Smith, 1975:27-45).

The difference requirement of the myth construction process is built into issues surrounding crime and justice. There is a conven-ient supply of unpopular people—those whom society labels criminal. Criminals are probably the most unpopular minority in any society, although they are difficult to identify visually aside from the undesirable conduct.

Another requirement for myth development is that "helpless" or "innocent" victims (people like ourselves) must be depicted as suffering the brunt of the newly found social evil. The more "innocents" perceived as being affected by the myth, the greater the likelihood of public attention and support for the creation of crime myths targeting unpopular groups. Women, children, hetero-sexual victims of AIDS, law enforcement officers killed in the line of duty, or unwitting business people who become the victims of "organized" crime are often used as the common "virtuous" victim who suffers at the hands of the unpopular deviant. Sutherland (1950) observed, "The hysteria produced by child murders is due in part to the fact that the ordinary citizen cannot understand a sex attack on a child. The ordinary citizen . . . concludes that sexual attack on an infant or girl of six years must be the act of a fiend or maniac. Fear is the greater because the behavior is so incom-prehensible" (144).

This type of victim or the casting of victims as "innocents" allows for the implementation of stiff criminal sanctions against the deviants with accompanying feelings of moral superiority and even retributive satisfaction. It is not uncommon for the media to dwell on the virtues of the innocent victim to the exclusion of the offender (see Drechsel et al. 1980; Karman, 1978). After all, what parents do not feel their child is either a "good student," a "likable person," or "a good boy or girl." This is not to say that innocents do not become the targets of violent crime, but rather to illustrate that media coverage of crime stories often focuses extensively on the innocent person victimized by the evil stranger. As we shall see in later chapters on child abduction and abuse, strangers are not the greatest threat to our nation's children. In the construction of crime mythology there are no "ordinary" victims or criminals.

The subjects of myths are characterized as constituting a major threat to middle class values, norms, or lifestyle. Myths of crime and justice when blended with threats to religious belief, economic systems, sexual attitudes or orientation, the traditional family, or political preference become a volatile mix. These characterizations of crime myths serve to fuel emotionalism. The fear generated by this mixture of the unpopular offender, the innocent victim, and the perceived threat to traditional lifestyle can produce a formal and even violent social response. The argument is simple; a growing menace and threatening epidemic is plaguing society. Not only is the conduct a preference of a deviant group, it is affecting innocents and constituting a threat to tradition. "If we relied solely on the evidence of the mass media, we might well believe that every few years, a particular form of immoral or criminal behavior becomes so dangerous as almost to threaten the foundation of society" (Jenkins, 1988:1).

The idea that "normal" life might break down adds to the value of a crime myth and provides for its continued existence long after media attraction has vanished. These characterizations ensure that major social institutions become involved in the reform process, since the conduct is perceived as not only a physical threat but a substantial threat to existing social arrangements and institutions. Jenkins and Katkin's (1988) study of the McMartin school affair notes that during the investigation of the child molestation incidents, specific attention was given to parents' regrets that they had departed from traditional parenting roles by relying on alternative child care. Such a focus reinforces traditional values and allows for blame to be placed on the deviant parents rather than the absence of positive alternatives to traditional child rearing practices. "If only she had not worked outside the home," instead of "if only the government supported and monitored alternative child care industries."

Mythmaking and the characterization of crime problems as major threats to traditional values and society serve important political functions for law enforcement. Consider organized crime and vice. Leaders in the law enforcement community testifying before Congress and state legislators can present the issue in one of two ways. They can present a relatively safe myth which suggests that organized crime is a foreign conspiracy (Italians, Colombians, Jamaicans, etc.) which has invaded America and threatens the peace and security of a homogeneous and righteous society. Organized crime brings with it numerous evils. It corrupts otherwise incorruptible politicians and police; it makes people gamble away their life savings; it introduces drugs into the schools; it uses prostitutes to seduce family men. Even worse, organized crime is an intricate, highly structured foreign conspiracy which can only be eliminated with more money, more justice personnel, and more enforcement power. The myth is safe and convenient. It points to the different ones as the source of a problem, so we do not have to change our lifestyle or take responsibility for the problem. Finally, it explains why law enforcement has yet to win the war against organized crime in America. The alternative would be to expose the myth. Organized crime is an integral part of American society. It could not exist if the citizenry did not wish to have ready access to drugs, pornography, prostitution, gambling, no-questions-asked loans, or stolen goods. Many of the "crimes" of organized crime would not be important or profitable if the business community did not collaborate in money laundering, the illegal disposal of toxic wastes, and the fencing of stolen goods. Organized crime would find itself quite harried if an array of politicians, law enforcers, and others were not willing to "grease the skids" of organized crime. To uncover the myth of organized crime and vice, however, carries no bureaucratic rewards for law enforcement; it would offend people and end law enforcement careers. A rational bureaucrat or politician will find characterizing myths in terms of different ones and threats to traditional values more useful than fact.

Techniques of Myth Characterization

Mythmakers do not simply uncover crime and transmit information; they serve to structure reality by selecting and characterizing events—thereby cultivating images of crime (Lang and Lang, 1969; Gerbner, 1972; Schoenfeld, Meier and Griffin, 1979). The characterization of criminal events into myth is largely a process of bias and distortion. This distortion is often an unintended consequence of the process by which information is collected, processed, and prepared for dissemination by mass media. Research on the media, the news particularly, concludes that misrepresentation and distortion is not an uncommon practice (see Marsh, 1991:72).

The collection of crime events for public presentation is often shaped by reporters' perceptions. Journalistic accounts are rarely the product of actual observation; when they are, they are often conducted by reporters largely untrained in field research. More often than not, reporting of crime is based on secondhand information a reporter gleans from witnesses. The process of listening and interviewing witnesses and crime victims invites bias. Frequently, the wrong questions are asked, essential questions are omitted, and sensationalism becomes the reporter's focus. After all, journalists are in competition when creating a product for audience consumption. The untrained observer or journalist who is driven by the competitive nature of the modern mass media may selectively observe or interview with the end product in mind. Outcome and conclusion may already have been drawn before the investigator begins collecting information. Thus, from the selection and first investigation of a criminal event, there is the possibility of distortion, bias, and sensationalism.

Following a journalist's selection of a topic and initial investigation of a potential media story, the reporter's observation must make a transformation to communicable material. It must be written for dissemination or presentation. In this process of moving from observation to presentation, several problems arise. First, there is the possibility of selective memory or even the injection of personal preference by the reporter. Forgotten statements or observations may later be recalled by the journalist in the process of constructing a crime story. As information is recalled, initially insignificant observations may take on new meaning as the story unfolds. Second, after initial drafts of the presentation are constructed, they must be edited. In this editorial process a story can change considerably. Reports are often edited by a series of people who are guided by numerous constraints. Editorial constraints often include the time available to present a story, the page space available, and the marketability of the final product. The audience and editorial ideology also influence decisions. This process requires persons often unassociated with the initial crime to make judgments about what should be said or what should be shown. Editorial decisions are not always made in conjunction with the advice of the original observer.

The selection of which stories eventually appear in the news is based upon the ordering of stories into media themes. Fishman (1976) notes that:

> The selection of news on the basis of themes is one ideological production of crime news. . . . This procedure requires that an incident be stripped of the actual context of its occurrence so that it may be relocated in a new, symbolic context: the news theme. Because newsworthiness is based on themes, the attention devoted to an event may exceed its importance, relevance, or timelessness were these qualities determined with

> reference to some theory of society. . . . Thus, something
> becomes a "serious type of crime" on the basis of what is going
> on inside newsrooms, not outside them (536).

Finally, after the presentation of a story there is the possibility of selective observation and retention on the part of the audience. Many will only remember the bizarre or hideous part of a communication to the exclusion of other information. While media attention with crime myth is often short-lived, the images created by intense media focus may linger in the minds of those exposed to them.

There are, however, other techniques used in the manipulation of information and the construction of crime myths. There is a rich history of research and literature on the use of propaganda by the media and government. Propaganda is a technique for influencing social action based on intentional distortions and manipulation of communications. While not all media and government presentation, or even a majority of it, is a conscious attempt at propaganda, many crime myths are the product of propaganda techniques. "One important point to remember is that objective reporting is a myth. Every reporter brings to the story his/her own biases and world view. Each reporter has to make choices in writing the story: what to include, what to leave out, what sources to use. A few well-placed adjectives, a few uses of 'alleged' or 'so-called' can cast a definite ideological twist" (Hynds, 1990:5). These techniques tend to shape the presentation of a crime, create images for the uncritical audience, and promote social reaction. Some of the most common techniques employed by the media and government officials for characterizing crime myths include:

- *Creating criminal stereotypes*: This practice amounts to presenting crime as a unidimensional and non-changing event. Certain phrases such as "crime against the elderly," "child abduction," "street crime," and "organized crime" group wide varieties of behavior into single categories that have been previously characterized by the media. The use of stereotyped phrases links broad and popular conceptions of crime to diverse criminal behavior. For example, "organized crime" often creates the image of large "well-structured" groups of foreign-born individuals who engage solely in criminal enterprise.

- *Presentation of opinion as fact*: This practice involves injecting personal opinion into media presentations without a factual basis. Phrases that contain such opinions that are presented as fact might include: "the police are doing all they can to prevent this crime" or the "community is in a state of panic."

- *Speaking through sources*: This activity involves collecting opinions of others that closely match the proponent's viewpoint on a given issue. A reporter may select people to interview on the basis of how well their opinion fits the theme of the story.

- *Biased attribution and labeling*: Value-loaded terminology is used to characterize crime, criminals, or victims. A serial murderer may "stalk" the victim; a group of individuals may be referred to as a "crime family"; or a group of youths may become a "gang" that "preys" on "unsuspecting" victims.

- *Selective presentation of fact*: Presenting certain facts to the exclusion of others strengthens a biased argument. To emphasize the issue of child abduction, a proponent could cite that thousands of children are missing each year without presenting the fact that the vast majority of children are runaways.

- *Information-management*: The editorial process by which a particular news story is shaped and selected for presentation to the exclusion of other stories is one way to manage information. Presenting stories about sensational crimes like serial murder, crack babies, and child abduction to the exclusion of stories on corporate crime, securities fraud, and other more common crime are examples of the results of such management.

- *Undocumented sources of authority*: Vague references including statements like "many police officials feel" or "many people are saying" without specific reference to who is saying what and what constitutes "many" is a misleading reference to authority.

- *Stripping fact from its context*: A variation of the characteristic above is using facts or statements of authorities taken from the actual context in which they were made to support a particular position or injecting facts that are unrelated to the issue. A media presentation on drug abuse that focuses on statistics about the high school drop-out rate without considering whether or not there is an empirical link between the two is stripping fact from its original context.

- *Selective interviewing*: A final method of portraying a position as more solid than the facts indicate is interviewing one or two authorities on a topic and presenting their remarks as the generalized expert opinion on a given topic. For example, interviewing one or two criminologists and giving the audience the impression that those views are reflective of the criminological community.

In the chapters that follow, we will address specific myths of crime and criminal justice. Each myth or series of myths presented in this text differ in the fashion in which they rely on these practices and other characterizations to create a crime myth.

On Analyzing Crime Myths

There are no traditional or standard crime myths. Myths have at their origin unique events that may or may not be noticed by the mythmakers in society. A criminal event or series of events cannot become a myth unless a sufficient number of people contribute to its transformation. The story that is conceived but never told does not become an issue or a crime myth. Crime myths are unique in that they are a product of the social, political and economic atmosphere of a time. That is to say that the audience must be ready or made ready to accept a crime myth. A criminal event that has the potential for becoming a crime myth at one given moment may not be a viable myth at another point in time.

As mentioned earlier, mythmakers are varied and their roles are not static. Sometimes the government is the mythmaker and the media responds to the official myth. Other times the government responds to the myths created by the media or special interest groups. These varied mythmakers and shifting roles all make crime myths unique. Crime myths also differ in their purposes and consequences. Some myths result in the criminalization of behavior while others die quietly without social or political response. Some myths serve the interests of powerful groups in society or serve a needed social function, while others serve no useful social purpose.

The uniqueness of the origins, detection, construction, and consequence of crime myths does not lend itself well to traditional criminological analysis. There are no master keys or magic statistical bullets to understanding and solving all crime myths. There is no blanket sociological theory that explains the development and purpose of all crime myths. Each crime myth requires individualized treatment and analysis. Such a situation is an invitation for criticism. It is, however, also a strength. Wedding oneself to a particular theory, perspective, or method of knowing is like relying on a single sense to describe a garden of flowers. This work is grounded in a variety of perspectives and supports its numerous contentions with varying means of understanding. We shall leave it to the reader to judge whether we have described a rose or merely wandered into the bramble bush.

Sources

Best, J. and Horiuchi, G. T. (1985). The Razor and the Apple: The Social Construction of Urban Legends. *Social Problems*, 32:488-99.

Drechsel, R., Netteburg, K. and Aborisade, B. (1980). Community Size and Newspaper Reporting of Local Courts. *Journal Quarterly*, 57:71-8.

Editorial Staff (1991). Halloween Candy Hotline. *Police Chief*, (September): 70.

Fishman, M. (1976). Crime Waves as Ideology. *Social Problems*, 25:531-43.

Galliher, J. and Walker, A. (1977). The Puzzle of the Social Origins of the Marijuana Tax Act of 1937. *Social Problems*, 24:371-73.

Gerbner, G. (1972). Communication and Social Environment. *Scientific American*, 227: 153-60.

Hallin, D. (1990). Whatever Happened to the News? *Media & Values*, 50:2-4.

Hynds, P. (1990). Balance Bias with Critical Questions. *Media & Values*, 50:5-7.

Jenkins, P. (1988). Myth and Murder: The Serial Killer Panic of 1983-5. *Criminal Justice Research Bulletin*, 3:1-7.

Jenkins, P. and Katkin, D. (1988). Protecting Victims of Child Sexual Abuse: A Case for Caution. *Prison Journal*, 58(2):25-35.

Karmen, A. (1978). How Much Heat? How Much Light: Coverage of New York City's Blackout and Looting in the Print Media. In *Deviance and Mass Media*, Winick, C. (ed.). Beverly Hills, CA: Sage Publications.

Kraska, P. B. (1985). Personal Communication. Sam Houston State University, Huntsville, TX.

Kraska, P. B. and Kappeler, V. E. (1988). Police On-duty Drug Use: A Theoretical and Descriptive Examination. *American Journal of Police*, 7:1-28.

Lang, K. and Lang, G. E. (1969). *Television and Politics*. Chicago: Quadrangle Books.

Mannheim, K. (1936). *Ideology and Utopia*. New York: Harcourt, Brace and World, Inc.

Marsh, H. L. (1991). A Comparative Analysis of Crime Coverage in Newspapers in the United States and Other Countries From 1960-1989: A Review of the Literature. *Journal of Criminal Justice*, 19(4):67-79.

Medalia, N. Z. and Larsen, O. N. (1958). Diffusion and Belief in a Collective Delusion: The Seattle Windshield Pitting Epidemic. *American Sociological Review*, 23:180-86.

Pepinsky, H. E. and Jesilow, P. (1985). *Myths that Cause Crime*, 2nd ed. Cabin John, MD.: Seven Locks Press.

Pfohl, S. J. (1977). The Discovery of Child Abuse. *Social Problems*, 24:310-23.

Quinney, R. (1970). *The Social Reality of Crime*. Boston: Little, Brown and Company.

Ryan, W. (1976). *Blaming the Victim*. New York: Vintage Books.

Schoenfeld, A. C., Meier, R. F., and Griffin, R. J. (1979). Constructing a
    Social Problem: The Press and the Environment. *Social Problems,*
    27:38-61.
Smith, D. (1975). *The Mafia Mystique.* New York: Basic Books.
Sutherland, E. H. (1950). The Diffusion of Sexual Psychopath Laws.
    American Journal of Sociology, 56:142-48.

The Myth and Fear of Child Abduction
Defining the Problem and Solutions*

To be unaware of the issue of missing children in America is to be totally isolated from newspapers, television, mail, or other forms of communication. During the early 1980s, barely a week went by when the public was not exposed to photographs, stories, and debates on this issue of missing and abducted children. Virtually every form of media was used to circulate the faces and stories of missing children. From milk cartons to flyers in utility bills to television documentaries, Americans were made aware of the child abduction "epidemic." The notion of missing and exploited children commands public attention and causes emotional response in even the most callous individuals. One cannot be exposed to the stories and images of these unfortunates and not feel some emotion. Shedding the issue of emotionalism, however, produces serious questions concerning the true magnitude of the missing children problem and the necessity of drastic social changes aimed at its prevention.

Several factors have culminated in the creation of an unprecedented level of fear and concern about the possibility of child

*Adapted from Kappeler, V. E. and Vaughn, J. B. (1988). *The Justice Professional*, 3(1):56-69.

abduction in America. Combining the concepts of missing children and exploited children precipitates increased emotionalism and concern. The thought of a child being abducted conjures images of strangers hiding under cover of darkness, waiting to whisk away someone's child, intent on committing some hideous crime. Undisputedly, there are hideous acts committed against children. These incidents often receive great media attention and remain embedded in the public's mind for extended periods of time. The media has focused extensively on sensational cases like the murder and abduction of Adam Walsh and the serial murders of children in both Atlanta and Texas. The horror of such examples becomes the key ingredient in the public's perception of the child abduction problem. However, children can be missing without being the victims of exploitation. Conversely, exploitation and abuse can occur in the child's own home and unfortunately are not limited to strangers.

The issue of child abduction is further complicated by the lack of a clear criteria for defining the term "missing children." While this may seem to be a trivial point, an analysis of the issue illustrates that the ambiguity of the definition "missing" distorts the public's perception of the "reality" and "extent" of the missing children problem. In order to understand the magnitude and nature of the problem, one should examine the latent social effects, both functional and dysfunctional, resulting from increased attention and fear of child abduction based upon these distorted perceptions.

The Missing Children's Assistance Act (MCA) of 1983 defines the term missing child as:

1) any missing person thirteen years of age or younger, or;

2) any missing person under the age of eighteen if the circumstances surrounding such person's disappearance indicate that such person is likely to have been abducted (Sec. 272).

Persons encompassed by this definition may be missing for a variety of reasons unrelated to stranger abductions. Children can be taken by strangers or abducted by a parent who does not have legal custody, an act commonly termed "child stealing" (McCoy, 1978). They may be missing because they ran away from home, or they may be suffering from some form of illness such as amnesia. Clearly, not all children counted as missing are lost as a result of some stranger's criminality. It is with this broad definition of missing children that the reality of the problem becomes distorted.

The failure to formulate clear typologies of missing children combined with law enforcement's merging of both exploited and missing children's units contribute to the public's perception of the extent and context of the problem. Taken together, these two factors produce a situation conducive to imprecise reporting of statistics to the public, often in such a fashion as to exaggerate the potential danger of a child being abducted by strangers.

For the purposes of clarity, the terms child stealing, child snatching and parental abduction (often used interchangeably) are defined as the taking of a child by a parent in violation of a court's custody order. Child kidnapping is defined as a stranger's abduction of a child in violation of criminal law. With these distinctions in mind, let's begin considering how the "reality" of missing children is created and how the problem has become defined in American society.

Creating Reality and Defining the Problem

The public is exposed to statistics on missing children published by sources varying from newspaper articles and private organizations to governmental reports. These reports generally indicate that anywhere between 1.5 and 2.5 million children are missing from their homes each year (Treanor, 1986; Regnery, 1986; Congressional Record—Senate, 1983; Dee Scofield Awareness Program, 1983a). Of those reported missing, it is predicted that as many as 50,000 children will never be heard from again (Schoenberger and Thomas, 1985). It is also estimated as many as 5,000 of these missing children will be found dead (Congressional Record—Senate, 1983).

These are the statistics distributed by various sources for public consumption. A more critical examination of these statistics finds that within some jurisdictions between 66 and 98 percent of those children listed as missing are in reality runaways and were not abducted at all (Treanor, 1986; Schoenberger and Thomas, 1985). Police departments receive many more reports of missing runaways than other types of missing cases. Regnery (1986) estimates that nearly 1 million of the reportedly 1.5 million missing children are runaways. As many as 15 percent of the missing children may be parental abductions (Schoenberger and Thomas, 1985). In fact one author has maintained that about one out of twenty-two divorces ends in child theft (Agopian, 1981). Others estimate that between 25,000 and 100,000 incidents of missing children are parent abductions (Foreman, 1980; Congressional Record, 1983).

In the case of a Michigan study (Schoenberger and Thomas, 1985), the researchers found that 76 percent of the 428 entries examined in Michigan's lost children files should have been removed because the persons entered as missing had been located. These 325 children had been found but were not removed from the active files. Similarly, the Massachusetts State Police Missing Persons Unit estimates that 40 percent of their computer listings on missing persons are in reality solved cases that have not been removed from the data base (Crime Control Digest, 1985). These files along with data from other states are used to support contentions about the scope of the missing children problem. The extent of the missing children problem has been dramatically overestimated by the presence of inaccurate data in many law enforcement record systems.

More conservative figures were presented by Bill Treanor (1986), Director of the American Youth Center in Washington who contends that:

> Up to 98 percent of so-called missing children are in fact runaway teenagers. . . . Of the remaining 2 percent to 3 percent, virtually all are wrongfully abducted by a parent. That leaves fewer than 200 to 300 children abducted by strangers annually. . . . . The merchants of fear would have you believe that 5,000 unidentifiable bodies of children are buried each year. In truth, it's less than 200 dead from all causes, such as drowning, fire and exposure, not just murder (BI).

At the same time, statistics are presented regarding the number of children abducted and murdered each year. It is maintained that approximately 2,500 children are murdered yearly including homicides committed by ". . . psychopathic serial murderers, pedophiles, child prostitution exploiters and child abusers (Regnery, 1986:42)." However, of these 2,500 children murdered, the number reported missing prior to their victimization was not determined. Additionally, it is not reported how many of these victims were killed by their parents. These distinctions are easily blurred in the public's eyes. Statistics, often without qualification, are distributed to the public from official governmental sources. Such findings raise serious doubts as to the accuracy of the statistics presented to the public concerning the number, nature and ultimate fate of missing children in America. Growing public awareness and concern over the missing children issue has been promoted through the use of inconsistent and inaccurate statistics. Such statistics and the effect they have on the public and its perception of the extent of the missing children problem have both obvious and unintended consequences.

Latent Functions of Prevention

The primary obvious function of increased awareness of the problem of child abduction is prevention. The preoccupation with child safety has become evident in the proliferation of children's literature addressing safety and the prevention of abduction. With increased frequency, books and other forms of literature are becoming available to children, illustrating the dangers of social contact with persons who are not considered a member of the family or extended family unit. These texts often inform the child of the danger of speaking or having contact with strangers.

Children's books of this nature can have at least three negative latent functions. First, through children's literature the feelings of danger are equated with social contacts outside the family unit. This perception can result in increased social isolation and alienation of children from the community. As both parents and children begin to equate social contact outside the family with danger and impending harm, community interaction will decrease.

The fear of child abduction, while limiting social interaction, may reduce the family's dependence on third parties for child care. Parents may begin to rely less and less on day care facilities, in-house sitters, and other third party child care sources. As parents take greater responsibility for the care of their children, the contact within the family unit may increase and greater dependence will be placed on the interactions of family members. The family unit may gain greater solidarity as social interaction with community decreases, but the cost may be increased fear and stunted social development.

Second, these texts often give questionable information to children. A specific case in point is a children's book entitled *Never Talk to Strangers* (Joyce, 1967), which advises children through the use of animal characters that they should never talk to strangers, but that it is acceptable to become friendly with acquaintances of the family. This notion is reinforced by a government program sponsored by the National Child Safety Counsel (NCSC). According to H. R. Wilkins of the Michigan based NCSC, millions of milk cartons are being printed that will utilize animal characters to instruct children of the dangers of contact with strangers (Juvenile Justice Digest, 1985a). Yet, the literature and research on both sexual abuse of children and child abduction indicates that children are more often victimized by acquaintances rather than strangers. As children are taught to run from unfamiliar persons, they are also being taught to run into the arms of those most often engaged in child abuse. These mediums also promote the notion that if properly educated, children can distinguish between those individuals who are "safe" and those persons to avoid, a distinction even criminologists are reluctant to make.

The fear invoked by the spread of prevention literature and the indoctrination of children with safety tips like avoiding strangers may be a zero sum game. Such prevention measures only replace the unfounded fear of child abduction with a new and equally unfounded fear of strangers. These approaches to prevention may confuse children and promote paranoia and insecurity. Where would a child abused by a family member turn given such mixed messages—to a stranger?

Third, the proliferation of literature on child safety stresses that it is the duty of the parents to educate their children. This responsibility in itself is not damaging and may very well contribute to prevention. However, placing blame on parents for failing to educate their children allows the responsibility for child safety to be shifted from social control agencies such as the police and society as a whole to individual family members. In effect, what these texts suggest is that if parents fail to educate their children and if children fail to heed their warnings, they will be abused or abducted and the responsibility rests on them alone, rather than the offender or society as a whole. We in effect begin to "blame the victim" and shift focus from the offender and crime control agencies to the child and nonvigilant parent.

The link between literature and the behavior of adolescents has been well illustrated by the works of David McClelland (1961). He found that the economic performance of a culture varied with the degrees of achievement portrayed in literature. Parallels were drawn between the declines and increases in achievement, and the decline and increase of literature depicting economic success. This research shows that literature has an effect on behavior; whether it is motivation to excel economically or motivation to withdraw socially, the effect is profound. By depicting strangers as the persons to fear and avoid due to the possibility of abduction and exploitation, we circumvent serious consideration of the extent to which relatives, friends, and family members are involved in child abuse and abduction. We also divert attention away from the fact that most missing children are runaways.

The concern for child safety and fear of child abduction has not been limited to children's literature. The fear of child abduction is beginning to motivate legal reform designed to criminalize a vast scope of behavior involving children. Society is turning to solutions to a problem which has been defined based on fear and inaccurate information.

Legal Reform: Creating Crime and Criminals

The emotional furor and fear of child abduction has created an atmosphere conducive to the creation of a new crime and class of criminals. In California, prior to 1976, if a parent took his or her child in violation of a custody order, it was not considered a criminal offense. Since October 1, 1977, legislation in California has been enacted making it a criminal offense for parents to take custody of their own children in violation of a court custody order (Agopian, 1980; 1981).

The state of New York has enacted similar legislation, making parental child abduction a felony offense. In February of 1985, the National Association of Governors called for all states to adopt legislation making child snatching a felony offense, regardless of whether the violator was a parent or stranger to the child. As of 1983, forty-eight states have adopted the Uniform Child Custody Jurisdiction Act and forty-two states classify child snatching as a felony (Silverman, 1983). The legal response to this behavior has also been addressed at the federal level.

Prior to 1983, the United States Department of Justice restricted the issuance of warrants for the arrest of parents who took illegal custody of their children and subsequently crossed state lines. As of December 23, 1982, federal and local law enforcement officials were able to seek federal arrest warrants for child snatching even if there was no evidence to suggest the child is in physical danger (United States Attorney Bulletin, 1983). In the Sixth Report to Congress on the implementation of the Parental Kidnapping Prevention Act of 1980, the Department of Justice indicated that during 1982, thirty-two "fugitive parents" were arrested by the Federal Bureau of Investigation (FBI). These arrests took place prior to removal of the warrant restrictions imposed by the Department of Justice. During the first nine months of 1983, after the removal of restrictions, the number of parents arrested by the FBI doubled to sixty-four (U.S. Department of Justice, 1983). With these reforms at both the state and federal levels, we have created the crime of child stealing and the criminal classifications of "fugitive parents" and "custody criminals."

While in some circles this easing of restrictions on the FBI and the criminalization of custody violations may be viewed as a positive step in solving the problem of child abduction by parents, there are certainly negative effects associated with the increased arrests of fugitive parents. An undetermined number of these children are physically and emotionally better off with the parent who committed the illegal act. This point was illustrated in the case of a Long

Island girl who was abducted by her mother after the father was awarded custody. After lengthy consideration of the case, New York Justice Alexander Vitale ordered that the mother should retain custody of the child, having decided that this was in the best interest of the child's welfare. The best interests of the child are not always paramount in the court's decision-making process; jurisdictional concerns are often given equal importance in deciding custody cases after an abduction has occurred (*In re Nehra v. Uhlar*, 1977).

The second problem arises out of labeling as criminal the parent who, with good intentions, removes his or her child from an abusive atmosphere. While not all parents who abduct their children do so with such noble intentions, these parents often have little recourse. Such parents must decide either to comply with the law and allow their children to endure further abuse or to violate the law in the best interest of the child. Legal avenues are often closed to parents. Fees associated with custody battles often restrict a parent's ability to obtain legal redress in these matters. Regardless of the individual's ability to access the courts, child abduction is often seen as the last alternative to maintaining a full-time parental relationship (Agopian, 1980). While some degree of formal social control may be required to prevent parental abductions, better screening and investigation by the courts before awarding custody could reduce the incidents of well meaning child abduction. We can only speculate as to the motivations of a parent who would abduct a child or children from an apparently stable family, but obviously the abducting party must feel that an adequate custody arrangement had not been made in the judicial process. More equitable custody arrangements may be one way of reducing child abduction by parents.

A more pragmatic consideration is the utility of fugitive warrants. A fugitive warrant does not allow the FBI to take a child into custody or even to return the child to the parent with legal custody. These children are often kept in foster homes or other community shelters while courts review the custody arrangements. In some cases these environments may be more damaging than staying with the abducting parent. Arrests on fugitive warrants do not reflect the number of children who are actually returned to their legal guardians as a result of arrest. Furthermore, the warrant does not allow agents to effect arrests of persons other than those named on the warrant, who may have materially participated in the abduction or currently have physical custody of the child.

The emotional atmosphere created by increased publicity of the dangers of child abduction has been used as a political tool to advocate stiffer punishments for offenders. In the cases of true stranger abductions, this may be a desirable prevention measure. It is, however, questionable whether stiffer sanctions would prevent hideous crimes against children. The desire to control and sanction stranger abduction often becomes politicized with calls for stiffer penalties for all offenders who commit crimes against children. Calling for legislative "reform," Congressman Henry J. Hyde advocated mandatory life sentences for persons who kidnap a child and the death penalty for child abduction that results in death. The Congressman stated, "I do not feel it is too harsh to say that one who kidnaps or murders a child has forfeited his right to freedom forever" (Juvenile Justice Digest, 1985b: 4). A call for the death penalty for child snatchers has not been limited to the political arena. Private organizations devoted to the location of missing children have also called for legislative "reform." Dee Scofield Awareness Program (1983b), a private organization located in Tampa, Florida, recommends that child abduction should be elevated to a federal offense punishable by either death or life imprisonment. The most disturbing point here is that the proposed reform fails to make a clear distinction between the parent custody violators and stranger abduction.

Conclusion

McClintock and Haden (1970) have pointed out that the manner in which a problem is defined is related to the type of social control systems available to address that problem. The problem of missing children in America is no exception to their contention. It becomes clear from the analysis of the missing children problem that the issue has been defined as epidemic in proportion and criminal in nature. Given this definition and perception of the issue, the current course of action — the criminalization of this behavior — is clearly a logical consequence. As a society, we have defined the problem as an abnormal behavior on the part of a select group of individuals we have chosen to call criminal. We have chosen social control agencies and criminal sanctions as the solutions for this epidemic. In an attempt to prevent this behavior, we have subsequently created a new classification of crime and criminals without distinguishing the motives and reasoning behind this behavior. In short, we have defined missing children in America as a legal problem with legal solutions.

As long as this definition and solution dominate the missing children problem, a solution is not forthcoming. The legal "solution" is merely a reaction to an undesirable behavior. However, if we define the scope of the problem more accurately and develop a clear understanding of the various types of incidents that collectively compose the problem, an alternative solution may yet emerge.

As previously mentioned, the missing children problem includes runaways, parental abductions, and stranger abductions. Incorporating runaways into missing children statistics produces the perception of an epidemic. The inclusion of stranger abduction in the composite figures permits the problem to be defined as criminal. Incorporating parental abductions and then criminalizing all abductions furthers conceptualization of the issue as both epidemic and criminal.

In order to begin to address the problem of missing children in America, we must come to understand the problem in a social rather than a legal context. Only then can we begin to take preventive rather than reactive measures. The nature of family relationships must be explored in order to begin to understand why 1.5 million children flee their homes each year. We must also begin to realize that our legal system, both criminal and civil, is not a panacea for all social problems. We must begin to separate the missing children problem into its parts—social and legal. The fact that thousands of children each year are abducted by their parents raises serious questions about our legal system's ability to define family relations equitably through divorce and child custody orders.

Our adversarial trial system, so often alluded to in the criminal process, is ever present in civil courts as well. The adversarial process creates what amounts to custody battles. These events can only be seen as creating conflict, setting the stage for continued discord between the winners (those awarded custody) and the losers (those denied custody). Unless a more equitable process is developed—one void of the conflicts resulting from the current system—child stealing will remain a result of custody battles. If we cannot adequately understand the behavior of runaway children and the reaction of parents who are denied the custody of their children, or develop workable solutions to custody arrangements, how can we hope to understand or prevent child abductions by strangers?

While this chapter has attempted to address some of the latent and manifest functions of the fear of child abduction, the true effects of increased awareness, fear, and use of prevention programs may not become evident for some time. It is too early to speculate on the possible effects the promotion of these fears will have on future generations of parents, children, and legal reforms.

The preliminary indications are that we will continue to attempt to handle the issue through increased legislation and stiffer penalties for offenders. However, it is evident that the campaign against missing children, while well intended, will have negative effects socially. It would appear prudent to consider the social effects of prescribing criminalization and prevention in mass dosages. It is readily apparent that critical research designed to reflect accurately the scope of the problem of missing children in America is desperately needed. Furthermore, we can no longer afford to implement prevention programs without first giving critical thought to both the manifest and latent social functions of these policies.

Sources

Agopian, M. W. (1981). *Parental Child Stealing.* Lexington, MA: Lexington Books.

_____. (1980). Parental Child Stealing: Participants and the Victimization Process. *Victimology: An International Journal,* 5:263-73.

Congressional Record—Senate (1983). Statements on Introduced Bills and Joint Resolutions. (October 27):S14787.

Dee Scofield Awareness Program (1983a). Federal Legislation: The First Steps. (Educational Report No. 5) Tampa, Florida.

_____. (1983b). Estimated Annual-Missing Children. (Educational Report, November) Tampa, Florida.

Foreman, J. (1980). Kidnapped! Parental Child-Snatching, A World Problem. *Boston Globe,* (March 16):B1.

In re Nehra v. Uhlar, 43 N.Y. 2d 242 (1977).

Joyce, I. (1967). *Never Talk to Strangers: A Book About Personal Safety.* Racine, WI: Western Publishing Company.

McClelland, D. C. (1961). *The Achieving Society.* New York: Free Press.

McClintock, F. H. and T. B. Haden (1970). Law and Social Control Systems: A Functional Analysis. *The Division and Classification of the Law,* J. A. Jolowicz (ed.). London: Butterworth.

McCoy, M. (1978). *Parental Kidnapping: Issues Brief No. ID 77117.* Washington, DC: Congressional Research Service.

Missing Children's Assistance Act of 1983, 28 U.S.C. 534.

National Governor's Association (1985). Policy on Missing and Exploited Children. Authors.

Regnery, A. A. (1986). A Federal Perspective on Juvenile Justice Reform. *Crime and Delinquency,* 32:39-51.

Schoenberger, R. W. and W. A. Thomas (1985). Missing Children in Michigan: Facts, Problems, Recommendations. *Juvenile Justice Digest,* 31:7-8.

Silverman, B. S. (1983). The Search for a Solution to Child Snatching. *Hofstra Law Review,* 11:1073-117.

Staff (1985). Massachusetts' New Missing Children Law Requires Immediate Reports, Investigations. *Crime Control Digest,* (January 14):10.

_____. (1985a). National Campaign to Locate Abducted Children Enters Phase II. *Juvenile Justice Digest,* (February 25):2.

_____. (1985b). Kidnapping and Abuse: Rep. Hyde Seeks Life in Prison or Mandatory Death Sentence for Crimes Against Children. *Juvenile Justice Digest,* (July 1):4.

Treanor, B. (1986). Picture Our Missing Children: The Problem is Blown Far Out of Proportion. *The Houston Chronicle*, (February 1).

United States Attorneys Bulletin (1983). (April 29): 31.

U.S. Department of Justice (1983). *Sixth Report to Congress on Implementation of the Parental Kidnapping Prevention Act of 1980.* Washington, DC: U.S. Department of Justice.

GRAND JURY INDICTS
Day Care Employees Arrested

Camp Counselors Indicted

Teacher charged with abuse

The *Unspeakable* Crime

chapter **3**

Protecting Victims of Child Sexual Abuse
A Case for Caution*

In the last decade, the sexual abuse of children has become a very prominent issue in the United States, with many state legislatures proposing various measures to protect and assist victims. One major problem in assessing such measures is that we do not really know how common child molestation is. Estimates of the annual number of victims nationwide range from a few thousand to many millions; there are some who argue that abuse— the "best kept secret"—is the common experience of literally tens of millions of Americans. The issue of frequency is important for policymakers. If indeed this type of offense is so common, there must be reasons why it is so rarely detected and prosecuted. Some suggest that molesters frequently escape prosecution because of the numerous obstacles placed in the way of the victim and of those who seek to help him or her.

In this view, authorities should take a much more proactive stance in seeking out abuse cases, and the law should be amended

*Adapted from Jenkins, P. and Katkin, D. (1988). *The Prison Journal*, 68(2):25-35.

to make the courtroom experience less traumatic for victims. Successful prosecution could be enhanced by a series of measures, such as permitting children to testify from behind screens or on videotape ("Prosecuting Child Abuse," 1988). The right of cross examination might be limited in such cases, and standards of proof might even be relaxed to the disadvantage of the accused. All such proposals derive from the assumption that the normal child abuse case involves a real victim and a justly accused offender; the first necessity is to secure the conviction of the wrongdoer. The perception is that we are dealing with a vast social problem; action is urgently needed; and children virtually never make false accusations in molestation cases.

Legal changes of the nature described naturally arouse the hostility of a variety of groups, including legal conservatives and civil rights advocates who oppose the reduction of any legal safeguards. However, the proposed reforms can be criticized from a number of additional perspectives. Each of the fundamental beliefs of the reformers can be challenged on the basis of extensive recent experience. The scale of the child abuse problem is very dubious; the need for draconian measures is at best debatable; and child witnesses unquestionably have lied in court, often in consequence of prosecutorial manipulation. It is also subject to question whether some recent abuse cases have involved any real molestation whatever. It now appears that real injustices have occurred under the existing system of prosecuting abuse cases; far worse would be likely under a "reformed" system.

This chapter will examine the recent experience of mass child abuse cases to argue for caution in any reforms that may be proposed in the investigation or prosecution of child molestation. Child abuse does occur, and it is a peculiarly heinous crime; but it will not be solved by attacking the rights of the accused. Removing legal protections in such cases is likely to lead to wrongful convictions, and thus to discredit genuine cases with real victims. The debate over child abuse laws is a contemporary manifestation of an ancient debate over the balance of rights between accused and victim. Any changes must be made with caution, and with full awareness of the social roots of the present panic over child molestation.

The Child Abuse Panic

In 1985, a case was in progress in a courtroom in southern California, one of the most economically advanced and socially sophisticated areas in the world. A key witness was a ten-year-old boy, who told how a defendant had led him to a church where children were the center of satanic rites. At other times, animals were sacrificed, and there were tales of secret tunnels and diabolic apparitions. This, however, was only one part of a much larger trial that focused on massive sexual abuse that had allegedly gone on in a preschool for many years (Lindsey, 1984:6; Chambers, 1986:7).

That the allegations were outrageous does not in itself mean that they were untrue; nor does the fact that the stories depended on the testimony of children. However, it is now beyond question that much of the evidence in this case — the notorious McMartin school affair — was wholly unreliable. In March 1986, all charges were dropped against five of the seven defendants, and most of the "trimmings" in the case (Satanism, sacrifice, hot-air balloons, nuns, tunnels) were allowed to fade into oblivion. What was left by 1988 was a straightforward sexual molestation case, in which the guilt or innocence of the remaining defendants remains undecided at the time of writing (Jenkins and Katkin, 1986; Eberle, 1986; Chambers, 1986:7).

What is incredible about the McMartin case is the extent to which the allegations drawn from the children were believed, particularly in light of the paucity of corroborating evidence. To understand the widespread willingness to believe the veracity of these dark tales, we must put the McMartin case into its social and historical context. The case occurred during the major "moral panic" in the United States, a purported "crime wave" (of child abuse) that the scandal itself did much to spread. The McMartin case by itself would have been a scandal. However, it was only one of a number of incidents, some of which evolved into full-fledged trials — as in Jordan, Minnesota, and in Bakersfield and Sacramento, California. All involved not only massive child abuse, but outrageous charges of diabolism and human sacrifice. Recently, a number of books and articles have described at length these chilling events and the long trial of questionable prosecutorial and therapeutic decisions that produced such a confused mixture. By far the best is the Eberles' study of The Politics of Child Abuse (see also Coleman, 1984, 1986; Eliasoph, 1986; Jenkins and Katkin, 1986; Nelson, 1984; Crewdson, 1988).

Critics of the prosecution in mass abuse cases often draw analogies to the witch-trials, and the parallels are very suggestive — the term is not only intended as slander. In both eras, there were experts in this form of deviancy who believed that charges, once made, must have some substance, even if subsequently recanted. The charges should be pursued relentlessly, which will almost infallibly lead to an ever-increasing circle of indictments. The process develops its own juggernaut momentum, until either public opinion changes or superior authorities intervene to stop the manifest injustices. The experts in question were the "diabolists" of the 1690s and the psychologists today who hold that children are more or less incapable of lying about sexual abuse (see the debate on this topic in, for example, Goodman, 1984; Eberle and Eberle, 1986; Coleman, 1984,1986; Russell, 1984; Ennew, 1986; Ward, 1984; Hollingsworth, 1986). Both groups also denounced the protections provided by the law to manifestly guilty offenders (for the witch analogies, see Hansen, 1970; Demos, 1982).

The child abuse panic is far from over, and other cases are currently in process. In 1988, a woman was convicted of mass sexual abuse at the "Wee Care" day care center in New Jersey (Nathan, 1987, 1988). Some observers continue to argue that the crisis is real (Hollingsworth, 1986; Hawkins, 1986). The purpose of this chapter is not to provide a detailed examination of the notorious cases in which child testimony was clearly exaggerated or untrue, but to explore the atmosphere in which widespread credulity was possible; and then to consider the legal implications.

The Context

In order to understand the recent wave of concern about child abuse, it is vital to understand the broader social context. In particular, we must realize that child molestation has been only one of several concurrent "moral panics" in contemporary America. There has been intense concern about other types of savage and amoral predators, often with motives that are literally satanic. In 1983, for example, law-enforcement agencies and mass media began giving intense coverage to the issue of serial killers, multiple murderers who are (it is said) guilty of four or five thousand deaths each year in the United States alone. Such figures are grossly exaggerated; this panic blossomed and then faded away within a few years (Jenkins, 1988). However, the issue illustrates a great deal about contemporary concerns and fears.

Moreover, these panics tended to merge into each other, and all tended to support the idea that society was under siege by barbaric and alien predators, often with a frightening degree of organization (Terry, 1987). The abuse cases are a notable example of the change of perceptions. Child molestation is almost invariably the act of a lone individual, but the mid-1980s saw a shift of interest to organized gangs of "sex predators" (Shipp, 1984a). These operated through day-care centers nationwide and funded themselves through child pornography operations. Even serial murder entered this less than appetizing picture, as uncooperative children were murdered, sometimes in the hundreds, usually to the ignorance of the local community. Just as the serial killer panic was reaching its height in 1984 and 1985, the related question of missing children entered a new phase of intense public concern and awareness. Estimates of the number of such cases rose into the millions. Such figures tended to be immensely flexible because the definition of "children" included age cut-offs varying from fourteen to twenty-one or even older (Eliasoph, 1986; Scardino, 1985).

In 1983, two separate reports (by the Department of Health, Education, and Welfare [HEW] and the Justice Department) spoke of millions of missing children. HEW extrapolated evidence from Louisville, Kentucky, to claim that over a million children disappeared each year, a figure publicized by a new National Center for Missing and Exploited Children. Where did they all go? Some all-too-familiar perpetrators appeared to provide the answer, with an alleged 1.5 million under the age of sixteen involved in prostitution and child pornography. Pornographers, it seems, often killed their subjects upon completion of a project (child pornography was a particularly popular element in most of the leading child abuse trials). Some children fell victim to serial killers, like (the very real) Clifford Olson or Arthur Bishop, but the phenomenon was massively exaggerated by the media. The idea grew that child abuse led infallibly to child murder, the apparent lesson of the initial charges at Jordan, Bakersfield, and Sacramento.

Exaggeration of this kind did in fact produce some good, with the distribution of pictures of missing children in many forms of mass media as well as on milk cartons. However, the near-universal distribution of such images did much to support the idea of North America as a jungle where predators freely killed and abused their immature and defenseless prey. As Nina Eliasoph (1986) shows, the figure of "50,000 abducted children" came to be repeated as credulously as that of 4,000 annual victims of serial killers—and with as little substance.

The United States in the 1980s was (so it seems) a strange and deeply terrifying land. Each year, several thousand people of all ages were murdered by predatory wandering strangers, while 50,000 children were abducted by criminals and sex offenders, often for the purpose of sexual exploitation and pornography. A national network of day-care centers concealed an organized army of child molesters, who rented out their pupils to be molested or murdered. Even worse, many of these appalling offenders were united by a religious bond, the satanic rituals for which they regularly employed child victims prior to killing and cremating them (Kahaner, 1988; Terry, 1987). The abundance of available children was scarcely surprising in view of the millions missing from home at any given time. To quote one activist, "This country is littered with mutilated, decapitated, raped and strangled children" (Eliasoph, 1986:7).

This fantastic picture is a composite of the claims made for several separate "panics." However, each individual assertion was supported by some reputable source—not merely by either crank tabloids or religious eccentrics. Much of this picture is drawn from stories on national television programs, and a remarkable amount from agencies of the United States government, above all the Justice Department. Virtually every aspect of the picture given is utterly false.

Every advanced country has its child molesters, abductors, and serial killers. In the twentieth century, however, only the United States has so inflated these stereotypes into figures of such awesome power and so quantified their excesses. The related panics of the 1980s undoubtedly require considerable explanation in terms of social psychology and the sociology of mass movements. Here, however, our goal is to examine the impact of these events, especially on the justice system.

At any time, there are likely to be a few individuals who believe that a society is besieged by human predators of various kinds— witches, Jews, Jesuits, Illuminati, and so on. Once a panic begins, there are a number of ways in which it can be distracted or derailed. Here, the role of the media is central. If the panics of the 1980s had targeted the traditional scapegoats for child disappearances—Jews and Gypsies—then the media would surely have attempted to resist and to calm these fears. In fact, the media acted as accomplices in the contemporary witch-hunts, leaving the law and the courts as the much-criticized last refuge of the falsely accused. On all the major issues discussed, the role of the national media was provocative and generally unsavory. On serial murder, satanism, child abuse, and abduction, the most reputable television shows presented quite outrageous fantasies as sober fact. When the McMartin story first made the news in early 1984, magazine programs like "20/20" treated the charges as automatically correct, with the children as victims of appalling maltreatment. One report ended with the alleged remark of a child: "Daddy, when I die, will the memories go away?"

With the case judged and proved, there remained only the task of explanation, and here the pundits had recourse to a reassertion of traditional family morality. Just as pornography and easy sex had (it was claimed) created an epidemic of serial killers, so the

SPECIAL ORDER FOR:

NAME _____ MUNRO _____ ORDER NO. _____ **US 24497**

ADDRESS _____ 1946 Dorothea Avenue - St.Paul,MN

TITLE _____ Kappeler - MYTHOLOGY OF CRIME..........

PUBLISHER _____ AMOUNT _____ 13.50 2070

_____ DEPOSIT _____

_____ BALANCE _____

CLERK _____ mp _____ DATE _____ 6-3-94

inv 60804
date 6-7-94

"day-care predators" were taking advantage of parents increasingly entrusting their children to strangers. "McMartin families" were quoted as regretting that they had abandoned traditional nuclear family roles and left their children (Lindsey, 1984).

It was many months before notes of criticism began to appear. The fall of 1985 marked a real transition here, with major holes appearing in both McMartin and Escondido cases, attacks on the "missing children" theory, and sympathetic reports about VOCAL—a support group of people falsely accused of child abuse ("Victims of Child Abuse Laws"). November 1986 was also a fruitful time for media criticisms, with a "60 Minutes" program that derided the child abuse/Satanism link. In the same month, *1986* featured the story of an alleged abuse case which arose out of hotly contested custody hearings in a divorce case (Spiegel, 1987). Here, too, the message was that child abuse provided a vehicle for the malicious or incompetent to persecute the innocent.

Even so, "CBS News" followed these programs within a few days by an attack on the legal formalities which had (it was implied) prevented the conviction of the guilty in cases such as McMartin and Jordan. With rare exceptions, the media failed utterly in any role as public "watchdog." Throughout the perceived crisis, mass media of all varieties consistently promoted the sensationalist view of the new offender types as lethal "predators." The defense of those accused—and many innocent people were accused—was thus left wholly to the court systems of respective states. However, this defense was only accomplished under severe challenge.

The Legal Response

> In cases of the most atrocious crimes—that is, the least likely ones—the flimsiest conjectures are sufficient, and the judge is permitted to overstep the bounds of the law (Beccaria, 1986:24).

The child abuse panic produced a good deal of legislation and litigation, much of both being ill-conceived. However, many important legal issues were raised that have yet scarcely begun to be dealt with. One legal consequence of the furor was a challenge to traditional concepts of professional confidentiality, with some states requiring the disclosure of information about child abuse, even if this arose during patient-client discussions. The implications of such legislation remain very uncertain, as a number of widely reported cases involved the secrecy of the Catholic confessional. This will undoubtedly be the very last bastion of professional confidentiality, and one that will presumably not be renounced at any cost. Of thirty-three states with child protection laws requiring reporting, only three had specific exemptions for clergy; a number of 1985 cases (notably in Texas and Florida) led to important church-state confrontations. The issue was also debated in the civil courts, as in a 1984-85 Louisiana case where the Catholic church was found liable for failing to detect or prevent the abusive activities of a priest, Father Gilbert Gauthe (Goldman, 1985).

As the child-abuse panic progressed, there were repeated charges that the legal system was incapable of dealing with crimes of this nature. Almost invariably, such charges come from supporters of the prosecution, who cited the failure to convict accused offenders. Also, it was charged that the cross-examination of children constituted a new act of victimization perhaps even worse than the original one. As the first Jordan cases collapsed in late 1984, *New York Times* correspondent E. R. Shipp published a characteristic article about the "Jeopardy of Children on the Stand." In retrospect, it is now apparent that all the children who were discredited were in fact lying repeatedly and very seriously, but the lesson was not noted. In 1986, the publicity for a book about an allegedly true case of molestation stressed the evil of defense attorneys who sought to "break down" child witnesses (Hollingsworth, 1986).

That such cases present a crisis for the courts seems beyond controversy. Guilty or not, Ray Buckey of the McMartin case should not have served five years in pretrial detention; there is little question that expensive time-wasting has often occurred in cases like these. Having said that, it is by no means certain that the perceived "crisis" has at its root a failure to convict the guilty, as opposed to prosecutorial ineptitude or worse. Indeed, legal "niceties" have worked credibly to prevent the false convictions of hundreds of individuals. If laws are to be changed, it is certainly not a given that the reforms should benefit the prosecution.

Some of the proposed reforms are at worst anodyne, at best long overdue. As in the reform of rape laws during the 1970s, a new emphasis on the victim has had a number of effects that might well be seen as positive. It would not constitute a judicial revolution to permit evidence to be given by closed-circuit television, in order to take account of a child's sensitivity about public speaking. The reform has been widely legislated, but its legality seems questionable in the light of recent Supreme Court decisions (discussed below). Changes like these are becoming popular in other countries, including Great Britain (proposed reforms are discussed at length in Whitcomb, 1984, 1985). In the debate on this reform, however, there is a recurring confusion. Does televised testimony mean that a child should give only evidence in chief by such means, and then be available for cross-examination in person? Should cross-examination also take place at a distance? Or, should cross-examination not be permitted, a radical departure widely suggested during the mid-1980s (Whitcomb, 1984,1985)?

The attitude of appellate courts on such matters remains uncertain, but the Supreme Court was critical of a Kentucky decision (*Stincer*) barring an accused from attending pretrial hearings where a child was testifying. In 1988, the Court struck down an Iowa law permitting alleged child victims to testify behind screens (*Coy v. Iowa*). It seems that courts will not lightly renounce the right of the defendant to confront an accuser.

Discussion of child witnesses tends overwhelmingly to assume that alleged victims really have suffered molestation and must be encouraged to talk. Children are thus seen as almost infallibly truthful, though this is a highly unlikely view. In 1985, for example, a burgeoning abuse case began in Escondido, California, when a group of children accused a bus driver. Two months later, the children admitted that the charges were wholly without foundation, and the driver was exonerated. In Jordan, too, a group of children lied systematically, though apparently with the laudable aim of producing charges so fantastic that they would discredit earlier accusations they had been induced to make. Little credence can therefore be placed on the common view — expressed, for example, by Dr. Goodman — that "If you ask children what happened, virtually everything they tell you will be correct" (quoted in Eberle and Eberle, 1986:253). Unless, of course, the children are lying (Wrightsman, 1987:321-32).

There is a substantial literature on the psychology of witnesses (Wolfe, 1988; Ellison and Buckhout, 1981; Melton et al., 1983; Wrightsman, 1987). Much of the debate on the use of child witnesses has concerned topics like the memory abilities and reportorial skills of juveniles and that more subjective issue, truthfulness. However, this may be misleading. The problem may not be so much that children maliciously invent false charges but rather the manner in which testimony is developed through interactions with interrogators, whether these are police officers, prosecutors, or psychologists. In the McMartin and Jordan cases, therapists apparently believed immediately in the charges of widespread molestation and used this fact as a yardstick to measure the candor of child witnesses. If children denied victimization, then it was assumed they were concealing the truth, which must be drawn out by some inducement or reinforcement. The therapeutic process thus became an infallible generating mechanism for criminal charges, and we should not be amazed that so few McMartin children (10 percent) continued to deny molestation.

In addition, the cases since 1983 have shown that there are any number of ways in which wholly false charges can be produced or developed. In Jordan, a genuine molester named James Rud needed to produce a "child-sex ring" to support a plea bargain. Some prosecutors have been charged with using abuse cases for political or electoral advantage. Other cases arise through the malice of a group of children against a person in a responsible position; through bitter custody fights; or through fraudulent malpractice lawsuits. Once a motive is present, it only remains to find a therapist sufficiently credulous to draw forth the appropriate story.

Such experience strongly suggests that the critical phase in any abuse trial is the pretrial evidence gathering, and it is here that legal procedures are urgently needed. Above all, it seems essential that all contact between an alleged child victim and a therapist be videotaped in detail and be freely available to both sides during the trial. Without this minimum prerequisite, the only acceptable alternative must be an assumption that child witnesses have been "coached" to a specific end, and their evidence should be automatically discarded.

Another possibility — surely not acceptable — is that if children are assumed to know the difference between truth and falsehood, there must be a negative sanction to ensure truth. In earlier times, a judge would often refuse to admit the testimony of children unless they knew and accepted ideas of future supernatural rewards and punishments. In a more secular society, the only available sanction would be an extension of the law of perjury, regardless of age — surely a wholly unacceptable move. The extension of compulsory videotaped interrogation and therapy would be a very mild reform by comparison.

Paradoxically, the much-criticized McMartin case was characterized by some very professional and correct behavior on the part of the therapists. Particularly to the credit of the unit concerned — Children's Institute International (CII) — interactions between children and therapists were the subject of lengthy videos, which then permitted the court to assess the degree of coaching or manipulation allegedly used to create testimony. Also, it was the executive director of CII who stated concisely why evidence obtained from a therapeutic source was likely to be difficult to use in court.

She stated — even in late 1986 — that the bulk of the evidence against the McMartin defendants was true:

> I think the children's way of telling what they had to tell was based on very convincing information and there's very convincing medical evidence that backs up what the children were saying.

On the other hand, she was reluctant to claim that the testimony would stand up in court. "The procedures that we used were designed to provide treatment for the children that came here. They were not designed for a court of law" (interview on CBS "60 Minutes," 2 November 1986). If testimony is to be produced in a court of law, it must not be elucidated in a tainted atmosphere.

Specific procedural reforms can therefore be suggested, but the most significant impact of child abuse on the legal system is more abstract, yet far more vital. The panic of the last four years has served to illustrate at once the nature and the value of some core features of the Anglo-American legal system. Far from eroding these principles, the current "crime wave" has proved their enduring necessity.

During the debates on cases like McMartin, there have been repeated challenges to the most basic legal concepts, including the presumption of innocence. Clearly, it is necessary to reassert some fundamental principles: specific acts must be proven to have occurred at a particular time and place. A "pattern" of activity may be proposed (as in the RICO organized crime cases), but this must be made up of a series of individual proven acts. Two (or two thousand) unproven suspicions do not make a fact. It was during the very early years of the academic study of crime that scholars like Beccaria and Voltaire railed against the confusion between ill-fame and criminal conduct, especially when notoriety was founded on anonymous denunciations. Over two hundred years later, it seems that the principle must be reasserted. It is alarming to see the extension of anonymous denunciations, the use of hearsay, and the reduction of cross-examination presented as positive reforms in criminal justice; we seem to have progressed far toward pre-Beccarian theories.

This point is illustrated by interviews with the prosecutors in cases that have fallen apart, or with the "victims" and their families. The overwhelming impression was that the endless fantasies and contradictions of the child witnesses could never assail the almost metaphysical fact of molestation, which, having once been uttered, required neither proof nor corroboration. For example, the McMartin children testified to many impossibilities — about tunnels, flights to be molested in other cities, and so on. When challenged about these, prosecution figures repeatedly dismissed such problems as quibbles: "A very large number of children were molested at the school. I mean, I don't see that at this point whether one says it was fifty or a hundred or two hundred or three hundred, that really is beside the point at this point in time. Because what really is the issue is that children were molested at this school—whether there be two or whether it be a hundred " (Lael Rubin, interviewed on "60 Minutes," 2 November 1986).

A parent remarked to similar challenges: "Well, there's one issue that's avoided, and that's the overall evidence. You can't look at one specific instance and say we're going to analyze it by whether or not a plane ride occurred. . . . " Not to labor a point, the essence of the Anglo-American legal tradition is precisely to determine whether the plane ride did occur. That may well decide the value of a particular allegation. Cases have to be made on the strength of particular allegations, not "overwhelming suspicion."

The significance of this can be seen in the wave of cases in which charges have collapsed before or during trial. Acquittal does not in itself indicate prosecutorial incompetence, but what is distinctive about the current cases is that the failure of so many cases reveals very little evidence that was ever even marginally credible. More-over, the evidence depended entirely on the testimony of children. In terms of plausibility, the mass abuse cases recall both the witch trials and the Stalinist trials in the USSR. The reason why such outlandish charges have reached the courtroom is because prosecutors have too often relied on the general evidence that molestation occurred, with appallingly little attention to the need to prove specific incidents at particular times and places. This sort of detail may be difficult for child witnesses to recall but proof of specifics is essential if justice is to be preserved.

These principles—especially the presumption of innocence—have many implications. We may ignore the vulgar attacks on defense attorneys in child abuse cases for "defending Satan," but the presumption of guilt occurs in more reputable circles (Eberle, 1986). Throughout the process, the charge of child abuse is seen as so heinous as to preclude formality. Child protective services are entitled to take children into care on the suspicion of molestation, even when that rises from an anonymous letter or telephone call.

The issues here seem similar to those which in the 1970s led to an ever-widening range of defenses against improper and arbitrary psychiatric detention. Such detention was increasingly regarded as a form of punishment, necessitating legal safeguards. Surely, a similar argument can be applied to the removal of children from a family, an act "penal" in nature for both children and parents. Reforms needed in this area seem obvious: court process with legal representation prior to removal; a presumption of innocence on the part of parents; and the exclusion of anonymous information as grounds for proceeding.

In its present form, the system provides an ideal means of harassment or revenge against any individual with children or who associates with children. (The original McMartin charges came from a schizophrenic and thoroughly deranged woman whose subsequent behavior left no doubt of her character; yet the allegations formed the basis of police action.) The workings of child protection agencies seem as urgently in need of a "due process revolution" as ever the state mental hospitals were in the age of the *Snakepit* or the juvenile courts in the age of *Gault*. If the present series of judicial circuses promote a recognition of this fact, then they will at least have accomplished some good.

Conclusion

The recent track record of prosecuting child abuse can best be described as deeply disquieting. "Reforms" in this area must therefore be regarded with considerable suspicion. Even at present, it seems possible to be tried on charges invented by the mentally deranged and supported by the testimony of elaborately coached toddlers. With a little improvement, such as the elimination of cross-examination and the admission of hearsay, there would seem to be no remaining obstacles to the conviction of many "offenders" who currently remain immune. It is an appalling prospect. If procedures are indeed to be changed in this controversial area, then reform must come in full awareness of the troubling historical precedents and social context of our current panic. With this in mind, the central reforms for the next decade would appear to lie in the maintenance and expansion of defendant's rights and, above all, in a severe limitation on the therapist's role in the judicial process.

This does not mean that we accept the assertion of K. Morris (1980), the prosecutor in the Jordan, Minnesota, case that "this means we live in a society that does not believe children," but only that we live in a society that values the rule of law — even (perhaps especially) in those cases that inflame public passions. This principle was recognized by the Supreme Court in the 1988 case, *Coy v. Iowa*. Writing for a 6-2 majority, Justice Scalia struck down (as a violation of the Sixth amendment guarantee of the right to confront witnesses) a state law that permitted children to testify from behind a screen. He wrote, "It is difficult to imagine a more obvious or damaging violation of the defendant's right to face-to-face encounter" than the screen used in this case.

"(F)ace-to-face presence may, unfortunately, upset the truthful rape victim or abused child, but, by the same token, it may confound and undo the false accuser or reveal the child coached by a malevolent adult." He noted, "It is a truism that constitutional protections have costs."

We would argue that this is a step in the right direction—the preservation of the rule of law. But vigilance is still necessary to assure the protection of the rights of the falsely accused.

Sources

Beccaria, Cesare (1986). *Of Crimes and Punishments*. Edited and translated by David Young. Indianapolis: Hackett.

Brody, Jane E. (1987). Therapists Seek Causes of Child Molesting. *New York Times*. (January 13).

Bureau of Justice Statistics (1984). *Tracking Offenders: The Child Victim*. Washington, DC: Department of Justice.

Chambers, Marcia (1986). Numerous articles in *New York Times* on the McMartin case.

Cohen, Stan (1972). *Moral Panics and Folk Devils*. London: McGibbon and Kee.

Coleman, Lee (1986). Has a Child Been Molested? *Augustus*, 9 (14-17).

_____ (1984). *The Reign of Error*. Boston: Beacon.

Crewdson, John (1988). *By Silence Betrayed*. Boston: Little Brown.

Demos, John P. (1982). *Entertaining Satan*. New York: Oxford University Press, 1982.

DeYoung, Mary (1982). *The Sexual Victimization of Children*. Jefferson, NC: McFarland.

Eberle, Paul, and Shirley Eberle (1986). *The Politics of Child Abuse*. Secausus, NJ: Lyle Stuart.

Eliasoph, Nina (1986). Drive-in Morality, Child Abuse and the Media. *Socialist Review*, 90:7-32.

Ellison, Katherine W. and Robert Buckhout (1981). *Psychology and Criminal Justice*. New York: Harper and Row.

Ennew, Judith (1986). *The Sexual Exploitation of Children*. London: Polity.

Finkelhor, David (1984). *Child Sexual Abuse*. New York: Free Press.

Forward, Susan, and Craig Buck (1978). *Betrayal of Innocence*. New York: St. Martin's Press.

Fox, James A. and Jack Levin (1985). *Mass Murder: America's Growing Menace*. New York: Plenum.

Goldman, Ari (1985). 3 Cases Challenge Privilege of Talks with Clergy. *New York Times*, (August 27).

Goodman, Gail S. (1984). The Child Witness. Special issue of *Journal of Social Issues*, 40.

Hansen, Chadwick (1970). *Witchcraft at Salem*. London: Hutchinson.

Hawkins, Paula (1986). *Children at Risk*. Bethesda, MD: Adler & Adler.

Hertica, Michael A. (1987). Police Interviews of Sexually Abused Children. *FBI Law Enforcement Bulletin*, April 12-16.

Hollingsworth, Jan (1986). *Unspeakable Acts*. New York: Congdon and Weed.

Jenkins, Philip (1988). Myth and Murder: The Serial Killer Panic of 1983-85. *Criminal Justice Research Bulletin*, 3: 11.

Jenkins, Philip and Daniel Katkin (1986). From Salem to Jordan: A Historical Perspective on Child Abuse Trials. *Angustus*, 9:6, 14-24.

Johnson, Sandy (1985). False Reports of Child Abuse Endangering True Victims. *Centre Daily Times*, Pennsylvania, (December 18).

Kahaner, Larry (1988). *Cults That Kill*. New York: Warner.

Lindsey, Robert (1985). Boy's Responses at Sex Abuse Trial Underscore Legal Conflict. *New York Times*, (January27).

_____ (1984-86). Articles on McMartin case in *New York Times*.

_____ (1984). Sexual Abuse of Children Draws Experts' Increasing Concern Nationwide. *New York Times*, (April 4).

_____ (1984). Officials Cite Rise in Killers. *New York Times*, (January 22).

Linedecker, Clifford H. (1981). *Children in Chains*. New York: Everest.

Melton, Gary B.; Gerald P. Koocher; and Michael J. Saks (1983). *Children's Competence to Consent*. Beverly Hills, CA: Sage.

Miller, Jerome (1985). Child Abuse Hysteria. *Institutions Etc.*, (September).

NICCAN (1980). *Sexual Abuse of Children*. Washington, DC: Department of Health, Education, and Welfare.

Nathan, Debbie (1988). "Child Molester?" *Village Voice*, (August 2).

_____. (1987). Are These Women Child Molesters? *Village Voice*, (September 29).

Nelson, Barbara (1984). *Making an Issue of Child Abuse*. Chicago: University of Chicago Press.

Prosecuting Child Abuse (1988). Special issue of *Prosecutors' Perspective* (January 2).

Rush, Florence (1980). *The Best Kept Secret*. Englewood Cliffs, NJ: Prentice Hall.

Russell, Diana E. M. (1984). *Sexual Exploitation, Rape, Child Sexual Abuse and Sexual Harassment*. Beverly Hills, CA: Sage.

Scardino, Albert (1984). Experts Question Data About Missing Children. *New York Times*, (August 18).

Shipp, E. R. (1984-5). Articles on Jordan case in *New York Times*.

_____ (1984a). The Jeopardy of Children on the Stand. *New York Times*, (September 23).

_____ (1984b). Minnesota Townspeople Jolted by Sex Scandal with Children. *New York Times*, (September 6).

Spence, Gerry (1986). *Trial by Fire*. New York: Murrow.

Spiegel, Lawrence D. (1986). *A Question of Innocence*. New Jersey: Unicorn.

Stuart, Irving R. and Joanne G. Greer (1984). *Victims of Sexual Aggression*. New York: Van Nostrand.

Terry, Maury (1987). *The Ultimate Evil*. New York: Dolphin.

Ward, Elizabeth (1984). *Father-Daughter Rape*. London: Women's Press.

Whitcomb, Debra (1986). Prosecuting Child Sexual Abuse. *NIJ Reports*, (May).

_____ (1984). Prosecution of Child Sexual Abuse-Innovations in Practice. *NIJ Research in Brief*, (November).

Whitcomb, Debra, et al. (1984). *When the Victim Is a Child*. Report to National Institute of Justice.

Wolfe, David A., editor (1988). *Child Abuse*. Beverly Hills, CA: Sage.

Wrightsman, Lawrence (1987). *Psychology and the Legal System*. Belmont, CA: Wadsworth.

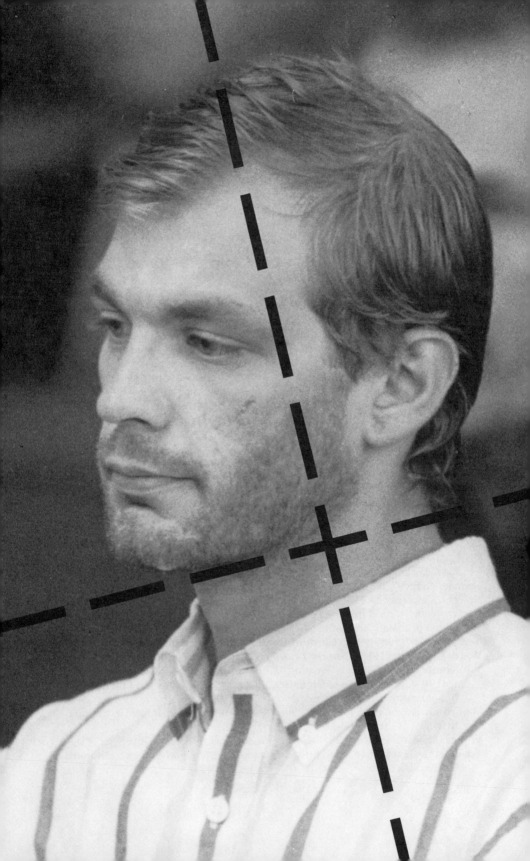

chapter 4

Myth and Murder
The Serial Killer Panic of 1983-85*

If we relied solely on the evidence of the mass media, we might well believe that every few years, a particular form of immoral or criminal behavior becomes so dangerous as almost to threaten the foundations of society. Some of these media scares or moral panics have been analyzed by social scientists, including the "dope-fiend" in his or her many guises (most recently, the crack enthusiast); the "sex-fiend" of the 1940s; and the white slavers of the Progressive era (Becker, 1963; Duster, 1970; Tappan, 1955).

These panics are important in their own right, for what they reveal about social concerns and prejudices—often based on xenophobia and anti-immigrant prejudice (Gusfield, 1981). Also, bureaucratic factors sometimes play a part when an agency promotes a panic in order to enhance its own power and prestige. An example often quoted in support of this theory is the view that Harry Anslinger and the Federal Bureau of Narcotics promoted a marijuana scare in the mid-1930s for just these ends. This particular theory has been disputed (Galliher and Walker, 1977), but a bureaucratic explanation for developments in criminal justice is widely accepted (Chambliss, 1976; Hagan, 1980).

---

*Adapted from Jenkins, P. (1988). *Criminal Justice Research Bulletin*, 3(11): 1–7.

Describing such issues as panics does not imply that they are without some real foundation. There were and are rapists and pimps, and drugs can cause immense damage to individuals and communities. However, such a "scare" period immensely inflates the perceived scale and prevalence of the original problem. In consequence, severe legislation is proposed which in turn fuels media fascination with the original issue.

The 1980s have been a particularly fruitful period for such media panics over crack, child sexual abuse, juvenile satanism, sex and violence in rock lyrics, and (in a rather different category) AIDS (Jenkins and Katkin, 1987). Each of these concerns had its particular stages of origin and growth, and deserves study. Here, the focus will be on the source of another modern panic—serial murder. This is a topic at least as old as Jack the Ripper and his contemporaries.[1] However, between 1983 and 1985, serial murder suddenly attained a major place in media attention, because of a number of specific incidents that we will examine.

It will be argued that the serial murder panic illustrates the way in which the media discover and publicize certain forms of criminality; but it also suggests certain important directions in contemporary views of the origins and causation of crime and deviancy.

Creating a Myth

Between late 1983 and mid-1985, serial murder was the topic of numerous stories in magazines and newspapers, as well as television programs. Most of these stressed the same group of themes, which can be conveniently summarized from a front-page *New York Times* article of January 1984 (Lindsey, 1984). The key concepts were that serial murder was an "epidemic" in contemporary America; that there were a great many such offenders active at any given time. The epidemic was new, and had grown immensely since the early 1970s; and that the new wave was qualitatively different from earlier occurrences, with more savage torture and mutilation of victims. Serial killers accounted for perhaps 20 percent of American murder victims, or some 4,000 a year, according to the accounts. It was also strongly implied that this appalling "disease" was largely a distinctive American problem.

According to Robert Lindsey, "the officials [quoted] assert that history offers nothing to compare with the spate of such murders that has occurred in the United States since the beginning of the 1970s." He quotes Robert O. Heck of the Justice Department for the view "that as many as 4,000 Americans a year, at least half of them under the age of 18, are murdered this way. He said he believes at least 35 such killers are now roaming the country." Many of their victims were to be found among the thousands of bodies that turned up each year unidentified and unexplained. As for the explanation of the new phenomenon, Lindsey quoted favorably the view that exposure to sexually explicit and sado-masochistic material tended to arouse the violent instincts of individuals already prone to extreme acts by an abusive upbringing.

The essentials of Lindsey's story were repeated extensively during 1984 and 1985, especially the estimate of 4,000 serial victims each year (Berger, 1984; Kagan, 1984). This was cited in a *Life* article, which placed particular emphasis in serial murder as an almost uniquely American problem, and in many leading newspapers and magazines (Darrach and Norris, 1984). In *Newsweek*, it was stated that "Law-enforcement experts say as many as two-thirds of the estimated five thousand unsolved homicides in the nation each year may be committed by serial murderers" ("Random Killers," 1984). Five thousand was also the estimate of an article in *Federal Probation* (Holmes and DeBurgos, 1985).

The "unsolved" category from the Uniform Crime Reports would be frequently quoted in this context. Sometimes, a story about the importance of serial murder would cite the number of "unsolved" killings (roughly 5,400) and then go on to estimate how many of these might be serial victims—anywhere from 10 percent to two-thirds, as here. Some stories, however, would simply state the number of "unsolved" homicides without comment. This left the reader with the impression that this *was* the serial victim category.

The visual media strongly reinforced the concept of a new and appalling menace, with each story—almost without fail—beginning with the estimate of 4,000 victims a year. Each of the major news magazines of the "60 Minutes" format had at least one story of this type, while an "HBO America Undercover" episode was a documentary focussing on three well-known serial killers of the last decade: Ted Bundy, Edmund Kemper, and Henry Lee Lucas. Interviews with all three were featured, as were harrowing (and controversial) reconstructions, using actors.

The Lucas Case

Lucas was the most frequent vehicle for a news story on this topic, which customarily referred to FBI sources for background on the scale of the murder wave. Lucas was a convicted murderer and arsonist, who began confessing numerous murders in the fall of 1983. By the end of the year, his alleged "kill" had exceeded three hundred, and he did much to shape the stereotype of the multiple murderer.

Lucas gave plausibility to the estimate of thousands of victims each year. His case also placed emphasis on the serial killer as a wanderer, a drifter who travelled between many states and regions. The roaming killer was much cited in 1983-85, especially when media attention was focused on the nationwide murder spree of Christopher Wilder in the spring of 1984 (eleven victims in six states). This suggested the need for new federal or interstate agencies to combat the menace, for which local agencies were clearly inadequate. Finally, Lucas and his partner Otis Toole claimed responsibility for the murder of a number of child victims including Adam Walsh, a notorious case that gave rise to national concern about missing children. This helped ensure publicity and linked the murder issue with other contemporary panics in which unsubstantiated figures were being severely misused (for child abuse as a comparable panic, see Eberle and Eberle, 1986; Jenkins and Katkin, 1986,1987).

During 1985, the Lucas case effectively collapsed, under investigation from a number of journalists. The estimate of three hundred murders had fallen to about ten, spread over several states. The basis of at least part of the panic had disappeared. It should be noted incidentally that the credence given to Lucas had never been universally shared, and the *New York Times* had published a very critical article as early as November 1983 (Joyce, 1983). However, the case continued to be a media event well into the following year.

To return to the substance of the issue: how accurate were the claims made by writers on serial murder in these years? The Lucas affair does not discredit the existence of a real phenomenon, and the media were drawing very heavily on the opinions of major official agencies, above all in the Justice Department. The figure of 4,000 seems to have been orthodox opinion, but none of these reports recognized how far such a view departed from established views on the nature of murder. That in itself certainly would not disprove the idea, but it is a statistic with remarkable consequences. Each year (it appears), one American murder in five is committed by a serial killer like Ted Bundy or John Wayne Gacy — perhaps forty thousand victims between 1976 and 1986. If this is correct, then clearly our views of violent crime need to be radically reformed. So would our policies and funding priorities in law enforcement. This was also an important argument for a growing federal role in law enforcement, as only national coordination could prevent the depredations of a Wilder or a Lucas.

The Reality of Serial Murder

There are a number of questions about this "murder wave" that must be handled separately. That this type of crime had become much more common is not in dispute. However, its numerical impact on the murder statistics may be challenged. Finally, how may this sudden concern about serial murder be explained, especially when reports of notorious multiple murder cases were no more frequent in 1983 than five or ten years previously?

In studying the reality of serial murder, there are a number of important problems. There is a sizeable literature on multiple murder, but it has important gaps and discontinuities. We have a distinguished psychiatric literature on the causation of this type of offense, and there is a superb and accessible synthesis of theories and typologies (Nettler, 1982; see Abrahamsen, 1945, 1960, 1973; Lunde, 1976; Toch, 1969). We have many case-studies of killers, some of the *True Crime* type, but many rising above it to real insight; but the real lack is in systematic or "epidemiological" studies of the phenomenon. Without such a broad survey, it is impossible to understand changes in the frequency or distribution of serial murder. Only in 1985 did a scholarly work of this nature appear (Fox and Levin, 1985) and even it made no attempt to compare the frequency of serial murder reports in the period studied (1974-79) with earlier periods (for the growing academic interest in the topic, see Egger, 1984,1986; Vetter and Rieber, 1986; Hickey, 1986; Leyton, 1986).

The present study is based on secondary studies of serial killers, together with a search of the *New York Times* since 1960. Only serial murder cases are noted, rather than mass murderers, and killing for profit or political motive has been excluded—a decision that would by no means be accepted by all students of the topic. Such exclusions are sometimes difficult, as in the case of Joseph Paul Franklin, reported in 1984 as a suspect in fifteen murders in eight states between 1977 and 1980. This would appear to be a "serial" case, but there is strong evidence that Franklin acted out of his political beliefs as a white supremacist who used violence against biracial couples. He was thus excluded from the present study, as were black racists Mark Essex and the "Zebra" gang (for works consulted, see footnote 2. Other books used include Abrahamsen, 1985; Godwin, 1978; Keyes, 1986; Klausner, 1981;

Lunde, 1976; Nettler, 1982; Olsen, 1983; Wilson, 1972; Wilson and Seaman, 1983; Caute and Odell, 1979).

There are obvious problems in using news media as sources for determining the frequency or scale of serial murder. The nature and quality of reporting is likely to change over the years, while newspapers concentrate on what is likely to interest a local readership. From its prominence in the media, one might well think that the "Son of Sam" case of 1976-77 was uniquely serious or remarkable. In fact, the affair received so much attention chiefly because it occurred in the New York area, and thus near the headquarters of so many news organizations. This geographical bias might lead to the under-representation of offenses occurring in areas of the country that would be considered remote by the important news media; and our knowledge of serial murder would be slanted.

On the other hand, it is possible to defend the view that a media search is likely to produce a reasonably accurate list, at least of extreme serial offenders who killed (say) ten or more victims. Throughout the century, there has been intense media attention on any such case, suggesting that public interest is steady, if not precisely constant from decade to decade. In the 1920s and 1930s, massive publicity was devoted to the cases of American serial killers like Albert Fish, Earle Nelson, Joe Ball, Carl Panzram and Gordon Stewart Northcott. In fact, coverage was more intense than for any comparable modern case, because of the greater rarity of the offense in that era. It is not claimed that the present study can be truly comprehensive, but it is also unlikely that many cases have been omitted. The combination of newspaper records and secondary accounts is likely to yield a sizeable majority of the serial murder cases that actually occurred.

Assessing the scale of the problem and calculating a figure for the victims of serial murder are also real problems. In part, this is because serial offenders remain such a tiny proportion of the population that statistical comparisons are of little use. We are often dependent on the offenders themselves for estimates of their "kill," the number of victims. False confessions sometimes appear to be part of the psychological make-up of such criminals.

Law enforcement agencies themselves play a vital part in shaping our perceptions here, and this may work in different cases either to swell or diminish the alleged total of victims. In the late 1960s, for example, the still-anonymous "Zodiac" killed several people in northern California. Recently, a journalist published a well-argued case for believing that the "Zodiac" attacks have continued into the present decade, with the consequence of almost fifty deaths (Graysmith, 1987). If this view is correct, the case would be a classic example of "linkage blindness"—the failure to perceive connections between incidents. On the other hand, bureaucratic self-interest might have the opposite effect, as there is so much pressure to avoid having uncleared cases—especially such glaring and publicized crimes. Law enforcement agencies wish to clear as many murders as possible as "solved" even if this means rather tenuous attributions of the crimes to currently notorious figures.

We are rarely in as reliable a position to estimate the number of victims as in the John Wayne Gacy case, where almost thirty bodies were found in his house. However, there are problems in as apparently clear a case. In 1985, extensive remains were found at the California home of Leonard Lake, but the conclusions of the forensic investigation were variously interpreted. Lake thus appeared to be connected with the murders of somewhere between six and thirty people—hardly precise figures. Lake has been included in the following study of extreme multiple murderers, but subsequent research may well prove this to be incorrect.

But even when these problems are taken into account, there is strong evidence for a dramatic increase in the scale and prevalence of serial murder in the United States since the end of the 1960s. This can be seen if we compare cases between 1950 and 1970 with those since 1971. Between 1950 and 1970, there were only two cases in the United States where a serial murderer was definitely associated with over ten victims (these were Charlie Starkweather in 1958 and the "Boston Strangler" case of 1962-64). There were other celebrated serial cases, but these tended to involve at most eight or nine victims. This was true of the cases of John Norman Collins, Melvin Rees, the notorious Manson "family," and probably Ed Gein. No serial case in this era involved over thirteen victims (for the celebrated murder cases of the 1950s and 1960s, see for example Allen, 1976; Bugliosi and Gentry, 1974; Frank, 1967; Freeman, 1955; Godwin, 1978; Keyes, 1977; Sanders, 1972; Wilson and Seaman, 1983; Graysmith, 1987).

This is in sharp contrast with the years between 1971 and 1987. There have been at least nine cases where offenders were generally credited with over twenty victims in this period (see footnote 2). The number of extremely "successful" serial killers rises still further if we include the very controversial case of Wayne Williams, blamed by authorities for many of the Atlanta child murders of 1979-81 (though see Detlinger and Prugh, 1983). There were also twenty-eight cases where people are believed to have killed between ten and twenty victims in the same period. We therefore have a total of thirty-seven cases, involving thirty-nine individuals (in at least two cases, the crimes were committed by pairs of killers).

The Justice Department appears to have underestimated the number of active serial killers. A 1983 study claimed that since 1973, there had been at least thirty individuals who had killed six or more victims serially. The present author would put the figure at well over forty for that same decade. However, while understating the number of killers, the same study appears to have grossly exaggerated the number of their victims. A subsequent Justice Department estimate gives a figure of thirty-five serial murderers active at any one time. Let us assume that this is correct. It is rare for such an offender to kill more than six victims in any particular year, which suggests that the real annual total for serial victims is unlikely to exceed three hundred, and may well be under two hundred. Even that may be far too many. In the present study, seventy-one cases were found where six or more people were killed serially between 1971 and 1987. Certainly, cases have escaped attention; but these seventy-one cases account for only 950-1000 victims in all—or about 50 to 60 each year.

There are occasional cases where a killer engages in a rampage—Paul Knowles in 1974, Christopher Wilder in 1984—but these usually attract major law enforcement attention, and are soon stopped. In other words, someone who kills more than ten or so people in a single year is unlikely to continue his career for more than that one year.

Even if our estimate for the number of active killers is too small, as it may be, then serial murder might account for at most three or four hundred victims each year. This is a terrible figure, but it is far short of the much-quoted "four thousand." In other words, even during a wave of serial murder like the last seventeen years, this type of crime accounts for perhaps 2 or 3 percent of American homicides, rather than the 20 percent suggested in 1984. Multiple murder remains an extreme fringe of American crime.

Distribution of Multiple Murder

Other conclusions can be drawn about serial murder. If we take extreme multiple murders—those credited with at least ten victims—we find that, generally, they do not "roam." James Fox and Jack Levin correctly note that such killers tend to act fairly close to home, often in or around one city, and this view can be confirmed from the cases listed here. Ted Bundy killed in four states, but this was unusual. Of the thirty-nine killers in our sample, only ten killed in more than one state. Two (Wilder and Knowles) went on short-lived "murder sprees," and three were active in

neighboring states. The stereotype of "roaming killer" applies best
to the case of William Christensen, who was accused in 1985 of
fifteen murders in the northeastern United States and in Canada.
A much more common pattern is the killer who finds and kills most
of his victims in one city, or even a small area of that city — from
East London in the 1880s to the Sunset Strip in the 1970s.

Generally, killers do not "roam" — or at least, not far from their
home base. Moreover, it is worth stressing that serial murder is a
regional problem rather than a national one. Of the thirty-seven
cases, fifteen were active almost entirely in California; four more
killed their victims in the states of California, Washington, and
Oregon. Extreme multiple murder appears to be found
overwhelmingly in the Pacific states, a picture that is strengthened
by the inclusion of Robert Hansen of Alaska (seventeen victims).
(Not included in this study is British Columbia's Clifford Olson.)

Elsewhere, we find two cases each in Florida, Texas, and Illinois.
The East Coast is severely under-represented, with New York's
Calvin Jackson a rare exception. In this area, there are of course
serial cases, but they rarely achieve the "success" of their western
counterparts. In populous states like Pennsylvania, serial killer
activity appears to be rare in the period, with no known cases of
an extreme offender claiming ten or more victims.

It is true that serial murder is much more prevalent in the United
States than in comparably advanced European countries. In Great
Britain, for example, there have only been four examples since 1960
where a killer claimed over ten victims (Jenkins, forthcoming). In
other European countries, there have certainly been waves of
notorious serial murder cases, as in Germany of the 1920s and
1930s. However, such incidents have been much rarer since 1950.[3]
Cases like those of Kemper or Bundy have been rare in the recent
history of Europe — but they have been common only in certain
areas of the United States.

It is beyond the scope of the present paper to attempt an
explanation of this curious distribution. It should be noted though
that the abundance of extreme serial cases in the West does not
correspond closely to the distribution of "normal" murder in the
United States. The frequency of murder in the South has often been
discussed in the literature on violent subcultures; but the Pacific
Northwest has not usually been seen as possessing such a culture
(Wolfgang and Ferracuti, 1967). Frontier theories would also fail
to explain why Seattle rather than Denver or Tucson should appear
to be so productive of such killers. The problem serves to remind
us of the rudimentary state of our knowledge about serial murder.

However, the concentration of such cases in the West represents a "wave" with close historical parallels; and this reminds us that serial murder on this scale is by no means an American peculiarity, as was so often claimed in 1983 and 1984. The "wave" of the 1970s bears very close resemblances to the string of German serial cases of the 1920s and 1930s mentioned above. There were a number of appalling murder cases, in some of which offenders claimed as many as fifty or more victims. These cases were associated with extreme perversion—cannibalism, rape, necrophilia, mutilation. Bruno Ludke, for example, is believed to have killed eighty-five women between 1928 and 1943, continuing to operate even under the Nazi police state (Wilson and Pitman, 1962). Serial murder is neither new nor distinctively American.

Explaining a Panic

Serial murder thus has to be placed into context. It may well be a growing menace, and steps to curb it should be vigorously encouraged. However, the official view of the problem in recent years has been badly flawed. The reasons for misinterpretation are complex, and include an element of pure accident. Lucas's confessions tended to cause both media and law enforcement agencies to lose perspective in examining the topic. The way in which a "murder epidemic" was created is an illuminating example of the relationship between media and official agencies. Also required is an explanation of why Lucas's statements met with the credulity they did.

One consistent theme in the media coverage of 1983-85 was the misuse of Uniform Crime Reports (UCR) murder data, by both experts and lay people alike. Put simply, the argument suggests that motiveless murders have risen dramatically in recent years. The UCR stated that in 1966, there were 11,000 murders in the United States. Of these, 644 (5.9%) involved no apparent motive. In 1982, there were 23,000 murders, but the number of "motive-less" killings was now 4,118 (17.8%) the figure quoted by Lindsey. By 1984, this "motiveless" category had risen to 22 percent. It has been suggested that the increase represents "serial" activity, and that serial killers may be claiming thousands of lives every year in the United States alone. It may even be that the figure for recorded murders (some 20,000 a year) actually understates the total, as many victims are not proven to have been murdered until many years later. The total of 4,000 serial victims annually therefore seemed plausible. Other sources took the "unsolved" figure from UCR statistics. In 1983, 28 percent of murders fell into this category.

Both categories—unsolved and motiveless—require serious qualification, based on an understanding of how UCR data are compiled by individual police departments. When a murder occurs, the police will file a UCR report, with the deadline being the first five days of the month after the crime is reported. They also submit a supplementary homicide report, addressing topics like characteristics of the victim and offender; weapon; relationship of victim to offender; circumstances surrounding death; and so on. "Offenders" can be single, multiple, or unknown. At this early stage, the police might well know neither the offender, a motive, nor the exact circumstances of the death. All these would thus be recorded as unknown.

Weeks or months later, the situation might well change, and the correct procedure would be for the department to submit a new report to amend the first. Here though there is enormous room for cutting corners. The death has been reported, and whether a further correction is submitted depends on many factors. A conscientious officer in a professional department with an efficient record system would very probably notify the reporting center that the murder was no longer "unsolved" or "motiveless" especially in an area where murder was a rare crime. Other officers in other departments might well feel that they have more important things to do than to submit a revised version of a form they have already completed. This would in fact represent a third form on a single case.

The chance of follow-up information being supplied will depend on a number of factors: the frequency of murder in the community; the importance given to record-keeping by a particular chief or supervisor; the organizational structure of the department (for instance, whether records and data are the responsibility of a full-time unit or of an individual); and the professional standards of the department. The vast majority of departments are likely to record the simple fact of a murder being committed; only some will provide the results of subsequent investigations, though these are crucial to developing any kind of national statistical profile of American homicide.

Murders depicted in the UCR as having a suspect and motive are likely to be those where there is a very clear-cut situation with the offender immediately identified. Any delay, and it is likely to fall into the limbo of "motiveless" crimes. If a suspect is not found within the same month as the murder, then the case is likely to be entered as "no suspect," and to remain so despite subsequent events. In this case, it is even likely that the later in the month a particular murder takes place, the more likely it is to be described as 'motiveless" or lacking a suspect.

Even when no suspect is ever found, it does not necessarily mean that a serial killer is to blame. Chicago, for example, has had over a thousand unsolved Mob murders in the last half-century, and Miami is contributing its quota to this category. Put another way, the remarkable fact about the UCR is the number of murders *with* an immediate motive and suspect. As to the sharp rise in the number of murders lacking this information, a variety of explanations is possible. These include an increase in homicides arising from narcotics trafficking and gang activities, and perhaps deaths resulting from an increase in violent robberies. Although some of the murders indeed indicate serial activity, this is far less than has been suggested.

The nature of the increase in homicides by strangers is suggested by a survey of Bridgeport, Connecticut, during 1986, though it is not claimed that this city is in any sense typical. There were forty-one known homicides during the year, including seven that remained open by the start of 1987. The murder rate had risen since the mid-1970s, but the most dramatic change had come in the increase in homicides outside the immediate family circle. Intrafamily homicide accounted for over 60 percent of murders in 1976, only 10 percent by 1986. The increase in murders by strangers or unknown parties was a striking fact, and there was strong evidence that this was explained in large part by the drug trade, specifically in cocaine. Drug deals were believed to account for thirteen of the cases where motives were known, while drugs were presumed to explain several of the open cases (Johnson, 1987).

To equate either "motiveless" or "unsolved" crimes with the number of serial victims is wholly to misunderstand the nature and composition of that much-criticized set of data. It is remarkable that some (by no means all) of the Justice Department sources so frequently quoted tended to continue this confusion, with the results we have witnessed.

As the Justice Department was the source of so much of the information and interpretation about serial murder during 1983-85, it is necessary to ask exactly what was the nature of their interest in the topic. In order to understand the context, it should be recalled that the 1983 work on serial murder became a justification for a new center for the study of violent crime at the FBI Academy in Quantico, VA, with a new Violent Criminal Apprehension Program (VICAP). In the previous two years, attempts to expand FBI databanks had met serious challenges, both from civil libertarians and from local law enforcement agencies. Similar opposition might well have been expected to the new federal interest in violent criminals.

In practice, the serial killer panic helped to justify the new proposals, and the creation of a National Center for the Analysis of Violent Crime (NCAVC) was announced by President Reagan in June 1984, with an explicit focus on "repeat killers" (Michaud, 1986). Early NCAVC publicity emphasized how frequently serial crimes "transcend jurisdictional boundaries," while serial murderers were characteristically "highly transient criminals" (NCAVC, 1986). However, it was mentioned that in the future, the new databank would expand its attention—to "rape, child molestation, arson and bombing" (NCAVC, 1986). Serial murder thus provided a wedge for an expansion of the federal role in law enforcement intelligence.

It would be the worst sort of conspiracy theory to claim that the Justice Department created or promoted the post-Lucas murder panic. This is especially true when some FBI officials placed the estimated number of serial victims at several hundred rather than several thousand, contradicting what was quickly becoming orthodoxy. But it was in the interests of the agencies and spokesmen concerned to emphasize certain themes that did in fact emerge strongly in media coverage: the sudden and extreme danger posed by a murder wave, and above all, the national and interstate character of the "new" serial killers. Henry Lee Lucas—at least as he portrayed himself—was tailor-made for such a campaign. The media should thus be criticized for failing to recognize this element of self-interest, as well as for their striking misuse of UCR data.

Finally, it can be predicted with some probability that the next three or four years may well see an apparent upsurge in serial killer activity, a still worse "murder wave." The VICAP report forms are lengthy and detailed documents, with over 180 separate questions on each particular case. Once they begin to be collated, some points of similarity between geographically separated cases are bound to be noted, and there will certainly be speculation about links. Unless care is taken, dozens or even hundreds of murders will be blamed on unknown hypothetical killers. The "panic" is likely to be self-sustaining. There are already warning signs to this effect from the British experience with that country's equivalent of VICAP, the Home Office Large Major Enquiry System, or HOLMES. In the last two years, use of this system has produced claims of the existence of hypothetical serial child-murderers, by the linkage of what appear to have been very dissimilar cases. And the one ensuing arrest led to a rapid and embarrassing realization that at least one string of cases was in fact unrelated (Ballantyne, 1987).

Apart from the bureaucratic interests involved, the new emphasis on serial murder also suggests a shift in popular attitudes to crime and criminals. These attitudes have changed dramatically in the last two decades, and the serial killer represents an extreme image of the newer and more conservative stereotype of the offender. The central element in the new concepts can perhaps be described as a quest for evil, a need to understand crime in terms of objective evil. Relativist ethics and environmental theories of causation are both discounted.

In the 1960s, environmental theories were widely held among the educated—though of course, by no means universally. An understanding of the sociology of crime and justice did much to condition the attitudes of the Warren and early Burger Supreme Courts on issues such as capital punishment or defendants' rights. Environmental determinism undermined concepts of absolute responsibility, while rehabilitation was seen as an appropriate response for deviancy. "Evil" fitted poorly with such an intellectual climate.

By the late 1970s, ideas had changed considerably, though it is always a temptation to regard the writings of a few experts as indicating universal trends. Broadly, though, scholars of criminality tended to place more emphasis on the offender as a rational, responsible creature who could be deterred by the certainty and scale of punishment (Wilson and Herrnstein, 1985). Retribution was therefore more suitable than rehabilitation, which was seen as a failed goal. In the new political agenda, criminals were less victims of society than ruthless predators upon it. Solutions to crime were to be found in the justice system, rather than in social or family policy. In the more conservative tone of the 1980s, there was a series of cases where offenders appeared to be not only predators but creatures of extreme, pathological evil. Apart from the serial killers, there was concern about the mass sexual abuse of children, and even suggestions that some such offenses might be connected to devil-worship (Eberle and Eberle, 1986). A recent book entitled *The Ultimate Evil* suggests that a satanic cult was responsible for numerous serial murders, including those of the Manson family and "Son of Sam" (Terry, 1987).

If ever a moral panic was personified in one individual, then the concerns of the Reagan era were focused in the case of Richard Ramirez. In September 1985, he was arrested as a suspect in sixty-eight offenses, including fourteen murders attributed to the "Night Stalker" over the previous year. The allegations were those of a classic serial murder case, while Ramirez himself seemed to be an archetypal "external enemy"—a drifter accused of brutal sexual violence against women. In court, he made apparently satanic references—a horned hand, and a cry of "Hail Satan!" The attention paid to this case—and the continuing Green River case in Seattle—did much to prevent any public doubt that might have arisen as the Lucas case fell apart in the following month or two.

Perhaps inevitably, the accounts of the collapse of many of Lucas's claims in late 1985 received nothing like the national attention of his initial boasts. Probably the American public will long recall the transparent myth that "serial killers account for one-fifth of all murder victims in the United States." The myth is important because it confirms a traditional notion of an overwhelming threat by lethal predators and because it distracts attention away from the reality of most homicide—as an act committed between relatives or acquaintances, often in a domestic setting. Crime is thus transformed from the problem of individuals and groups in a particular environment to a war fought by semi-human monsters against society.

Social scientists often find cause to bemoan the myths portrayed by the media, especially in the area of crime and justice. The tendency is to blame sensationalist editors and journalists, but the current study of serial murder suggests a much more complex explanation. There was sensationalism, and also manipulation of the media by official agencies; but the media "panic" also resulted from a more subtle and general shift in public attitudes. The credulity apparent from reactions to the Lucas case is indicative of what has been described here as a "quest of evil," and this attitude forms the context of both public and official responses to a variety of legal and social issues in contemporary America. Understanding this attitude is an essential prerequisite to approaching the political debate over crime, law, and order in the 1980s.

Conclusion

This study has presented conclusions that might seem to be contradictory. On the one hand, it has been suggested that serial murder is not as serious a problem as has been claimed; but at the same time, the list presented here of serial killers active in recent years is, I believe, more comprehensive than any now in print (compare Leyton, 1986; Brooks et al., 1987). Paradoxically, this list also suggests that the Justice Department may actually have underestimated some of the figures on which recent debate was based. In other words, this article is emphatically not an attempt to trivialize or wish away the problem of serial murder, still less to carp at the schemes proposed to combat this harrowing type of offense. If nothing else, the recent concern (or panic) has fostered debate; persuaded agencies to establish better lines of mutual communication; and helped to create in NCAVC the nucleus of what may come to be an invaluable resource for law enforcement.

If so much good has been produced, why then should we be concerned about the inaccuracies so often heard about serial murder? Put in an extreme way, it may be asked whether the misstatements matter if only one life is saved as a result of the new networks of communication and intelligence. But there are reasons why we should demand the highest standards of accuracy in the portrait of crime that is presented to the public both by law enforcement professionals and by academic researchers in this area—one that is quite literally a matter of life and death. Most clearly, there is the question of resources and the political priorities given to different areas. For example, it might be that a focus on serial murder might have an impact on this type of homicide, here estimated as accounting for perhaps two or three percent of homicides annually. It might also be that the homicide rate could be reduced still more dramatically by devoting the same resources to (for example) drug interdiction or anti-gang activities. To put the problem in proportion: the total number of victims of serial murder across the United States in a particular year is considerably less than the annual total of homicide victims in Detroit alone. Should resources and activity be directed to a perceived national problem, or might they be better employed in a highly focussed way in one or two major metropolitan areas?

In other words, the problem of serial murder raises many of the perennial issues of criminal justice: public perceptions of the threat of crime as opposed to the very different reality; the tendency of agencies to direct resources to issues in the public view; and the role of the media in forming public perceptions of the crime problem. That much of the recent debate was based on misinformation will come as no surprise to anyone familiar with journalistic treatments of many problems in the area of crime and justice. But where this debate was different was in the extreme character of those inaccuracies. This indicates many inadequacies in our knowledge of the topic and the previous lack of a systematic literature—a gap that is now being filled by work of researchers like Leyton, Egger or Fox and Levin. Finally, serial murder is emerging as a field of very reputable scholarship. With this new foundation, we may reasonably hope that serial murder will not readily form the basis for another panic like that of the early 1980s. But that other scares of this sort will occur on other issues appears quite inevitable.

Notes

[1] In this article, I have taken what now appears to be the standard United States definition of serial murder, as several killings committed over a period of time. It should be noted that there are problems with this. Opinions differ on how frequently a person must kill to be counted in this category (four and six victims have both been suggested). Also, the "period of time" remains undefined. If someone kills repeatedly over some hours, this is a mass murder. If days elapse, then it might be seen as a "serial" offense, though the exact dividing line is not clear. Finally, there is the problem of an individual committing one murder, and then another mass killing at a later date. Does he become a serial killer?

These points may appear pedantic, but they are important in developing a taxonomy of multiple murderers. It might be suggested that a mass murderer like Richard Speck was no different behaviorally or psychologically from a serial lust-murderer. It merely happened that he found himself with the opportunity to carry out so many of his fantasies at one place and time. Generally, though, there are substantial differences between mass killers like James Huberty and Patrick Sherrill and their serial counterparts, so the distinction is a useful one.

[2] Killers alleged to have claimed twenty or more victims are:

Name	Source
Ted Bundy	(Rule, 1980; Michaud and Aynesworth, 1983)
Dean Corll/Elmer Henley	(Olsen, 1974)
Juan Corona*	(Kidder, 1974)
Bruce Davis	
John Wayne Gacy	(Sullivan and Maiken, 1983; Cahill, 1986)
Donald Harvey	
Patrick Kearney*	(Godwin, 1978)
Gerald Stano	
"Green River Killer"	
Wayne Williams	(Detlinger and Prugh, 1983)

Those associated with between ten and twenty killings are:

Kenneth Bianchi/	
Angelo Buono*	(O'Brien, 1983; Schwartz, 1982)
William Bonin*	
William Christensen	
David J. Carpenter*	
Douglas D. Clark*	
Carroll Cole	
Robert Diaz*	
Larry Eyler	
Gerald Gallego	
Robert Hansen	
Frederick Hodge	
Calvin Jackson	(Godwin, 1978)
Edmund Kemper*	(Lunde, 1967; Cheney, 1976)
Paul Knowles	(Fawkes, 1978)
Randy Kraft*	
Leonard Lake*	
Bobby Joe Long*	
Henry Lee Lucas	
Bobby Joe Maxwell*	
Sherman McCrary	
Herbert Mullin*	(Lunde and Morgan, 1974)
Marcus Nisby*	
Richard Ramirez*	
Daniel Lee Siebert	
Coral Watts	

Christopher Wilder
Randall Woodfield   (Stack, 1984)
"South Side Slayer"*

(Asterisks denote individuals chiefly active in California)

3   Between 1920 and 1940, there were five particularly celebrated serial murder
    cases in Germany—those of Fritz Haarman, Peter Kurten, Adolf Seefeld, Karl
    Denke and Bruno Ludke. Since 1950, there have only been two comparable cases
    in Germany, those of Rudolf Pleil and Heinrich Pomerencke.

Sources

Abrahamsen, D. (1985). *Confessions of Son of Sam*. Columbia U.P.

_____ (1973). *The Murdering Mind*. New York: Harper & Row.

_____ (1960). *The Psychology of Crime*. Columbia U.P.

_____ (1945). *Crime and the Human Mind*. Columbia U.P.

Allen, W. (1976). *Starkweather: The Story of a Mass Murderer*. Boston: Houghton Mifflin.

Ballantyne, Aileen (1987). Man Released in Child Deaths Inquiry. *Guardian*, (London) 1 May.

Becker, Howard (1963). *Outsiders*. New York: Free Press.

Berger, Joseph (1984). Traits shared by mass killers remain unknown to experts. *New York Times*, (August 27).

Brooks, Pierce R., Michael J. Devine, Terence J. Green, Barbara L. Hart and Merlyn D. Moore (1987). Serial Murder: A Criminal Justice Response. *Police Chief*, 54:37-45.

Bugliosi, Vincent and Curt Gentry (1974). *Helter Skelter*. New York: W.W. Norton.

Cahill, Tim (1986). *Buried Dreams: Inside the Mind of a Serial Killer*. New York: Bantam.

Capote, Truman (1965). *In Cold Blood*. New York: Random House.

Caute, J. H. and Robin Odell (1979). *The Murderers' Who's Who*. London: Pan.

Chambliss, W. (1976). The State and Criminal Law. In W. Chambliss and M. Mankoff, *Whose Law What Order?* New York: John Wiley.

Cheney, Margaret (1976). *The Coed Killer*. New York: Walker.

Darrach, Brad and Joel Norris (1984). An American Tragedy. *Life*.

Detlinger, Chet and Jeff Prugh (1983). *The List*. Atlanta: Philmay Enterprise.

Duster, Troy (1970). *The Legislation of Morality*. New York: Free Press.

Eberle, Paul and Shirley Eberle (1986). *The Politics of Child Abuse*. Secaucus: Lyle Stuart.

Egger, Steven A. (1986). Utility of Case Study Approach to Serial Murder Research. Paper presented to ASC, Atlanta, GA, (November).

_____ (1984). A Working Definition of Serial Murder. *Journal of Police Science and Administration*, 12(3):348-357.

Fawkes, Sandy (1978). *Killing Time*. London: Hamlyn.

Fox, James A. and Jack Levin (1985). *Mass Murder: America's Growing Menace*. New York: Plenum.

Frank, Gerold (1967). *The Boston Strangler*. London: Pan.

Freeman, Lucy (1955). *Before I Kill More*. New York: Pocket.

Galliher, John and A. Walker (1977). The Puzzle of the Social Origins of the Marijuana Tax Act. *Social Problems*, 24:367-376.

Gardiner, Muriel (1976). *The Deadly Innocents*. New York: Basic.

Gelb, Barbara (1975). *On the Track of Murder*. New York: William Morrow.

Godwin, John (1978). *Murder USA*. New York: Ballantine.

Graysmith, Robert (1987). *Zodiac*. New York: Berkley.

Gusfield, Joseph (1981). *The Culture of Public Problems*. Chicago U.P.

Hagan, John (1980). The Legislation of Crime and Delinquency. *Law and Society Review*, 3:603-628.

Hazelwood, Robert and John E. Douglas (1980). The Lust Murderer. *FBI Law Enforcement Bulletin*, 49(4):18-22.

Hickey, Eric W. (1986). The Etiology of Victimization in Serial Murder. Paper presented to ASC, Atlanta, GA, (November).

Hillberry, Conrad (1987). *Luke Karamazov*. Detroit: Wayne State University Press.

Holmes, Ronald M. and James DeBurgos (1985). Profiles in Terror. *Federal Probation*, 49(3):29-34.

Jenkins, Philip (forthcoming). Serial Murder in England 1940-1985. *Journal of Criminal Justice*.

Jenkins, Philip and Daniel Katkin (1987). Benefit of Law. Paper presented to the American Society of Criminology, Montreal, (November).

_____ (1986). From Salem to Jordan. *Augustus*, 9(6):14-24.

Johnson, Dirk (1987). Bridgeport Hit by Sharp Rise in Murder Rate. *New York Times*, (January 26).

Joyce, Fay S. (1983). Two Suspects' Stories of Killings Culled. *New York Times*, (November 4).

Kagan, Dan (1984). Serial Murderers. *OMNI*.

Keyes, Daniel (1986). *Unveiling Claudia*. New York: Bantam.

Keyes, Edward (1977). *The Michigan Murders*. London: New English Library.

Kidder, Tracy (1974). *The Road to Yuba City*. New York: Doubleday.

Klausner, Lawrence D. (1981). *Son of Sam*. New York: McGraw-Hill.

Leyton, Elliott (1986). *Compulsive Killers*. New York University Press.

Lindsey, Philip (1958). *The Mainspring of Murder*. London: John Long.

Lindsey, Robert (1984). Officials Cite a Rise in Killers Who Roam US for Victims. *New York Times*, (January 22).

Lunde, D.T. (1976). *Murder and Madness*. New York: W.W. Norton.

Lunde, D. T. and Jefferson Morgan (1980). *The Die Song*. New York: W.W. Norton.

Lundsgaarde, Henry P. (1977). *Murder in Space City*. New York: OUP.

McIntyre, Tommy (forthcoming). *A Wolf in Sheep's Clothing*. Detroit: Wayne State University Press.

Michaud, S. G. and H. Aynesworth (1986). The FBI's New Psyche Squad. *New York Times Magazine*, (October 26).

_____ (1983). *The Only Living Witness*. New York: Simon and Schuster.

NCAVC (1986). The National Center for the Analysis of Violent Crime. Behavioral Science Services, FBI Academy, Quantico, VA ("revised 4/7/86").

Nash, Jay Robert (1973). *Bloodletters and Bad Men*. New York: M. Evans & Co.

Nettler, Gwynn (1984). *Explaining Crime*. 3rd ed. New York: McGraw-Hill.

_____ (1982). *Killing One Another*. Cincinnati: Anderson.

Newman, G. (1979). *Understanding Violence*. Philadelphia: Lippincott.

O'Brien, Darcy (1985). *Two of a Kind*. New York: New American Library.

Olsen, Jack (1983). *Son: A Psychopath and His Victims*. New York: Dell.
_____ (1974). *The Man with the Candy*. New York: Simon and Schuster.
The Random Killers (1984). *Newsweek*, (November 26).
Rule, Ann (1980). *The Stranger Beside Me*. New York: NAL.
Sanders, Ed (1972). *The Family*. London: Hart-Davis.
Schreiber, Flora Rheta (1984). *The Shoemaker: Anatomy of a Psychotic*.
    New York: Signet.
Schwarz, Ted (1982). *The Hillside Strangler*. New York: Signet.
Stack, Andy (1984). *The 15 Killer*. New York: Signet.
Sullivan, Terry and Peter T. Maiken (1983). *Killer Clown: The John Wayne
    Gary Murders*. New York: Grosset and Dunlap.
Tappan, Paul (1955). Some Myths About the Sex Offender. *Federal
    Probation*, 19:1-12.
Terry, Maury (1987). *The Ultimate Evil*. Garden City, NY: Dolphin.
Thompson, Thomas (1979). *Serpentine*. New York: Dell.
Toch, H. (1969). *Violent Men*. Chicago: Aldine (revised ed. 1980).
Vetter, Harold and Robert Rieber (1986). Dissociative States and Processes.
    Paper presented to ASC, Atlanta, GA, (November).
Wilson, Colin (1984). *A Criminal History of Mankind*. London: Granada.
_____ (1972). *Order of Assassins*. London: Rubert Hart-Davis.
Wilson, Colin and P. Pitman (1962). *Encyclopaedia of Murder*. New York:
    Putnam.
Wilson, Colin and Donald Seaman (1983). *Encyclopaedia of Modern
    Murder*. New York: Perigee.
Wilson, James Q. and Edward Herrnstein (1985). *Crime and Human
    Nature*. New York: Simon and Schuster.
Wolfgang, Marvin and Franco Ferracuti (1967). *The Subculture of Violence*.
    London: Tavistock.

chapter 5

Blue Smoke and Mirrors
The "War" on Organized Crime

There are few social phenomena that attract as much public attention as organized crime. It has been the subject of countless novels, magazine articles, movies, newspaper reports, criminal investigations, congressional hearings, and public inquiries by criminal justice agencies. The American fascination with the covert world of organized crime has created a popular view of this phenomenon that has elevated it to legend. But, if federal law enforcement officials are to be believed, the glamour of organized crime and those things of which legends are made are undergoing drastic changes.

After years of frustration, the tide of the battle has turned according to Justice Department officials. Former United States Attorney Rudy Giulani reported: "This has been the Mafia's worst year . . . eventually they [will] become just another street gang" (McFadden, 1987). The official in charge of the Justice Department's organized crime section added: "Their standing as a powerful and untouchable entity in the United States is in serious trouble and may well be a thing of the past in terms of their power" (Kahler, 1986). Philadelphia's District Attorney was ready to claim victory. According to him, recent indictments against southeastern

Pennsylvania Mafiosi, ". . . will bring an end to organized crime in the Philadelphia-South Jersey area as we know it" (Linder, 1987). Most recently, the conviction of John Gotti was heralded as bringing chaos to the Cosa Nostra (see chapter 12 for further discussion).

As optimistic as these claims may sound, the fact is that they are quite misleading. For more than half a century, law enforcement agencies have pursued, prosecuted, imprisoned and even executed organized criminals. Professional, well-funded agencies have been established to investigate organized crime and expose its many intricate conspiracies. Billions of dollars have been spent on "closing the borders" to the drug trade, on "stinging" labor racketeers, and on auditing the tax returns of gamblers. And still organized crime continues to conduct business-as-usual. There is little or no evidence to show that organized crime activities have been or are being significantly disrupted. In fact, most of the available evidence points to the contrary. With all of the time, effort, and money that has been expended in this area, we are still confronted with the basic questions of what can be done about organized crime and how will we know if we have been successful?

The answers to these questions are contingent upon a more basic question: What is organized crime? For the most part policy makers have answered this question by pointing to a myth of organized crime in America.

The Official Myth of Organized Crime

What do we know about organized crime in America? How much empirically verified information do we have and how much data is simply based on myth and misconceived belief? How dependent is criminal justice policy on a "set of disputable facts" rearranged into a set of " 'proofs' of a criminal conspiracy" (Smith, 1975:77)? As Charles McCaghy and Stephen Cernkovich (1987) comment:

> During the medieval ages Christian theologians pondered the question, How many angels can dance on the point of a needle without jostling one another? Although we might argue the subject's importance, we must at least marvel at any attempt to solve such a problem. After all, there is little evidence on angels' width and dancing abilities. The modern-day equivalent of angel counting is "syndicate structuring." Today's Mafia watchers have about as much data as the angel counters did as they debate the nature of organized crime's organization (1987: 265).

Many federal law enforcement officials and some scholars think they know how many angels are dancing on the point of organized crime's needle. For them the answer is simple. Organized crime in the United States is a conspiracy of outsiders ". . . a group of men motivated by criminality and a sense of loyalty foreign to an open, democratic society" (Smith, 1978:168). Organized crime was imported to the United States during the late nineteenth and early twentieth centuries in the wave of Italian immigration. With these foreign immigrants came secret, outlaw, feudal societies such as the Mafia and the Camorra, the seedlings planted on American soil from which organized crime sprouted (Bequai, 1979). In 1931, these secret, feudal societies went through a catharsis, the Castellamarese War, which successfully wiped out the last vestiges of feudal Sicilian rule in the mob, removed illiterates from power and placed Americanized, business-oriented, Italian gangsters in charge of organized crime. By 1932 organized crime, years ahead of the business world, had become a sleek, modern, bureaucratized Italian crime corporation, made up of 24 (or 25, or 27) "families" based on Italian lineage and extended family relationships, and governed by a national commission.

This massive, alien conspiracy was first called to our attention in a systematized manner by the Federal Bureau of Narcotics in 1946 (Smith, 1976). In later years, Senator Kefauver's Committee on interstate gambling (1951); Senator McClellan's Committee on labor racketeering (1957); investigations of the "Apalachin Meeting," and the testimony of Joe Valachi (1963) formed the cornerstones of the alien conspiracy theory. Following the lead of the law enforcement community, ambitious politicians, presidential commissions, journalists, academics, and writers of novels and screenplays eagerly advanced the theory. The President's Crime Commission (Task Force on Organized Crime, 1967) and Donald Cressey's *Theft of the Nation* (1967) gave the theory scholarly credibility and presented it in terms useful to policy makers. Since then, virtually every journalistic account and a host of academic treatises have championed the myth of an alien conspiracy (see, for example: Chandler, 1975; Cook, 1973; Demaris, 1981; Hammer, 1975; Pace and Styles, 1975, among many others).

The myth of alien conspiracy is relatively simple. First, organized crime groups are viewed as criminal equivalents of legitimate corporate sector enterprises, exhibiting similar structural features and bureaucratic organization. Instead of president, vice-president, chairman of the board, general managers, personnel directors and the like, we have "bosses," "underbosses," "counselors," "captains," and "soldiers" (Salerno and Tompkins, 1969:84-85).

Authority and discipline in the organization are based on violence, bribery, and a clan-based feudal hierarchy. Second, organized crime "families" exhibit an inexorable tendency toward monopoly and the formation of massive international cartels to dominate illicit goods and services (Task Force on Organized Crime, 1967:6-8). Third, group membership is determined by ethnic identity. As the Task Force Report on Organized Crime tells us, "their membership is exclusively men of Italian descent" (Task Force on Organized Crime, 1967:6). If anyone else, unlucky enough not to have been born Italian, wishes to engage in the provision of illicit goods and services, they do so only at the sufferance of the Mafia. And finally, organized crime groups attack the very foundations of democracy by their corrupting of otherwise upstanding and loyal public servants. They are an alien force perverting sound economic and political institutions (Salerno and Tompkins, 1969; Pace and Styles, 1975).

Of course, times change, and myths must be adjusted to new realities. In the case of the alien conspiracy theory, drug trafficking by non-Italian groups presented a particularly thorny problem. So, in the last decade, the official depiction of organized crime in the United States underwent a pluralist revision. Federal, state, and local law enforcement organizations began noticing a growing number of new organized crime groups. The "traditional" Mafia was joined by "forceful new competition from Asian and Latin American underworld groups that specialize in heroin, cocaine, and marijuana" (Rowan, 1986:26). By the end of 1986, various law enforcement agencies had added to the list: Jamaicans, Colombians, Cubans, Japanese, Canadians, Irish, Vietnamese, Mexicans, blacks, Russians, the pornography syndicate, and outlaw motorcycle gangs (*Organized Crime Digest*, 1986a:1; Pennsylvania Crime Commission, 1986:2; President's Commission on Organized Crime, 1986).

What is most intriguing about this shift in the official myth of organized crime is not how much it has changed but how stead-fastly it clings to the fundamental assertions of the alien conspiracy myth. First, the pluralist revision is true to the conspiracy myth in that all of the new groups are defined as racially, ethnically, or culturally homogenous. They have "alien" origins and are inevitably described in terms of some kind of culturally delineated "family" structure that resembles a corporate bureaucracy, but which is rooted in the foreign customs of their homelands. They are all rabidly expansionist in their marketing strategies and inevitably are described as "more violent," "more secretive," and "more closely knit" than the traditional Mafia. In fact, the primary explanation that has been used for the decline of Mafia power is that it has been Americanized. That is, younger Italians have adopted mainstream American values — presumably making them less violent, less secretive, and less closely-knit (Ianni, 1972; 1974; Rowan, 1986:24). According to this view, the Mafia has lost its edge because of declining interest in high-risk ventures by new leadership and moderation in the use of violence.

> The leadership is old, and the next generation of managers seems to lack spirit, dedication, and discipline. "Today you got guys in here who have never broken an egg," a New Jersey Mafia leader complained in a conversation bugged by the FBI (Rowan, 1986:24).

So, in the tradition of corporate America, at least as interpreted by law enforcement officials, Italian organized criminals have elected to make deals in lieu of using intimidation. And, of course, these same law enforcement officials point with pride to their role in debilitating the Mafia through intense surveillance and prosecution under the Racketeer Influenced and Corrupt Organization (RICO) statute (Rowan, 1986:26).

This is the federal law enforcement version of Darwin's theory of natural selection. Old groups give way to new and better adapted ones. The new groups assume the old Mafia functions, and the Mafia moves on into new enterprises such as the disposal of toxic wastes, securities fencing, and fraud. Essentially, the same alien conspiracies remain; the only difference is that occasionally they involve new aliens.

It is interesting to note that as federal law enforcement agencies scramble to account for new forces in illicit markets without seriously impairing their myth of organized crime, they have not only relied on the tenets of an old myth, but they have also relied on old tactics. In the early twentieth century the same kind of alien conspiracy was touted as being responsible for America's drug problems. The temperance movement, for example, was a part of a nativist panic over the diminution of traditional rural, middle-class, white Protestant, native lifestyles in America. As Joseph Gusfield (1963) comments:

> The power of the Protestant, rural, native Americans was greater than that of the Eastern upper classes, the Catholic and Jewish immigrants, and the urbanized middle class. This was the lineup of the electoral struggle. In this struggle the champions of drinking represented cultural enemies and they had lost . . .
>
> Increasingly the problem of liquor control became the central issue around which was posed the conflict between new and old

cultural forces in American society. On the one side were the
Wets—a union of cultural sophistication and secularism with
Catholic lower-class traditionalism. These represented the new
additions to the American population that made up the
increasingly powerful political force of urban politics. On the
other were the defenders of fundamental religion, or old moral
values, of the ascetic, cautious, and sober middle class that had
been the ideal of Americans in the nineteenth century (Gusfield,
122-23, 124).

So, like organized crime in the 1990s, liquor in the 1890s was a
foreign, alien impingement upon an otherwise righteous society.

The same fear of alien influence can be seen in discussions
surrounding early narcotics legislation. Despite the fact that the
250,000 addicts in the United States at the turn of the century were
predominantly middle-aged, middle-class, white women (Brecher,
1972:17-18; Musto, 1973:5), the problem of drugs was laid squarely
at the feet of aliens.

In the nineteenth century addicts were identified with foreign
groups and internal minorities who were already actively feared
and the objects of elaborate and massive social and legal
restraints. Two repressed groups which were associated with
the use of certain drugs were the Chinese and the Negroes. The
Chinese and their custom of opium smoking were closely
watched after their entry into the United States about 1870. At
first, the Chinese represented only one more group brought in
to help build the railroads, but, particularly after economic
depressions made them a labor surplus and a threat to American
citizens, many forms of antagonism arose to drive them out, or
at least to isolate them. Along with the prejudice came a fear
of opium smoking as one of the ways in which the Chinese were
supposed to undermine American society.

Cocaine was especially feared in the South by 1900 because of
its euphoric and stimulating properties. The South feared that
Negro cocaine users might become oblivious of their prescribed
bounds and attack white society. . . .

Evidence does not suggest that cocaine caused a crime wave
but rather that anticipation of black rebellion inspired white
alarm. Anecdotes often told of superhuman strength, cunning,
and efficiency resulting from cocaine. One of the most terrifying
beliefs about cocaine was that it actually improved pistol marks-
manship. Another myth, that cocaine made blacks almost
unaffected by mere .32 caliber bullets, is said to have caused
southern police departments to switch to .38 caliber revolvers.
These fantasies characterized white fear, not the reality of
cocaine's effects and gave one more reason for the repression
of blacks.

> By 1914 prominent newspapers, physicians, pharmacists, and
> congressmen believed opiates and cocaine predisposed habitues
> toward insanity and crime. They were widely seen as substances
> associated with foreigners or alien subgroups. Cocaine raised
> the specter of the wild Negro, opium the devious Chinese,
> morphine the tramps in the slums, it was feared that use of all
> these drugs was spreading into the "higher classes" (Musto,
> 1973:5-7, 65; cited in McCaghy and Cernkovich, 1987).

Musto links similar fears toward Mexicans with the passage of the
Marijuana Tax Act of 1937 (1973:219-25).

The fear of immigrants and repressed racial and ethnic groups
in the United States was used to construct a conspiracy myth of
drug use, just as it was used to construct a conspiracy myth of
organized crime. The argument has always been the same: forces
outside of mainstream American culture are at work which seek
to pervert an otherwise morally sound, industrious, and democratic
people. It is a convenient and easily understood argument. It is, in
fact, the only depiction of organized crime that could gain
widespread popular appeal. To suggest that righteous citizens are
being perverted, intimidated, and forced into vice by alien forces
is far more palatable than suggesting that "native" demands for
illicit drugs, sex, and gambling invite the creation of organized
crime groups. So, despite the minor alterations in the alien
conspiracy myth, we can clearly discern that its revisionist form
is neither new, clever, nor very different from the Mafia myth.

Historical Myths of Organized Crime

The "constructed proofs" used to justify the alien conspiracy
myth range from the dubious to the preposterous. First, the
assertion that the Sicilian Mafia was transplanted to America in the
waves of Italian immigration is open to question. Research on the
Mafia in Sicily indicates that it was never a highly structured
criminal conspiracy, rather it was an intermediary and fragmented
force of mercenaries providing local control of the peasantry for
absentee landlords (Blok, 1971). In addition, it is more than a little
curious that other nations which received waves of Italian
immigrants at the same time as the United States failed to develop
anything even close to the American version of the Mafia (Potter
and Jenkins, 1985:iii). The importation myth derives from a
combination of press sensationalism and nativist sentiments in the
United States (Smith, 1975; 1976). The great revolution in
organized crime, the Castellamarese War, never happened. Rather

than the forty assassinations credited to the "young turks" led by Lucky Luciano, only four possibly related murders have been turned up by serious research efforts. In addition, serious questions have been raised about the logistical improbabilities of such an uprising (Block, 1978; Nelli, 1976). The Kefauver Committee heard a great deal of testimony about organized crime and its role in gambling. However, it failed to produce a single knowledgeable witness who even mentioned the Mafia (Albini, 1971; Smith 1975). The investigation of the Apalachin conclave was so tangled in New York state politics that no one really knows what happened there, who was there, or what they were doing. The sparse information which is available is amenable to many more credible explanations than that of an international Mafia conclave (Morris and Hawkins, 1970; Albini, 1971; Smith, 1975). Finally, the 1963 testimony of Joe Valachi and subsequent statements by alleged Mafia turncoat, Jimmy "the Weasel" Fratianno, have been shown to be riddled with contradictions, factual errors and uncorroborated assertions. In addition, neither of these informers was in any position to provide the insights credited to them (Albanese, 1985; Albini, 1971; Morris and Hawkins, 1970; Smith, 1975).

Rather than substance, the alien conspiracy myth is supported by the testimony of a few government-sponsored informants and public release of heavily edited and carefully selected police files and surveillance transcripts—all tied together by official speculation. Peter Reuter (1983), in his meticulous research on organized crime, has questioned both the knowledgeability of the government (pointing to problems and inaccuracies in the monitoring of legal, open, and public industries) and the inherent bias in the data collection process utilized by law enforcement agencies which seek only evidence to support their own basic assumptions about organized crime. If other groups had been subjected to the same level of wire-tapping, surveillance, interrogation, arrest and comprehensive investigation as groups of aged Italians, federal officials would no doubt have been startled to learn that "new" organized crime groups were not new at all— some have been active for the past century.

Empirical Evidence and Organized Crime

Quite apart from the historical problems with the alien conspiracy myth are problems revealed by the current body of empirical research on organized crime. Virtually every empirical study of organized crime conducted in the past twenty years has reached conclusions diametrically opposed to those in the official myth. Studies have demonstrated that rather than being a tightly structured, clearly defined, stable entity, organized crime operates in a loosely structured, informal, open system. Organized crime is made up of a series of highly adaptive, flexible networks that readily take into account changes in the law and regulatory practices, the growth or decline of market demand for a particular good or service, and the availability of new sources of supply and new opportunities for distribution. It is this ability to adapt that allows organized crime to persist and flourish. The inflexible, clan-based corporate entities described by law enforcement agencies could not survive in this turbulent environment.

It makes far more sense to conceive of organized crime as a partnership arrangement, or a patron-client arrangement, rather than as an immutable bureaucratic structure with a clearly defined hierarchy. Mark Haller's (1987) research reveals that organizations such as those surrounding the Capone gang and Meyer Lansky's extensive operations were in reality a series of small-scale business partnerships, usually involving several senior "partners" (Capone, Nitti, Lansky) and many junior partners who sometimes conducted business in concert with one another and often conducted business separately. Organized crime was not directed by Lansky or Capone in any bureaucratic sense but was merely a series of investment and joint business ventures. Joseph Albini (1971), as a result of his study of organized crime in Detroit, concluded that organized crime was made up of certain criminal patrons who traded information, connections with government officials, and access to a network of operatives in exchange for the clients' economic and political support. The roles of client and patron fluctuated depending on the enterprise; combinations were formed, dissolved and reformed with new actors. William Chambliss' (1978) study of organized crime in Seattle depicts an overlapping series of crime networks with shifting memberships highly adaptive to the economic, political and social exigencies of the community—without a centralized system of control. Alan Block's (1979b) study of the cocaine trade in New York concluded that the drug trade was operated by "small, flexible organizations of criminals which arise due to opportunity and environmental factors" (94-95). John Gardiner's (1970) study of corruption and vice in "Wincanton," Ianni's (1972, 1974) two studies of organized crime in New York, and a study of organized crime in Philadelphia (Potter and Jenkins, 1985) reach similar conclusions. Peter Reuter's (1983) study of Italian organized crime in New York found that no group exercises control over entrepreneurs in gambling and loansharking. Reuter concludes that rather than the officially depicted view of organized crime as a monolithic conspiracy, it is in fact characterized by conflict and fragmentation.

The empirical research clearly reveals that organized crime is made up of small, fragmented, and ephemeral enterprises. There are very practical reasons for this. First, small size and segmentation reduce the chances of getting caught and prosecuted. Since employees in illicit industries are the greatest threat to those operations, and make the best witnesses against them, it is an organizational necessity for organized crime groups to limit the number of people who have knowledge about the group's operations. This is achieved by small size and segmentation so that employees only know about their own jobs and their own level of activity in the enterprise. Such arrangements are clear in the gambling and drug industries. In gambling, runners and collectors are distanced from the bank itself (Potter and Jenkins, 1985; Reuter, 1983). In drug trafficking, production, importation, distribution, and retail activities are kept as discrete functions, often performed by completely different organized crime groups, most of which are both temporary and small (Hellman, 1980; Laswell and McKenna, 1971; Wisotsky, 1986).

For the same reasons that organized crime groups choose to limit the number of employees, they also tend to limit the geographic areas they serve. The larger the geographic area, the more tenuous communication becomes, requiring either the use of the telephone (and the threat of electronic surveillance) or long trips to pass on routine information in person, a most inefficient means of managing a business. In addition, the larger the geographic area served, the greater the number of law enforcement agencies involved and the higher the costs of corruption (Reuter, 1983; Wisotsky, 1986). In his study of New York, Reuter (1983) found no evidence of centralization in gambling and loansharking, and he argues persuasively that in drug trafficking even less permanence and centralization is found (184).

The evidence also calls into question the assumption in the official myth that organized criminals act as the corrupters of public officials. Available evidence indicates that a more accurate perspective is that organized criminals, legitimate businessmen, and government officials are all equal players in a marketplace of corruption. Each brings to the market things wanted by the others and routine series of exchanges occur. The purveyors of illicit goods and services wish to exchange their products, money, and influence for protection, selective enforcement against competitors, and favorable policy decisions by government authorities. Public officials for venal reasons, or in recognition of a need to regulate and constrain illicit activity, put their policy-making and enforcement powers on the market. Who initiates such a deal depends upon circumstances, and the initiator is as likely to be the "legitimate" actor as the "criminal."

It is not uncommon for a series of exchanges between the under- and upperworlds to develop into a long-term corrupt relationship. Studies have shown that in some cases those who occupy positions of public trust are the organizers of crime (Gardiner, 1970; Chambliss, 1978; Gardiner and Lyman, 1978; Block and Scarpitti, 1985; Potter and Jenkins, 1985). Investigations of police corruption in Philadelphia and New York have demonstrated how thoroughly institutionalized corruption can be among public servants. In the private sector, respected institutions such as Shearson/American Express, Merrill Lynch, the Miami National Bank, Citibank, and others have eagerly participated in illicit ventures (Lernoux, 1984; Moldea, 1986; *Organized Crime Digest*, 1986a; 1986b; 1987a; 1987b; President's Commission on Organized Crime, 1984:31-42). For example, in the infamous "Pizza Connection" case, in which Southeast Asian heroin was distributed through a series of pizza parlors located in the United States, tens of millions of dollars were laundered through New York City banks and then transferred by those banks to secret accounts in Switzerland, the Bahamas and other countries. In addition to using banks to launder money, the "Pizza Connection" heroin traffickers also used the brokerage firm of Merrill Lynch Pierce Fenner and Smith, depositing $5 million (all in $5, $10, and $20 bills) over a six-week period. Merrill Lynch not only accepted these highly dubious deposits but provided the couriers carrying the heroin money with extraordinary security for their transactions. At the same time, couriers from the "Pizza Connection" were laundering $13.5 million through accounts at another brokerage house, E.F. Hutton, which also provided protection for the couriers (President's Commission on Organized Crime, 1984:31-42). Contrary to the official myth, under- and upperworld criminals form close, symbiotic bonds. Public officials are not the pawns of organized crime; they are part of its fabric — the part found in America's respected institutions.

Finally, the role of ethnicity in determining the structure of organized crime is misinterpreted and overstated by the alien conspiracy myth. There is ample evidence that many organized crime groups are made up of individuals of varied ethnic backgrounds or cooperate on a regular basis with individuals of various ethnic backgrounds (Block, 1979b; Pennsylvania Crime Commission, 1986; Abadinsky, 1985; Potter and Jenkins, 1985).

As Haller's (1987) study of Lansky's and Capone's enterprises makes clear, organized criminals who wish to survive and prosper quickly learn the limits of kinship, ethnicity, and violence, and proceed to form lucrative business partnerships on the basis of rational business decisions and common needs.

In those cases where organized crime networks do demonstrate ethnic homogeneity, it is merely a reflection of the exigencies of urban social life, not the machinations of a secret, ethnic conspiracy. It makes sense that vice in a black neighborhood is going to be primarily delivered by a black crime network. Similarly, illicit goods and services in an Italian neighborhood will probably be delivered by entrepreneurs of Italian lineage. This is not an organizational design but merely a reflection of the constituency of small, geographically compact, organized crime networks.

Headhunting

The alien conspiracy myth has dictated an enforcement strategy based on its precepts. Since Prohibition, the federal effort against organized crime has involved identifying and prosecuting group members for *any* available offense. Many times, these offenses are unrelated to illicit entrepreneurship and are often comparatively minor infractions. This strategy is predicated on the assumption that the actual conspiracy is too complex and well organized to be proved in court. As we shall see, this rationale is also part of the myth; the actual structure of organized crime operations is not as complex as the myth asserts. The myth of conspiracy actually becomes an excuse for a lack of success in controlling organized crime. In the headhunting strategy, success is calculated in the form of a body count. Arrests, indictments and convictions are used to justify budgets and ask for new enforcement powers. Because the conspiracy myth places a high premium on position in the hierarchy, the assumption has been that the farther up that hierarchy an arrest goes, the more disruptive it is to the business of organized crime. The most prized catch is the "boss" of a Mafia family. If the alien conspiracy myth is correct, and these groups are tightly structured and disciplined, the incapacitation of a "boss" should be debilitating to the organization.

Of course, because of the myth of an insulated hierarchy, the culture of violence, the code of silence, and the fidelity of clannish conspirators, successful headhunting requires a massive arsenal of law enforcement powers, powers that must be continually augmented and expanded. In addition, new laws, creating new criminal categories (i.e., "drug kingpin," "racketeer") must be created so that heavy sentences and fines can be imposed on those convicted. Simply convicting them of the crimes with which they are charged would not be a sufficient deterrent, additional penalties must be included. All of this and more was provided by the Racketeer Influence Corrupt Organization Act in 1970. RICO provided for special grand juries to look for evidence, created a more potent immunity law, eased requirements for proving perjury, provided for protective custody of government witnesses, weakened the defense's capacity to cross-examine and exclude illegally obtained evidence, expanded federal jurisdiction to cover conspiracy to obstruct *state* law, and increased prison sentences (Chambliss and Block, 1981). It is a curious, but seldom noted fact, that the Nixon administration, which was responsible for the passage of RICO, chose to ignore organized crime and used the provisions of the act to prosecute anti-Vietnam war protesters (Chambliss and Block, 1981). In addition, RICO has civil provisions that allow the government to pursue what the Justice Department has called a "scorched earth" approach to organized crime — seizing assets and "leaving the mobster with nothing but a return address in federal prison" (Kahler, 1986).

As is the case with many law enforcement programs, rigorous assessments of the headhunting strategy are not available (President's Commission on Organized Crime, 1986:205). When organized criminals are successfully prosecuted, this is used as evidence that the strategy is working. When convictions are not forthcoming or when the penalties imposed seem mild, law enforcement complains that "its hands are tied" — that it lacks sufficient resources or legal authority to implement the headhunting strategy.

Despite the fact that comprehensive statistics are not kept on how many organized criminals have been put away, some fragmentary data is available to suggest the scope of the headhunting effort. A 1986 *Fortune* magazine article listed the "top 50" Mafia bosses (based on interviews with law enforcement officials). The article showed that fifteen of the fifty were in jail, ten were indicted or on trial, and one was a fugitive (Rowan, 1986). This included eight of the top ten. Since the publication of that article twenty-four of the remaining "free" crime leaders have been indicted or jailed. If we look specifically at the fabled five families of New York, we find that all of the top leaders of the Colombo, Bonnano, and Lucchese groups have been incapacitated, along with half of the Genovese group's leaders. From 1981-1985, seventeen of the twenty-four alleged Mafia bosses across the country were indicted or convicted

(President's Commission on Organized Crime, 1986:47). In 1984 alone, organized crime indictments totaled 2,194, almost exclusively alleged Mafia group members.

In addition, conviction rates and sentences have also been going up. The General Accounting Office (GAO) estimated that the conviction rate rose from 56 percent to 76 percent in the period from 1972 to 1980 (Albanese, 1985). The GAO also noted a concomitant increase in jail terms handed down for convictions.

The problem with all of this is that the government has failed to produce any evidence that these prosecutions have resulted in a diminution of organized crime's illicit ventures. The federal government simply has no measures of the amount of harm caused by organized crime with which to measure such an impact (President's Commission on Organized Crime, 1986:203). But other indicators seem to suggest that organized crime is alive and quite healthy despite the prosecutorial efforts.

For example, prosecutions of a major gambling syndicate in Philadelphia in the early 1980s had the result of spawning at least two dozen other criminal networks in the same neighborhood as replacements for the targeted crime groups (Pennsylvania Crime Commission, 1985; 1986). Major enforcement efforts directed at "syndicate heads" in Seattle and "Wincanton" resulted in minimal restructuring of street-level operations with no discernible impact on the provision of illicit goods and services (Chambliss, 1978; Gardiner, 1970). Major prosecutions in New York directed at labor racketeering and drug trafficking have had the effect of weeding out inefficient and highly visible operators, leaving more viable organized crime groups in their wake (Chambliss and Block, 1981). Recent prosecutions aimed at the pornography syndicate have resulted in the creation of at least six new, major organized crime groups and the revival of one group that had been closed down a decade ago by successful prosecution (Potter, 1986). Studies of the organization of vice have demonstrated consistently that prosecutions have only negligible impact on the provision of illicit goods and services and the operation of organized crime groups (Reuter, 1983; Albini, 1971; Reuter, Rubinstein and Wynn, 1983).

The reason that no impact on organized crime can be demonstrated as a result of the headhunting approach is that it is based on myth. Organized crime groups learned long ago that to be successful in a threatening legal environment they must be prepared to adapt their structures and practices. The irony of the situation is that the more successful federal prosecutors become in incarcerating organized crime leaders, the more the industry responds by decentralizing and maintaining temporary and ephemeral working relationships. Because the headhunting approach never disables more than a small proportion of the total number of organized crime entrepreneurs at any given time, it actually strengthens and rewards some organized crime groups by weeding out their inefficient competitors.

It should also be pointed out that headhunting often involves targeting the easiest cases. Successful prosecutions of highly visible and public, but not overly influential, crime figures is good press, but will have very little impact. The selection of "Little Nicky" Scarfo, the alleged boss of Philadelphia's Cosa Nostra "family," for special federal treatment has left the field open for far more powerful and dangerous crime figures. While Scarfo has been designated as the head of organized crime in Philadelphia by federal investigators and the press, his actual role and influence are highly suspect. The differences between Scarfo and his associates who were prosecuted (with mixed success) and those who have been left more or less alone are important to understanding the failure of the federal enforcement effort. Scarfo is a small-time hood who lacks political influence and has a minuscule share of the illicit market (considerably less than the 25 percent of the gambling market which was credited to his vastly more competent predecessor Angelo Bruno) (Potter and Jenkins, 1985). In addition, Scarfo's vision of criminal enterprise (among other things) is decidedly limited, highlighted by such capers as an extortion scheme directed at hot dog vendors in Atlantic City (DeMaris, 1986). However, also active in Philadelphia during the same time as "Mafia Boss" Scarfo were individuals identified by a variety of sources as controlling a great deal of political clout and a large share of the illicit market. At least one gambler had run a $35 million a year numbers bank virtually unmolested for three decades. A major attorney, identified several times in print as the emissary of Meyer Lansky and later of Alvin Malnik continued to grant favors from his plush offices as allegedly the sole license-granting authority for illicit activities in Atlantic City (Demaris, 1986). A local realtor whose cocktail parties for judicial candidates are among the premier events of the political season continued to be the primary landlord for the pornography syndicate (Potter, 1986). Not to belabor the point, there are at least two dozen other operatives of similar stature who operated with relative immunity, while the federal government pursued "Little Nicky" with a vengeance far in excess of his importance or his capacity for future importance (Demaris, 1986; Potter and Jenkins, 1985). It is the relative immunity of major figures in organized crime, such as money launderers, corrupt public officials, and other individuals who serve as bridges between the underworld and the upperworld, that so clearly demonstrates the deficiencies in the myth of organized crime on which headhunting strategies are based.

One other issue needs to be discussed before moving on—headhunting does not always result in successful prosecutions. For example, charges against Jack Nardi, Jr., a Teamsters Union official, were dismissed on October 9, 1985. In May 1986, all six defendants in the celebrated trial of "Matty the Horse" Ianniello were acquitted in a RICO prosecution in New York. The defendants had been charged with trying to defraud Con Edison. The jury found that charge either laudable or impossible and acquitted the defendants. On March 13, 1987, John Gotti and six alleged accomplices were acquitted on charges that they ran the Mafia. In this case, as prosecutors admitted, the jury simply refused to believe turncoat criminals who had been given very lenient sentences in return for testimony. And on December 12, 1987, "Little Nicky" Scarfo and four of his alleged "family" members were acquitted in a drug case. The summation from the jury was simple: "the jury looked at this case that they put on and it stunk" (*Organized Crime Digest*, 1985, 1986b, 1987a). The point of this litany of defeats is not to suggest that federal prosecutors are incompetent but merely to demonstrate that the credibility of the alien conspiracy myth is weakening with juries around the country.

The idea that vigorous prosecution and stiff criminal penalties will win the war against organized crime is at variance not only with current research on organized crime but with historic precedent as well. Literally thousands of cases in which organized crime figures have been arrested, convicted, and imprisoned in the last fifty years could be cited here. The fundamental question remains—so what? There is no evidence that these successful prosecutions have in any way negatively impacted or altered the activities of organized entrepreneurial groups in illicit markets.

Controlling Organized Crime

Our efforts to control and eradicate organized crime have failed. They have failed for two basic reasons: the headhunting strategy is predicated on false assumptions about the importance of "bosses" to the illegal market and the alien conspiracy myth which dictates organized crime policy is bankrupt in its understanding of illicit enterprises. Organized crime groups operate in a complex web of interrelated and tangled environments. They are impacted by the opportunities and constraints of the market, the legal system, politics, "upperworld" commerce, and the community in which they operate. Most attempts to analyze organized crime focus almost exclusively on *criminal* actions. Traditionally, analyses of organized crime have concentrated attention on the deviant aspects of organized crime rather than on its institutionalized and normative aspects. In Chambliss' (1978) words this emphasis has "obscured perception of the degree to which the structure of America's law and politics creates and perpetuates syndicates that supply the vices in our major cities" (6).

Empirical research on organized crime suggests that in order to understand it, we must understand its social context. That social context is defined by two consistent threads running through the organization of crime: official corruption and the exigencies of the political economy. The evidence is compelling that organized crime should not be conceptualized as a dysfunction in society, nor as an alien force impinging upon society. Rather, organized crime is part and parcel of the political economic system. Once again, Chambliss (1978), in commenting on the organization of vice in Seattle, makes the degree of integration clear:

> Working for, and with, this cabal of respectable community members is a staff which coordinates the daily activities of prostitution, gambling, bookmaking, the sale and distribution of drugs, and other vices. Representatives from each of these groups, comprising the political and economic power centers of the community, meet regularly to distribute profits, discuss problems, and make the necessary organizational and policy decisions essential to the maintenance of a profitable, trouble-free business (6).

This point of view has compelling implications for policy. The argument advanced here suggests that policy makers have been attacking the wrong targets in their battle against organized crime.

Dwight Smith (1978) observes that law enforcement strategy traditionally "has rested on the belief that acts of crime are the sole responsibility of the perpetrator, and that as a consequence of removing him from society, the criminal acts would disappear" (162). However, the evidence suggests that the existence of illicit drug dealers, loansharks, gamblers, and other illegal entrepreneurs is due to the fact that the legitimate marketplace leaves a number of potential customers for these services unserved. The control of organized crime can be achieved only with a greater understanding of organizational and market behavior, by "learning how to reduce the domain of the illicit [entrepreneur] . . . and a wider appreciation of the entire market spectrum, and a deeper analysis of the dynamics that nurture its illicit aspects" (Smith, 1978:175-76). Smith argues that an understanding of the "task environment" of particular enterprises will promote a better and more comprehensive understanding of how such illicit enterprises emerge, survive, and make a profit from crime.

In rethinking strategies to control organized crime, we must begin by conceptualizing organized crime as a business, not an alien conspiracy. Doing so will direct us to efforts that will improve our understanding of the causes of organized criminal behavior and the means used to organize illicit enterprises. In addition, this view directs our attention toward the elimination of arbitrary distinctions between legal and illegal goods and services (particularly in gambling, lending, drug distribution and sexual services) and the importance of corruption in the ability of organized crime to prosper. Chambliss (1978) supports this view in his study of organized crime in Seattle.

> Money is the oil of our present-day machinery, and elected public officials are the pistons that keep the machine operating. Those who come up with the oil, whatever its source, are in a position to make the machinery run the way they want it to. Crime is an excellent producer of capitalism's oil. Those who want to affect the direction of the machine's output find that the money produced by crime is as effective in helping them get where they can go as is the money produced in any other way. Those who produce the money from crime thus become the people most likely to control the effectively working political economy. Crime is, in fact, a cornerstone on which the political and economic relations of democratic-capitalistic societies are constructed.

> In every city of the United States, and in many other countries as well, criminal organizations sell sex and drugs, provide an opportunity to gamble, to watch pornographic films, or to obtain a loan, an abortion or a special favor. Their profits are a mainstay of the electoral process of America and their business is an important (if unrecorded) part of the gross national product. The business of organized crime in the United States may gross as much as one hundred billion dollars annually . . . the profits are immense, and the proportion of the gross national product represented by money flowing from crime cannot be gainsaid. Few nations in the world have economies that compare with the economic output of criminal activities in the United States (1-2).

So, rather than directing control efforts in an enforcement direction aimed at specific individuals or groups, a realistic view of organized crime points to the importance of the market and the political arrangements which sustain organized crime.

The way we conceptualize and understand organized crime dictates the means selected to control it. While detailed policy alternatives are beyond the scope of this discussion, several thematic departures from present policy are dictated by what we know about organized crime. The most important of those policy departures may well be consideration of steps necessary to shrink and control the market for the goods and services of organized crime.

Reducing Market Demand

The largest and most profitable organized crime enterprises are those that provide illicit goods and services to a significant segment of the public eager to obtain them, and among these, the most important are drug trafficking, gambling, prostitution, and loansharking. One approach to limiting the demand for these goods is to punish the consumer, but in addition to being practically and politically unpalatable, we have also seen that historically (especially with regard to drugs) such tactics have had precisely the opposite effect of the one intended.

Another approach is available, however. The first objective of control policies aimed at organized crime should be reducing the size of the illicit market and the profits emanating from that market—in other words, decriminalization. It is the very existence of these laws against consensual crimes that create such a remarkable opportunity for criminal entrepreneurs. The laws against vice are almost unenforceable. All of these behaviors require cooperation between buyer and seller. There is no victim to call the police, there is no complainant to instigate an investigation. As a direct result, these laws are enforced in a highly selective and discriminatory manner. Individuals who are unlucky enough to be arrested under the gambling, drug, and prostitution statutes are almost always the most visible and the easiest to catch. So enforcement of the laws fills the prisons with junkies and streetwalkers. Ironically, the enforcement of these laws serves to strengthen organized crime rather than to control it. Those who will be apprehended are the smallest operators—those with the least organization, the least power, and the least expertise. Organized crime groups find that the law weeds out the inefficient and small operators. Enforcing the law leaves the entire illicit market open to exploitation by better organized, more successful criminal enterprises. The law helps organized crime in a number of other ways as well. Since these types of goods and services are in demand but illegal, organized crime groups can charge dearly for their services. The profits reaped in the heroin and cocaine markets alone are staggering, and it is only the illegality of the drug which makes these profits possible. The immense sums of money realized from entrepreneurship in the illicit market makes possible a protective web of pervasive police and political corruption.

In view of the fact that the laws are dysfunctional and the markets enormous, it makes sense to end arbitrary distinctions between legal and illegal activities. Organized crime scholars have long argued that decriminalization or legalization is one way to reduce the market domain of organized crime (Albini, 1971; Albanese, 1985; Anderson, 1979; Luksetich and White, 1982; Smith 1980). Merely removing the criminal label from gambling, loansharking, prostitution, and drug trafficking—and even legalizing and regulating them—would not eliminate organized crime's involvement entirely. Legalized off-track betting in New York did not drive bookmakers out of business. It did, however, constrain their activity. They must offer odds within the limits of those being offered by the state. They must be restrained in their collection methods. But most importantly, bookmaking profits appear to have stabilized at between 5 and 10 percent (Reuter, 1983). Decriminalization would similarly constrain commerce in the most profitable enterprises in organized crime's portfolio. As long as the profits are high and the risks diffuse, criminal entrepreneurs will continue to engage in these activities. It simply makes sense to take some of the profit out these markets.

Decriminalization of the illicit goods and services which are at the core of the business of organized crime may be difficult to achieve. The same forces that gave rise to the alien conspiracy myth make decriminalization a difficult option for policy makers to exercise. Americans have historically been unwilling to acknowledge their own role in creating a market for prostitution, gambling, loansharking, drugs, and the like, preferring instead to label certain acts deviant and criminal rather than accepting them as social constants in society. Decriminalizing, or even legalizing, such activities might be seen as condoning them or as catering to moral "defects" in the "weaker" members of society. If the political reality remains such that the laws cannot be changed to shrink organized crime's market, then the focus of current law enforcement efforts must be changed to address the problem of organized crime more effectively. Specific policies should be formulated to address the "laundering" of illicit funds, corruption of officials, and improved intelligence and surveillance to target those in control of illegal operations.

Fighting Corruption

It is axiomatic to organized crime that it cannot flourish without a favorable political environment in which there are systematic abuses of the public trust. While there is no reason to believe that the customers of organized crime can be deterred from seeking out illicit goods and services, there is every reason to believe that corruption can be deterred. Instead of wasting valuable resources on surveillance of criminals with a "bad reputation," government should focus attention on finding individuals who serve as links between the underworld and the upperworld. The importance of such links is exemplified by the fact that 15 percent of all political contributions to local and state political campaigns come from organized crime figures (Task Force on Organized Crime, 1967). After all, these are the people who can guarantee that organized crime is able to continue uninterrupted operations with a minimum of official governmental interference, and these are the people who reap both political and financial rewards from those organized crime operations. At a minimum, increased and more comprehensive reporting of assets and sources of income should be required of public officials in key decision making positions. Governmental attention should maintain closer supervision of public officials and strengthen conflict of interest laws. Obviously, greater restrictions on contributions to political candidates could be enacted—for example, limiting private contributions to $100 or adopting public financing of political campaigns.

Cleaning Up the Money Laundries

The recent increase in drug trafficking profits has focused attention on the critical role of financial institutions in laundering illicit incomes. Organized crime groups have become dependent on bankers, stockbrokers, lawyers, realtors, and others close to the financial community (Demaris, 1986; Moldea, 1986; Lernoux, 1984). As a first step, there should be a standardized federal requirement for corporate reporting in order to avoid the great variance in state regulations. At a minimum, sufficient information should be required so that investigators will be able to follow money trails with greater ease. Second, the enforcement of existing reporting regulations should be increased in areas involving large sums of money transferred between and among banks. Interbank transfers and wire transfers to foreign banks and corporations should have to be reported. Foreign currency transactions should be subjected to reporting requirements detailing where the money is going and why. Certainly crimes committed by financial institutions and corporations as part of organized crime operations should be treated with the same severity as crimes committed by the organized criminals themselves. Surely, if the federal government can justify putting labor union locals into receivership based on the criminal records of their officers, the same should hold for brokerage houses. Federal prosecutors should recognize that a corrupt organization is a corrupt organization whether it is the Mafia or Merrill Lynch. The seizure of corporate assets under the RICO statute should become as common as the confiscation of a drug dealer's Cadillac.

Improving Intelligence

Following the money, rather than the perpetrator, should be the hallmark of effective organized crime investigations. By tracing the path of illicit profits, law enforcement agencies would gain valuable information on cash deposits, property transactions, fund purchases, real estate ownership, and foreign currency transfers. It is a reality of organized crime that the point at which illicit wealth accumulates is also the point closest to the most powerful underworld operators.

At the moment, law enforcement agencies' concept of intelligence gathering is primarily limited to preparing a "rogue's gallery" of ethnics with bad reputations. Obtaining useful intelligence on organized crime is admittedly difficult, but law enforcement agencies can vastly improve their understanding of organized crime by focusing on the development of an accurate picture of organized crime markets. Intelligence operations should follow the processes of distribution, supply, manufacturing and financing—regardless of who is involved, or whether they reside in the under- or upper-worlds. This approach to intelligence means that analysts should be more concerned with assessing market, production, and social conditions that shape the patterns of organized criminals' interactions.

In addition, intelligence-gathering operations must be separated from operations designed to produce arrests and convictions. Intelligence gathering, when done correctly, is unlikely to result in quick arrests and certain convictions. Agencies under pressure to show results calculated by numbers of arrests tend to choose the easiest cases, and to arrest the most obvious (and usually the least important) criminal operatives. These arrests inflate statistics and contribute little to our knowledge about organized crime. Intelligence gathering must be recognized as important on its own merits and success must be measured by the quality of data produced, not prosecutors' batting averages. Reactive intelligence-gathering strategies must be replaced by intelligence operations sensitive to shifts in law, enforcement patterns, technology, markets and social trends.

None of these suggestions for changes in policy are new, nor are they likely to be embraced by policy makers. Attacking white collar criminals is not as politically satisfying, nor as easy, as jailing highly visible and reasonably unimportant purveyors of vice on the street. The very fact that law enforcement agencies continue to base their control strategies on failed approaches and continue to reject a comprehensive attack on organized crime clearly demonstrates the poverty of present policies of control.

Sources

Abadinsky, H. (1985). *Organized Crime*. Chicago: Nelson-Hall.

Albanese, Jay (1985). *Organized Crime in America*. Cincinnati: Anderson.

Albini, Joseph (1971). *The American Mafia: Genesis of a Legend*. New York: Appleton-Century-Crofts.

Anderson, Annelise Graebner (1979). *The Business of Organized Crime: A Cosa Nostra Family*. Stanford, CA: Hoover Institution Press.

Bequai, August (1979). *Organized Crime: The Fifth Estate*. Lexington, MA: Heath.

Block, Alan A. (1979a). *East Side-West Side: Organizing Crime in New York, 1939-1959*. Swansea, United Kingdom: Christopher Davis, Publishers.

_____ (1979b). The Snowman Cometh: Coke in Progressive New York. *Criminology*, (May 17):75-99.

_____ (1978). History and the Study of Organized Crime. *Urban Life*, (January 6):455-74.

Block, Alan and Frank R. Scarpitti (1985). *Poisoning for Profit: The Mafia and Toxic Waste*. New York: William Morrow.

Blok, Anton (1971). *The Mafia of a Sicilian Village, 1860-1960*. London: William Clowes and Sons.

Brecher, Edward M. (1972). *Licit and Illicit Drugs*. Mount Vernon, NY: Consumers Union.

Chambliss, William (1978). *On the Take: From Petty Crooks to Presidents*. Bloomington: Indiana University Press.

Chambliss, William and Alan Block (1981). *Organizing Crime*. New York: Elsevier.

Chandler, David L. (1975). *Brothers in Blood: The Rise of the Criminal Brotherhoods*. New York: Dutton.

Cook, Fred J. (1973). *Mafia!* Greenwich, CT: Fawcett.

Cressey, Donald R. (1967). *The Theft of the Nation*. New York: Harper & Row.

Demaris, Ovid (1986). *The Boardwalk Jungle*. New York: Bantam.

_____ (1981). *The Last Mafioso*. New York: Bantam.

Gardiner, John A. (1970). *The Politics of Corruption: Organized Crime in an American City*. New York: Russell Sage Foundation.

Gardiner, John A. and Theodore R. Lyman (1978). *Decisions for Sale: Corruption and Reform in Land-Use and Building Regulations*. New York: Praeger.

Gusfield, Joseph R. (1963). *Symbolic Crusade: Status Politics and the American Temperance Movement*. Urbana, IL: University of Illinois Press.

Haller, Mark H. (1987). Business Partnerships in the Coordination of Illegal Enterprise. Paper presented at the annual meetings of the American Society of Criminology, Montreal, (November).

Hammer, Richard. (1975). *Playboy's Illustrated History of Organized Crime*. Chicago: Playboy Press.

Hellman, Daryl A. (1980). *The Economics of Crime*. New York: St. Martin's Press.

Ianni, Francis A. J. (1974). *Black Mafia: Ethnic Succession in Organized Crime*. New York: Simon and Schuster.

_____ (1972). *A Family Business: Kinship and Social Control in Organized Crime*. New York: Russell Sage Foundation.

Kahler, Kathryn (1986). The Mob is Winning: Organized Crime in the United States is Richer than Ever. *Gannett Westchester Newspapers*, (May 25):B1, B6.

Knapp Commission (1972). *Report of the Commission to Investigation Alleged Police Corruption*. New York: Braziller.

Laswell, Harold D. and Jeremiah McKenna (1971). *The Impact of Organized Crime on an Inner-City Community*. New York: Policy Sciences Center.

Lernoux, Penny (1984). *In Banks We Trust*. Garden City: Anchor/Doubleday.

Linder, L. (1987). Scarfo Charged with 2nd Murder. *Associated Press*, (April 11).

Luksetich, William A. and Michael D. White (1982). *Crime and Public Policy: An Economic Approach*. Boston: Little, Brown.

McCaghy, Charles H. and Stephen A. Cernkovich (1987). *Crime in American Society*. New York: Macmillan.

McFadden, R. D. (1987). The Mafia of the 1980s: Divided and Under Siege. *New York Times*, (March 11):A1.

Moldea, James (1986). *Dark Victory: Ronald Reagan, MCA, and the Mob*. New York: Viking.

Morris, Norval and Gordon Hawkins (1970). *The Honest Politician's Guide to Crime Control*. Chicago: University of Chicago Press.

Musto, David F (1973). *The American Disease: Origins of Narcotics Control.* New Haven, CT: Yale University Press.

Nelli, Humbert S. (1976). *The Business of Crime.* New York: Oxford University Press.

Organized Crime Digest (1987a). (March 25).

_____ (1987b). (December 23).

_____ (1986a). (May).

_____ (1986b). (August).

_____ (1985). (November).

Pace, Denny F. and Jimmie C. Styles (1975). *Organized Crime: Concepts and Control.* Englewood Cliffs: Prentice-Hall.

Pennsylvania Crime Commission. (1986). *Report.* Conshohocken, PA: Commonwealth of Pennsylvania.

_____ (1985). *Report.* Conshohocken, PA: Commonwealth of Pennsylvania.

Potter, Gary W. (1986). *The Porn Merchants.* Dubuque, IA: Kendall Hunt.

Potter, Gary W. and Philip Jenkins (1985). *The City and the Syndicate: Organizing Crime in Philadelphia.* Lexington, MA: Ginn Press.

President's Commission on Organized Crime (1986). *The Impact: Organized Crime Today.* Washington, DC: United States Government Printing Office.

Reuter, Peter (1983). *Disorganized Crime.* Cambridge, MA: MIT Press.

Reuter, Peter, Jonathan Rubinstein and Simon Wynn (1983). *Racketeering in Legitimate Industries: Two Case Studies.* Washington, DC: National Institute of Justice.

Rowan, Roy (1986). The 50 Biggest Mafia Bosses. *Fortune,* (November 10):24-38.

Salerno, Ralph and John S. Tompkins (1969). *The Crime Confederation.* Garden City, NY: Doubleday.

Smith, Dwight C. (1980). Paragons, Pariahs, and Pirates: A Spectrum-Base Theory of Enterprise. *Crime and Delinquency,* 26 (July):358-86.

_____ (1978). Organized Crime and Entrepreneurship. *International Journal of Criminology and Penology,* 6:161-177.

_____ (1976). Mafia: The Prototypical Alien Conspiracy. *The Annals of the American Academy of Political and Social Science,* 423 (January):75-88.

_____ (1975). *The Mafia Mystique.* New York: Basic Books.

Task Force on Organized Crime. (1967). *Task Force Report: Organized Crime.* Washington, DC: United States Government Printing Office.

Wisotsky, Stephen (1986). *Breaking the Impasse in the War on Drugs.* New York: Greenwood Press.

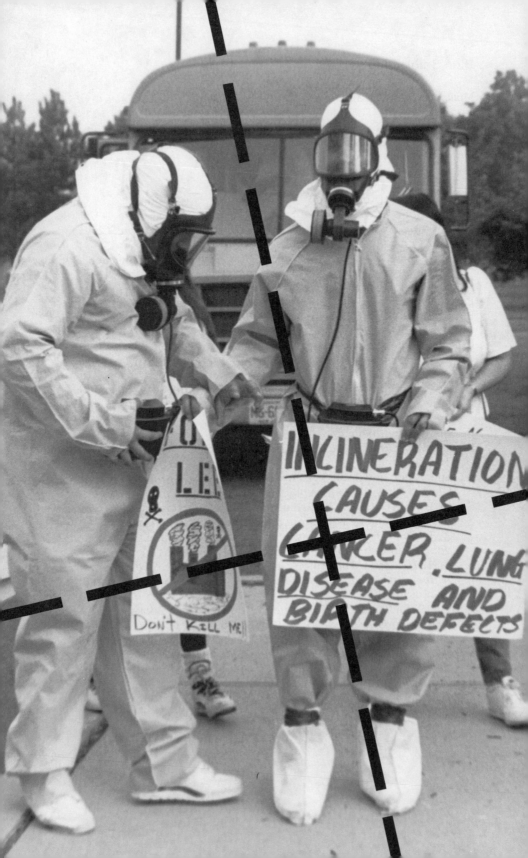

chapter 6

Myths that Justify Crime
A Look at White Collar Criminality

Myths of crime and criminal justice, for the most part, revolve around two central themes. First, there is a criminal act or behavior that stimulates public concern and interest. That behavior is seized upon by the media, law enforcement bureaucracies, and politicians as a way of attracting public attention and raising policy issues related to crime in general. In the ensuing discussion of the behavior, exaggerations, political rhetoric and often outright misconceptions and misunderstandings combine to create a distorted view of the threat to society and to individuals in that society. It is common for these myths to target groups with unpopular beliefs or minority population groups. So, throughout history, we have had crime scares about women and witchcraft, homosexuals and molested children, satanists and ritual murders, Italians and organized crime, blacks and drugs, and immigrants and political subversion. The second recurring theme which we find in exploring myths of crime and criminal justice is a massive law enforcement response to the behavior in question. New laws are passed outlawing certain aspects of the behavior, prison sentences are increased, new powers are granted to investigating agencies, and a proactive campaign of enforcement is launched in an attempt to control the perceived danger. In taking these steps we frequently overreact and make the problem we are trying to solve much worse than it was originally.

In this chapter, however, we will explore a myth of a different kind. This is a myth designed to downplay the importance of criminal behavior and justify a policy of lax enforcement. This is a myth which seeks to mitigate responsibility and excuse misconduct. This is a myth which argues for less enforcement, fewer laws, and less stringent punishment. This is a myth which protects those with political and economic power. In this chapter, we will explore the issue of white collar crime. We will address a series of neutralizations and explanations which have been used to justify political and criminal justice policies which some suggest go so far as to encourage criminality. The first of these myths is that white collar crimes cause less damage, both economic and physical than traditional "street crimes." Government officials have tried to present the issue of white collar crime in terms of embezzlement, or employee fraud, ignoring the more pervasive and dangerous criminality of corporations. The second myth is that white collar crimes are accidents or oversights, that they are unintended crimes lacking the criminal intent found in crimes of violence and theft. The third myth used to explain away white collar crime is that present laws and enforcement efforts are more than sufficient to deal with the problem. In fact, this argument is frequently carried a step further to suggest that present laws are too stringent and severe and out of proportion to the danger of the behavior. We will explore the actual patterns of enforcement and the punishments actually meted out to white collar criminals.

"Real" Crime and White Collar Crime

When most people think of crime they think of acts of interpersonal violence or property crimes. In the popular imagination, a crime is an act committed against an innocent victim by an uncaring perpetrator. A crime occurs when someone breaks into your house and steals your television set and stereo. A crime occurs when an anonymous mugger knocks you to the ground and steals your wallet and watch. A crime occurs when a serial killer goes on a rampage and slaughters innocent victims.

These images of crime are perpetuated by the media and by the law enforcement establishment. News reports carry nightly features on robberies at convenience stores, assaults, drug crimes, and murders. Television movies and police shows emphasize crimes of violence, with a particular bent toward the sensational (but rather rare) crime of murder. Police departments, the FBI, and other law enforcement agencies monitor the amount of street crime and gauge the threat of crime in society in that context. When politicians talk about crime, engaging in their ritualistic calls for law and order, they are careful to stress crimes of violence and theft. When George Bush raised the crime issue in the 1988 presidential election, he was careful to portray it in the personage of Willie Horton, a black criminal convicted of a violent offense. We spend billions of dollars a year, we employ over 500,000 police and thousands of other government officials and prosecutors in the battle against street crime.

Of course, we are all appalled by murder, rape, robbery, and the other predatory crimes in society. But our emphasis on these crimes is fundamentally misleading. It conceals two fundamental truths about crime in the United States. The first is that while we may worry about street crimes, there is very little the criminal justice system can do to control them and next to nothing the criminal justice system can do to prevent them. The second basic truth is that all the violent crime, all the property crime, all the crime we concentrate our energy and resources on combating is less of a threat, less of a danger, and less of a burden to society than the crime committed by corporations and crime "committed by a person of respectability and high social status in the course of his occupation" (Sutherland, 1940), or, more simply, white collar crime. As Bertram Gross (1980) has commented, these are society's "dirty secrets":

> We are not letting the public in on our era's dirty little secret: that those who commit the crime which worries citizens most — violent street crime — are, for the most part, products of poverty, unemployment, broken homes, rotten education, drug addiction, alcoholism, and other social and economic ills about which the police can do little if anything. . . . But, all the dirty little secrets fade into insignificance in comparison with one dirty big secret: Law enforcement officials, judges as well as prosecutors and investigators, are soft on corporate crime. . . . The corporation's "mouthpieces" and "fixers" include lawyers, accountants, public relations experts and public officials who negotiate loopholes and special procedures in the laws, prevent most illegal activities from ever being disclosed and undermine or sidetrack "over zealous" law enforcers. In the few cases ever brought to court, they usually negotiate penalties amounting to "gentle taps on the wrist" (110, 113-15, cited in Hagan, 1986:111).

The Costs of White Collar Crime

In simple dollar terms, there is no question that white collar crime does significantly more damage to society than all street crimes put together. The economic losses resulting from street crimes are generally estimated to be about $10 billion a year (Webster, 1984). The total monetary damage from white collar crimes is somewhere between $174 billion and $231 billion annually (Clinard and Yeager, 1980:8).

Some commentators are quick to point out that these economic losses are spread across millions of victims, the damages are diffuse, and the trauma to the victim less than in the case of street crimes. They are also quick to point out that crimes of violence entail losses that far exceed monetary damages in terms of injury and even death. The fact is that they are too quick to point to death and injury as an index of the seriousness of street crimes. White collar crimes kill and maim as well, and in staggering numbers. Consider the following:

- Every year approximately 14,000 workers in the United States are killed on the job.

- Annually 100,000 workers die from diseases contracted in the course of their occupations as a direct result of violations by corporations of health and safety codes.

- It is estimated that 140,000 people die each year from air pollution alone, most of which is the result of a violation of governmental regulations by corporations.

- Unsafe and defective merchandise produced by corporations and sold to consumers results in an additional 30,000 deaths and 20,000,000 serious injuries a year.

- About 2,000,000 workers a year are injured on the job because ·of dangerous working conditions maintained by their employers in violation of prevailing safety standards (Kramer, 1984: 19).

Compare this record of corporate carnage to the approximately 20,000 murders and 850,000 assaults a year committed in the United States; you can then begin to appreciate the extent of victimization from white collar crimes.

White Collar Crime and Criminal Intent

Despite the damage to society resulting from white collar crimes, government officials, corporate executives, and even some law enforcement experts argue that these crimes differ from street crimes in several important respects. They attempt to mitigate the impact of white collar crime by pointing to a lack of *mens rea* (criminal intent) (Clinard and Yeager, 1980:70). They say that unlike muggers, rapists, and murderers, corporate violators do not set out to commit crime. Violations simply happen in the context of occupational environments. They result from oversights, occasionally from negligence, and from the pressures inherent in the business world. These crimes and violations are not the result of a conscious decision to do harm or inflict injury.

The argument that corporate offenders lack criminal intent is one of a series of neutralizing myths employed by white collar criminals to excuse their conduct. Unfortunately, the facts simply belie the myth. Studies have shown clearly that injuries and deaths caused by corporate violations are not simply a matter of carelessness or neglect, many are the direct result of willful violations of the law. For example, James Messerschmidt, in a comprehensive review of research studies on job-related accidents, determined that somewhere between 35 and 57 percent of those accidents occurred because of direct safety violations by the employer (Messerschmidt, 1986:100). Laura Shill Schraeger and James Short, Jr. (1978:413) found that 30 percent of industrial accidents resulted from safety violations and another 20 percent resulted from unsafe working conditions. The Environmental Protection Agency estimates that of the 88 billion pounds of toxic waste produced annually by American companies, 90 percent of it is disposed of improperly and in violation of the law (Coleman, 1989).

Anecdotal evidence, while often hard to come by in considering white collar crime, further supports the contention that many of these crimes are willful and deliberate.

Consider the case of the asbestos industry in the United States (Carlson, 1979:25-52). Major asbestos manufacturers were aware as long ago as 1934, as a result of company-funded research, that asbestos-related diseases (commonly referred to as "white lung") were a distinct threat to their workers. Two of the largest asbestos manufacturers, Johns-Manville and Raybestos-Manhattan, not only knew of the danger but covered up their own research findings. Researchers hired by the asbestos industry were prevented from publishing their findings about the dangers of asbestos, and the Philip Carey Company even went so far as to fire its own medical consultant when he warned of the dangers of asbestos-related diseases. Rather than taking steps to protect workers in the asbestos plants, the companies engaged in a policy of quietly settling death claims from workers who died. Even more shocking is the fact that

Johns-Manville did not notify employees when their medical checkups revealed the presence of asbestosis ("white lung"), despite the fact that this is a progressive disease which can be treated successfully in its early stages but is fatal if left untreated.

The Ford Pinto case provides a similar and equally chilling example of a corporate decision to commit an act of violence against consumers. It is estimated that nine hundred people were incinerated due to the engineering of the Pinto gas tank which tended to burst into flames as the result of even a low-speed rear end collision (Dowie, 1977:20; Cullen, 1984). The decision to allow these people to die was a calculated one based entirely on Ford's profit outlook. Ford had rushed the Pinto into production in the 1960s in an attempt to compete with cheaper, more efficient, smaller Japanese imports. The company had made a substantial investment in modifying its assembly line to produce this new model car when it learned, as a result of its own crash tests, that the gas tank would explode in rear end collisions. Ford was faced with a dilemma: it could stop production and lose the money it invested in the Pinto, it could make a modification to the gas tank which would cost roughly eleven dollars per car and would correct the problem, or it could say nothing and allow a deadly automobile to be manufactured and sold. They chose the latter. Ford calculated that it would save about eighty-seven million dollars by settling death and injury claims rather than by making the modification in the gas tank. It was not until 1978 that the Department of Transportation finally got around to recalling the Ford Pinto.

Of course, Ford is not the only auto manufacturer who can be held accountable for producing unsafe automobiles. General Motors (GM) had a similar experience in the 1980s (Hills, 1987:7). GM began production of a new line of cars in 1980, known as X-cars. Its own tests indicated clearly that these X-cars had a tendency for the rear-wheel brakes to lock prematurely, causing the car to spin out of control. Even after fifteen people died in X-cars and at least seventy-one were injured, GM continued to fight government attempts to recall the X-cars for needed repairs.

GM did not limit its production of defective vehicles to cars. They also produced school buses with dangerous defects and delayed as long as possible in making the necessary repairs. When Ralph Nader, the well-known consumer advocate, raised the issue of dangerous school buses with GM, the company responded by hiring private detectives to investigate Nader's personal life in an attempt to blackmail him into silence (Heilbroner, 1973).

As if it were not bad enough that United States corporations produce unsafe cars and school buses, they also produce unsafe tires to put on those vehicles. Firestone produced a series of steel-belted radials in the 1970s known as the "500" series. The company received complaints from consumers about sudden blowouts occurring in these tires. Even after forty-one deaths related to the defective product, Firestone was still fighting to keep the tire on the market and was engaged in a "concerted campaign to keep the truth from the public" (Coleman, 1989:42).

While the highways are acknowledged to be a dangerous place, particularly if you have a Ford Pinto with Firestone steel-belted radials on it, the air is not much better. General Dynamics was warned by one of its engineers in the early 1970s that the cargo doors in its DC-10 aircraft were defective. The warning was ignored and 346 people were killed in a plane crash in France when the cargo door on their plane opened during flight (Nader, Green, and Seligman, 1976). In another case, B.F. Goodrich falsified test records and laboratory reports in an attempt to sell defective air brakes to the United States Air Force, a product which would have endangered the lives of thousands of fighter pilots (Heilbroner, 1973).

Other industries provide similar examples of deliberate criminal conduct by corporations. Hormel, one of the nation's largest meat-packing companies bribed a Department of Agriculture inspector to ignore violations in their production and packaging of meat (McCaghy, 1976:216). In fact, Hormel not only produced unsafe food products for original consumption, but the company recycled spoiled meat and sent it back to the market.

> When the original customers returned the meat to Hormel, they used the following terms to describe it: "moldy liverloaf, sour party hams, leaking bologna, discolored bacon, off-condition hams, and slick and slimy spareribs." Hormel renewed these products with cosmetic measures (reconditioning, trimming, and washing). Spareribs returned for sliminess, discoloration, and stickiness were rejuvenated through curing and smoking, renamed Windsor Loins and sold in ghetto stores for more than fresh pork chops (Wellford, 1972:69).

Other examples abound in virtually every industry. Consider the following examples from the pharmaceutical industry (Coleman, 1989; Braithwaite, 1984):

- William S. Merrell Company submitted false test results and records to the Food and Drug Administration (FDA) in order to avoid losing the money they had invested in developing what turned out to be a dangerous and defective drug.
- Eli Lilly and Company failed to report illnesses and at least fifty deaths associated with their arthritis medication Oraflex.

- The Richardson-Merrell Company, during testing for a cholesterol inhibitor called MER/29, noted serious vision problems caused by the drug and the deaths of laboratory animals. The company not only lied to the FDA about these findings but told the researchers to falsify their data to make the drug look safe and effective.

- In another case, Richardson-Merrell produced a drug called Benedectin, which was used to treat nausea. The company had research results which indicated that the drug caused serious birth defects. Despite the fact the company knew of the danger, it continued to manufacture and market the drug and withheld the data from the FDA.

Not all white collar and corporate crime endangers our health and our lives. Some of it merely endangers our finances. There can be little doubt that when corporations engage in price fixing and restraint of trade, they are engaged in deliberate and premeditated criminality. Estimates on the overall cost to the public from restraint of trade are difficult to arrive at, but there is a general consensus that the price we pay for this corporate misconduct is around $20 billion a year (Bequai, 1978:93). When we consider individual cases, it becomes clear that each violation places an enormous economic burden on society. For example, the Federal Trade Commission has estimated that the public pays $128 million a year in higher prices because of an agreement among four cereal companies to minimize competition, a conspiracy that has been in effect for over thirty years (Mayer and Bishop, 1976:79). The impact is even more pronounced in the automobile industry where consumers pay $1.6 billion in higher prices because of collusion to limit competition among the major automobile manufacturers (Green et al., 1972:4). Even local conspiracies to fix prices and limit competition are enormously costly. In Seattle and Tacoma, a local price-fixing conspiracy among bakers added four cents to the price of every loaf of bread, resulting in consumer losses of $35 million over the ten-year period the conspiracy was active. Price-fixing conspiracies have even impacted the most basic aspects of life. For example, in 1975 the Justice Department filed an antitrust suit against three of the largest plumbing fixture producers in the United States (Borg Warner, American Standard, and Kohler) for conspiring to fix prices in the amount of $1 billion on bathroom fixtures (Hagan, 1986:133). Everest and Jennings engaged in an illegal price-rigging conspiracy which raised the price of wheelchairs four times over the market value (McCaghy and Cernkovich, 1987:366-67). Of course, the most celebrated example of a price-fixing conspiracy involved twenty-nine corporations in the heavy electrical equipment industry, who conspired to fix prices on government contracts, costing consumers $1.75 billion per year over a seven-year period (Hills, 1971:162; Green et al., 1972:155).

Sometimes the devastating effects of white collar crime are harder to quantify and even more difficult to see. Consider the current crisis with regard to environmental pollution. Almost everyone is aware of the Three Mile Island incident in Pennsylvania which involved a nuclear accident that released radioactivity into the atmosphere and required the evacuation of children and pregnant women from the area around the plant. The company involved, Metropolitan Edison, pleaded guilty to using inaccurate testing methods and pleaded no contest to charges of destroying records and five other criminal counts (Hagan, 1986:139). Other environmental disasters have included the dumping of toxic chemicals at Love Canal, New York [where Hooker Chemical dumped twenty-one thousand tons of chemicals resulting in birth defects and cancer] and Times Beach, Missouri [where all the residents of the town had to move out because of dioxin levels one hundred times above those considered safe for humans] (Beirne and Messerschmidt, 1991:189). In fact, the Environmental Protection Agency (EPA) estimates that there are thirty-four thousand dump sites with "significant problems" where toxic wastes have been buried in the United States (Brown, 1982:305). Other cases of environmental crime by corporations abound:

- Olin Corporation illegally dumped thirty-eight tons of mercury, a chemical which causes damage to the human reproductive system and nervous disorders, into the municipal sewage system of Niagara Falls, New York, between 1970 and 1977 (McCaghy and Cernkovich, 1987:376).

- Kentucky Liquid Recycling, Inc. forced the shut down of the entire Louisville sewage system in 1977 by dumping toxic chemicals into that system (375-76).

- Allied Chemical Company dumped Kepone in Virginia's James River and in 1976 pleaded *nolo contendere* to 153 criminal charges (Hagan, 1986:140).

Occasionally, corporations actually commit crimes against the state. Once again, in the case of crimes such as defense contract fraud and trading with the enemy, there can be little doubt of the criminal intent of the actors involved. Corporate fraud committed in relation to defense contracts is almost legendary and the cases are too numerous to recount in detail, but a few examples are instructive (McCaghy and Cernkovich, 1987:366, 395-96). Swift and

Company, one of America's largest meat packers, sold hams contaminated with rat manure to the Walter Reed Army Medical Center. General Electric pleaded guilty in 1985 to overcharging the Air Force $800,000 on a $47 million contract. General Dynamics corporation charged the Air Force $9,609 for a twelve-cent wrench. In other cases, the Pentagon was charged $659 for an ashtray, $425 for a hammer, $7,622 for a coffee maker, $400 for a socket wrench, and $640.09 for toilet seats.

While these overcharges in defense contracts are outrageous and clearly deliberate examples of attempts to defraud the government by major corporations, they pale in comparison to charges of collaboration by United States corporations with the enemy during World War II. Charles Higham (1982), in his study of corporate misconduct during World War II charges that executives of Ford Motor Company authorized the production of trucks for German troops occupying France; that Chase Manhattan Bank continued to do business with the Nazis throughout the war, and that while gasoline and oil was stringently rationed in the United States to support the war, Standard Oil of New Jersey was shipping fuel to the Nazis through Switzerland.

The Criminogenic Corporation

As shocking as these cases may be, it is important to understand they are not aberrations—they are not merely a collection of apocryphal stories that deviate from the norm. Everything we know about corporate and white collar crime leads us to believe that crime is a way of life for many corporations. While it may be fashionable for government officials and corporate executives to claim that corporations behave responsibly and that these tragic cases are simply isolated incidents, the data conclusively indicate otherwise.

Consider Edwin Sutherland's (1949) findings in his groundbreaking research on white collar crime conducted almost fifty years ago. Sutherland searched the records of regulatory agencies and commissions, and federal, state, and local courts looking for adverse decisions handed down against the seventy largest corporations in America over a twenty-year period. His findings are enlightening:

> Each of the 70 large corporations has 1 or more decisions against it, with a maximum of 50. The total number of decisions is 980, and the average per corporation is 14.0. Sixty corporations have decisions against them for restraint of trade, 53 for infringement,

44 for unfair labor practices, 43 for miscellaneous offenses, 28 for misrepresentation in advertising, and 26 for rebates (15).

Sutherland found that major corporations engage in widespread violations and that these corporations are recidivists, committing their crimes both frequently and on a continual basis (97.1 percent of the corporations in his study were recidivists). These numbers are even more compelling when one considers that little effort is put into discovering and prosecuting corporate violations; therefore, adverse decisions represent only a tiny portion of the actual crime committed. Later studies have confirmed Sutherland's conclusions.

In 1980, Marshall Clinard and Peter Yeager published their findings with regard to crimes committed by the 477 largest manufacturing corporations and the 105 largest wholesale, retail, and service corporations in the United States in 1975 and 1976 (Clinard and Yeager, 1980:110-16). In that two-year period, these 582 corporations were the subjects of 1,553 federal cases initiated against them. Because these numbers include only cases brought against the corporations, they once again represent a major underestimate of the total amount of crime committed by these corporations. Clinard and Yeager suggest they had uncovered only "the tip of the iceberg of total violations" (Clinard and Yeager, 1980:111). They found that in just two years, 60 percent of the corporations had at least 1 action initiated against them, 42 percent of the corporations had 2 or more actions initiated against them, and the most frequent violators were averaging 23.5 violations per corporation (Clinard and Yeager, 1980:116). In the face of these numbers, it is extremely difficult to argue that corporate criminality is random and isolated.

An even more recent investigation of white collar crime by *U.S. News & World Report* (1982) found that during the decade of the 1970s almost 2,700 corporations were convicted of federal criminal charges. The cost to the public from price fixing, pollution, corruption of public officials, and tax evasion was $200 billion a year.

What these findings also suggest is that there is a double standard of justice operating in the United States. Consider the outrage that would be expressed by the public, politicians, and law enforcement officials if they identified a community of people in which 60 percent of the residents were convicted of a crime, 40 percent were repeat offenders, and a substantial number were committing almost a dozen crimes a year. There would be calls for preventive detention (lock them up before they commit more crimes), automatic add-on sentences for being career criminals (keep them in jail so they can't commit crime), as well as for stepped-up law enforcement efforts (increased patrols, sting operations, career criminal profiling). Every law enforcement measure that could be dreamed up would be placed on the public agenda and probably initiated on the streets. But does this happen when the criminal justice system confronts white collar crime? Are there calls for a massive crackdown on corporate violence? Do the police break down the front doors of Ford and General Motors in midnight raids? The answer is no. We make little effort to enforce the law against these criminals. When we do manage to catch them at their nefarious deeds, we tap them on the wrist, make them say they are sorry and send them about their criminal business. As Bertram Gross pointed out, the "big, dirty secret" about crime in America is that judges, prosecutors, police, and "law and order" politicians are soft on corporate crime.

Law Enforcement and White Collar Crime

The response to the thousands of deaths and injuries and the billions of dollars in damage caused by white collar crime has been to give official sanction to continued criminality. Instead of stepped-up law enforcement, more money for investigations and harsher penalties, the government has responded with precisely the opposite. What has the Federal government's "attack" on corporate crime consisted of (Isaacson and Gorey, 1981:22-23)?:

- The Consumer Product Safety Commission's budget has been slashed by 30 percent imperiling consumers more than ever;

- The number of inspectors in the Occupational Safety and Health Administration (OSHA) has been cut by 11 percent. OSHA has less than three thousand inspectors to "regulate" four million workplaces;

- The Federal Trade Commission's antitrust division had its funding, manpower, and enforcement powers cut, making restraint of trade easier than ever;

- The federal government repealed requirements that companies tell workers about dangerous chemicals they are exposed to on the job;

- The requirement that pharmaceutical manufacturers list the possible risks of their medicines to consumers was canceled by the Reagan administration as unnecessary interference with business;

- The requirement that auto manufacturers produce cars that were safe at 5 miles per hour was changed to a requirement that they demonstrate safety at 2.5 miles per hour, making us much safer in an automobile as long as its not moving.

As Frank Hagan (1986) notes:

> The enforcement divisions of many regulatory agencies are critically understaffed and can be cut back, as in the Reagan administration's plans for the EPA and other agencies, to inoperable levels (110).

The official response to corporate crime enforcement has roughly been the equivalent of a city experiencing a wave of homicides and pulling the police off the streets to prevent interference with the exercise of free will.

While there are fewer regulators and enforcers available to combat corporate crime, it is even more disturbing to learn who those regulators are and how the laws which govern corporate crime are written. One of the most frequently repeated canards associated with white collar crime is that business is overregulated, and that laws designed to control pollution, the quality of consumer products and worker health and safety are unwarranted interferences in the free enterprise system. Corporate officials and government officials are unrelenting in their claims that laws designed to prevent corporate crime adversely impact profits and, by implication, jobs. They charge that environmentalists, consumer advocates and other "do-gooders" conspire to regulate the free enterprise system out of existence. But the facts suggest otherwise.

First, the simple fact is that business has no objection to regulation and government interference when it benefits corporate objectives. The history of government regulation of business in the United States is one of business regulating itself for its own benefit. The earliest controls on corporate crime were the antitrust acts of the late 1800s. These early controls were in fact initiated and supported by the very businesses they ostensibly regulated (Weinstein, 1968; Pearce, 1976:84). Government regulations were used by the robber barons to stabilize the market and to make the economy more predictable. At the same time, they were useful for driving smaller competitors out of business by denying them the use of the same unsavory and illegal tactics that the large corporations had used with such skill in creating their dominant economic positions. The 1906 Meat Inspection Act is a classic case in point. Ostensibly, the act was passed to protect consumers from spoiled, contaminated meat products. But in fact, this "government interference" had full support from the large meat-packing companies because it kept imported meat off the United States market at government expense, and the new regulations hindered smaller meat-packing companies making it hard for them to survive and to compete with the major corporations (Kolko, 1963:99-108). The situation in contemporary America is no different. Industry welcomes governmental meddling with price competition, such as the Interstate Commerce Commission's fixed rates on rail and water freight charges, and distance (or "long-haul") charges on highway transportation which keep transportation costs artificially high (McCaghy and Cernkovich, 1987:399). It is simply impossible to reconcile business complaints of overregulation with demands for more controls on foreign imports, requests for government bailouts, and demands for government assistance to "beleaguered" United States companies.

Corporations in the United States have made the most of the protections provided them by regulatory statutes. They have used government regulations, which they help write and help enforce, to create what Mark Green, Beverly Monroe, and Bruce Wasserstein (1972:7) have called "shared monopolies," markets controlled by four or fewer firms. Shared monopolies can now be found in the the tire industry, the aluminum industry, the soap industry, the tobacco industry, cereals, bread and flour, milk and dairy products, processed meats, canned goods, sugar, soups, and light bulbs. In 1979, the 450 largest American corporations controlled 79 percent of all manufacturing assets and 72 percent of all profits (Simon and Eitzen, 1982:71).

Second, and more importantly, those few regulators and enforcers which the government employs to enforce laws against corporate misconduct are hardly in an adversarial relationship with the industries they regulate. The fact is that those in charge of many of the regulatory agencies and commissions are people who have come to government service from the same corporations they are supposed to be regulating. Contacts between the regulators and the regulated have been cordial and frequently collaborative. Regulators who have come to the government from private enterprise are often more concerned with the needs of the corporations they are regulating than with the safety or economic health of the public. The simple fact that many agency employees leave government service to work for the companies they regulated is compelling evidence of a very cozy relationship (Hagan, 1986:110). This conflict of interest has been apparent in several cases, but the most blatant example can be found in the Environmental Protection Agency during the Reagan administration. Rita Lavelle was appointed by the president to oversee the government's "superfund" program, designed to clean up the most threatening cases of corporate pollution resulting from improper disposal of toxic waste. She had previously been employed at Aerojet-General Corporation in California. During her tenure at the EPA, she participated in decisions relating to her former employer (a clear conflict of interest), entered in "sweetheart deals" with major polluters, and used the superfund allocations for political purposes. In 1983, Lavelle was convicted on four felony counts (Hagan, 1986:139).

Underenforcement and Nonpunitive Justice

"Law and order" advocates in politics are quick to argue that crime can be controlled by "sure, swift, and severe punishment." But in the case of white collar crime the opposite is true.

As we have seen, the lack of staff and resources which hampers regulatory agencies—along with the pervasive conflicts of interest in those agencies—makes the risk of apprehension for white collar criminals very low. The Federal Trade Commission (FTC) offers an excellent example (Cox, et al., 1969; Hills, 1971:180). On an annual basis, the FTC receives about nine thousand complaints. Of those nine thousand complaints, one is referred for criminal prosecution. Of those referred for criminal prosecution, some have been delayed as long as twenty years in going to trial by the corporations involved. The FTC only rarely uses its power to conduct hearings and has been extremely reluctant to use any of the enforcement mechanisms granted to it by law. This laxity in enforcement is not unique to the FTC but has been documented for other agencies as well (Benekos, 1983; Clinard et al., 1979; Hagan et al., 1980; Snider, 1982).

The lethargy of regulatory agencies is compounded by the fact that in order to make a successful case against a corporation, defendant cooperation is almost always necessary (Hagan et al., 1980:818). Unmotivated, understaffed, underfunded agencies are not able to litigate even those few cases of corporate crime that actually come to their attention. The result is one of the most bizarre remedial measures found in law, the consent decree. Under the terms of a consent decree, a defendant corporation negotiates with the government over the violations the corporation has committed. It agrees to alter its pattern of conduct. In return, the government agrees that the company will not have to admit guilt. The company does not have to admit its culpability with regard to a crime, but it does have to promise to stop committing the crime, thereby ending the prosecution. The irony of this "sanction" is made clear by Peter Wickman and Phillip Whitten (1980):

> Corporations that have been involved in polluting the environment sign consent decrees with the EPA and announce that they are working on the problem. Imagine the public reaction if a common street criminal were to be dealt with in this fashion. Here's the scene: Joe Thug is apprehended by an alert patrolman after mugging an eighty-five-year-old woman in broad daylight on the streets of Paterson, New Jersey. Brought down to police headquarters, he holds a press conference with the assistant police chief. While not admitting his guilt, he promises not to commit any future muggings and announces that he is working on the problem of crime in the streets (367).

No matter how serious the crime or how flagrant the violation, the fact is that criminal sanctions are rarely applied in the case of corporate criminals. In their study, Clinard and Yeager (1980:122-26) found that the actual sanctions applied to corporate criminals were weak at best. The most common sanction was a warning which was issued in 44 percent of the cases. Following warnings, corporate criminals were assessed fines 23 percent of the time, although those fines were negligible. In 80 percent of the cases, they were for five thousand dollars or less—hardly a significant sanction to corporations earning billions of dollars a year. The Senate Governmental Affairs Subcommittee (1983) noted an even more disturbing fact. Over a thirty month period, thirty-two thousand fines levied against white collar crime offenders had gone uncollected by the government. Not only are the fines minuscule in size, but offenders seem to feel free to ignore them altogether. In only 1.5 percent of the cases was a corporate officer convicted of a crime, and in only 4 percent of those convictions did the offender go to jail. Even so, their terms of incarceration were very light—averaging thirty-seven days (Clinard and Yeager, 1980:272). This pattern appears to be consistent throughout United States history. Albert McCormick, Jr. (1977) studied antitrust cases brought by the Department of Justice from 1890-1969 and found that only 2 percent of the corporate violators served any prison time at all.

A Dual System of Justice

This survey of white collar and corporate crime is cursory and incomplete at best. There are many other equally troubling patterns of criminality in evidence in corporate America which we will briefly mention.

- *Corporate Bribery*: There has been a pervasive pattern of bribes by corporations to foreign governments in return for preferential treatment and contracts. A similar pattern of bribes through illegal campaign contributions in the United States surfaced during the Watergate investigation. Such activities compromise national security abroad and threaten the foundation of democratic government at home.

- *Crime in the Professions*: Researchers who have studied lawyers, doctors, pharmacists, and others have isolated a long list of offenses committed by these professionals ranging from medicaid and medicare fraud, to overcharging for services, fee-splitting, unnecessary surgery, and many others.

- *Bank and Financial Institution Fraud*: There is a rich and growing literature on crimes committed by banks, savings and loan institutions, and stock brokerage houses. We have not discussed such common offenses as insider trading, money laundering, or financial fraud. The current crisis in the savings and loan industry will keep researchers busy for years to come merely recording the enormous numbers of crimes committed.

- *Tax Fraud*: We have also not been able to explore the massive area of illegal tax fraud and legal, but inequitable tax laws that protect corporate wealth, pilfer the public treasury, and add to the tax burdens of private citizens.

The available evidence on white collar and corporate crime leads to several clear conclusions. (1) Criminality in the corporate sector is widespread and pervasive; few corporate criminals are ever caught or prosecuted. (2) Corporate criminals are recidivists. They commit crimes over and over again with great frequency. They are truly career criminals. (3) When apprehended, they are treated with kid gloves. They are warned, given small fines, or allowed to bargain out of prosecution altogether. In those very rare cases where they are convicted of a crime and sentenced to prison, they are treated with far more consideration and leniency than traditional offenders.

This evidence leads us inexorably to one more myth about the American criminal justice system. Contrary to popular notions and official pronouncements, in opposition to slogans chiseled in marble on courthouses across the country, we do not have an equal system of justice in the United States. There are two very different justice systems. One is for the poor and defenseless, and the other is for the rich and powerful. As Ralph Nader (1985) has commented:

> The double standard — one for crime in the streets and one for crime in the suites — is well known. A man in Kentucky was

sentenced to 10 years in jail in 1983 for stealing a pizza. . . .
Dozens of corporations have been caught illegally dumping toxic
wastes. Yet, only small fines followed.

The double standard prevails in the Justice Department, which
has no corporate-crime equivalent to the Federal Bureau of
Investigation's Uniform Crime Reporting System. The Bureau
has its updated list of the 10 most wanted criminals, but has
no high-visibility listings for the most wanton corporate
recidivists (F3).

All other forms of criminal behavior in society do not begin to
equal the costs, both in terms of dollars and lives, of white collar
crime. Yet our government officials, from the President on down,
continue to protect wanton acts of criminality as long as they are
committed by "respectable society." Some forty years ago, C.
Wright Mills (1952) labeled this condition as "the higher
immorality," arguing that there was a peculiar and pathological
moral degeneracy among the most powerful in American society.
Mills argued that corrupt, unethical, and illegal practices by the
wealthy and powerful were institutionalized in American society.
Sadly, all the available evidence indicates that Mills was entirely
correct, as Clinard and Yeager (1980) indicate in a summary of their
research findings:

> Corporate crime provides an indication of the degree of
> hypocrisy in society. It is hypocritical to regard theft and fraud
> among the lower classes with distaste and to punish such acts
> while countenancing upper-class deception and calling it
> "shrewd business practice." A review of corporate violations and
> how they are prosecuted and punished shows who controls what
> in law enforcement in American society and the extent to which
> this control is effective. Even in the broad area of legal
> proceedings, corporate crime is generally surrounded by an aura
> of politeness and respectability rarely if ever present in cases
> of ordinary crime. Corporations are seldom referred to as
> lawbreakers and rarely as criminals in enforcement proceedings.
> Even if violations of the criminal law, as well as other laws are
> involved, enforcement attorneys and corporation counsels often
> refer to the corporation as "having a problem": one does not
> speak of the robber or the burglar as having a problem (21).

The evidence speaks clearly. Our political institutions and our
criminal justice system, in helping to perpetuate these myths about
white collar crime, have indeed institutionalized this "higher
immorality."

Sources

Benekos, P. J. (1983). Sentencing the White-Collar Offender: Evaluating the Use of Sanctions. Paper presented at the Academy of Criminal Justice Sciences annual meetings, San Antonio, TX, March.

Bequai, A. (1978). *White-Collar Crime: A 20th-Century Crisis.* Lexington, MA: Lexington Books.

Beirne, P. and J. Messerschmidt (1991). *Criminology.* New York: Harcourt Brace Jovanovich.

Braithwaite, J. (1984). *Corporate Crime in the Pharmaceutical Industry.* Boston: Routledge & Kegan Paul.

Brown, M. H. (1982). Love Canal and the Poisoning of America. In *Crisis in American Institutions,* Jerome H. Skolnick and Elliott Currie (eds.), 297-316. 5th ed. Boston: Little Brown.

Carlson, K. W. (1979). Statement before the Congressional Committee on Education and Labor, Subcommittee on Compensation, Health and Safety, Hearings on Asbestos-Related Occupational Diseases, 95th Congress, Second Session. Washington, DC: United States Government Printing Office, pp. 25-52.

Clinard, M. B. and P. C. Yeager (1980). *Corporate Crime.* New York: Macmillan.

_____ (1979). *Illegal Corporate Behavior.* Washington, DC: Law Enforcement Assistance Administration.

Coleman, J. (1989). *The Criminal Elite.* New York: St. Martin's Press.

Cox, E. R., R. C. Fellmuth, and J. E. Schultz (1969). *Nader's Raiders: Report on the Federal Trade Commission.* New York: Grove Press.

Cullen, F. T. (1984). The Ford Pinto Case and Beyond. In *Corporations as Criminals,* Ellen C. Hochstedler (ed.). Beverly Hills: Sage.

Dowie, M. (1977). Pinto Madness. *Mother Jones,* (September):18-32.

Green, M. J., B. C. Monroe, and B. Wasserstein (1972). *The Closed Enterprise System: Ralph Nader's Study Group Report on Anti-Trust Enforcement.* New York: Grossman.

Gross, B. (1980). *Friendly Fascism: The New Face of Power in America.* New York: M. Evans and Co.

Hagan, F. E. (1986). *Introduction to Criminology: Theories, Methods and Criminal Behavior.* Chicago: Nelson-Hall.

Hagan, J. L., I. Nagel, and C. Albonetti (1980). The Differential Sentencing of White-Collar Offenders in Ten Federal District Courts. *American Sociological Review,* 45 (September):802-20.

Heilbroner, R. L. (1973). *In the Name of Profit: Profiles in Corporate Irresponsibility.* New York: Warner Paperback Library.

Higham, C. (1982). *Trading with the Enemy: An Expose of the Nazi-American Money Plot, 1933-1949.* New York: Delacourte Press.

Hills, S. L. ed. (1987). *Corporate Violence*. Totowa, NJ: Rowman and Littlefield.

_____ (1971). *Crime, Power, and Morality*. Scranton, PA: Chandler.

Isaacson, W., and H. Gorey (1981). Let the Buyer Beware: Consumer Advocates Retrench for Hard Times. *Time*. (September 21):22-23.

Kolko, G. (1963). *The Triumph of Conservatism*. New York: Free Press.

Kramer, R. C. (1984). Corporate Criminality: The Development of an Idea. In *Corporations as Criminals*, Ellen Hochstedler (ed.). Beverly Hills: Sage.

Mayer, A. J. and J. Bishop (1976). Antitrust: Snap, Crackle and Pop. *Newsweek*. (June 14):14.

McCaghy, C. (1976). *Deviant Behavior*. New York: Macmillan.

McCaghy, C. and S. Cernkovich (1987). *Crime in American Society*. New York: Macmillan.

McCormick, A. E., Jr. (1977). Rule Enforcement and Moral Indignation: Some Observations on the Effects of Criminal Antitrust Convictions upon Societal Reaction Process. *Social Problems*, 25 (January):30-39.

Messerschmidt, J. W. (1986). *Capitalism, Patriarchy, and Crime: Toward a Socialist Feminist Criminology*. Totowa, NJ: Rowman and Littlefield.

Mills, C. W. (1952). A Diagnosis of Moral Uneasiness. In *Power, Politics and People*, Irving L. Horowitz (ed.), 330-39. New York: Ballantine.

Nader, R. (1985). America's Crime Without Criminals. *New York Times*, (May 19):F3.

Nader, R., M. J. Green, and J. Seligman (1976). *Taming the Giant Corporation*. New York: Norton.

Pearce, F. (1976). *Crimes of the Powerful*. London: Pluto Press.

Schraeger, L. S. and J. F. Short, Jr. (1978). Toward a Sociology of Organizational Crime. *Social Problems*, 25 (April):407-19.

Senate Permanent Subcommittee on Investigations, Committee on Governmental Affairs (1983). 98th Congress, First Session, August 3.

Simon, D. R. and S. D. Eitzen (1982). *Elite Deviance*. Boston: Allyn and Bacon.

Snider, L. (1982). Traditional and Corporate Theft: A Comparison of Sanctions. In *White-Collar and Economic Crime*, Peter Wickman and Timothy Dailey (ed.), 235-58. Lexington, MA: Lexington.

Sutherland, E. H. (1949). *White Collar Crime*. New York: Holt, Rinehart and Winston.

_____ (1940). White Collar Criminality. *American Sociological Review*, 5 (February):1-12.

U.S. News & World Report (1982). Corporate Crime: The Untold Story. (September 6):25.

Webster, W. H. (1984). *Crime in the United States*. Washington, DC: United States Government Printing Office.

Weinstein, J. (1968). *The Corporate Ideal in the Liberal State: 1900-1918.* Boston: Beacon Press.

Wellford, H. (1972). *Sowing the Wind: A Report from Ralph Nader's Center for Study of Responsive Law.* New York: Grossman.

Wickman, P. and P. Whitten (1980). *Criminology: Perspectives on Crime and Criminality.* Lexington, MA: D.C. Heath.

chapter 7

Battered and Blue Crime Fighters

Myths and Misconceptions of Police Work

The public and media have had a long running fascination with police officers and their work. This fascination is reflected in books, newspaper and magazine accounts, as well as television documentaries. Depiction of the police and their work has been especially well represented by the media industry in television shows and movies. From the *Keystone Cops* of the early cinema to *RoboCop II*, many of us have grown up with media portrayals of policing. These images of policing usually carry with them certain recurrent themes that promote and shape our view of the nature of police work in American society. Two prevalent media characterizations of police work are: policing as an exciting yet dangerous profession and the stressful life of a police officer has many negative side effects.

The danger and glamour of police work is revealed in movies like *Dirty Harry, Lethal Weapon I & II, Nighthawks, Fort Apache—The Bronx,* and *Silence of the Lambs.* These movies and other television accounts of policing show the autonomous police officer, single-handedly or sometimes with a minor partner, fighting diabolical, sophisticated and well-armed criminals. These are not run-of-the-mill criminals like the drunk driver, the thief or the check forger. More often than not, police officers are pitted against psychosexual killers, serial murderers, and international terrorists. In almost every depiction of Hollywood policing, officers are shown shooting it out with armed criminal suspects while simultaneously being locked in conflict with the police department they work for— as well as the unenlightened criminal justice system that is unwilling to understand the unique demands of police work.

Movies like the *Blue Knight* and television serials such as "Hill Street Blues" and "Hunter" have painted portraits of police officers and their work as exciting but personally destructive. These more sophisticated presentations often focus on the effects of being a police officer—how policing destroys officers' personal lives. Media portrayals often chime the theme of mental distress because of a growing dissatisfaction and frustration with the criminal justice system's emphasis on criminal rather than victim rights. Stress is rampant among television cops and suicide is always a possibility. Each side effect is presented as commonplace for television cops. More recently, media fascination with policing has even extended to what police officers and policing might be like in centuries to come. Movies like *RoboCop* show policing in terms of its crime fighting role and allude to the almost superhuman qualities needed by modern law enforcement officers.

Media depiction of policing is of course not the only source from which we draw our images of policing and police work. The law enforcement community and political leaders alike reinforce media created perceptions of danger, glamour, and stress. America's "war against crime" and more recently the renewed "war on drugs" have helped reinforce an image of police officers locked in mortal combat with sophisticated high-tech international criminals and drug dealers who will use all means available to them to prevent detection and effect their escape. These arch criminals are shown as far more numerous and better armed than the police and willing to use deadly force in an instant.

In an attempt to become more open with the public, police executives have given the media access to police operations, allowing them to film drug raids, gang sweeps and other high profile operations. Television shows like "Cops" reinforce the notion that police work is dangerous and exciting; camera crews selectively move from call to call filming officers' unique activities. The image is projected that police officers, our most visible symbols of justice, are under siege by drug-dealing kingpins, occupational stress, and even their own police departments.

The allure to study the negative side of police work has not gone unnoticed by scholars. Virtually hundreds of articles have been written about danger and stresses in police work and almost every introductory text in criminal justice or policing contains a section devoted to these topics. One work on policing has even been entitled *The Custer Syndrome*, alluding to the way police are severely out numbered by their criminal counterparts and the "belief that not losing ground [in the war against crime] can be counted as success" (Hernandez, 1989:2). How accurate are the depictions of American policing presented by the media and reinforced by the government and law enforcement community? How conclusive is the research on the dangers and stress of policing in America? This chapter will address a few of the common myths and misconceptions of crime fighting. We will conclude with a consideration of how the disjuncture between perceptions, expectations, and reality shapes the police as an occupational group as they live the myth of crime fighting.

Real Police Work

Despite the images and claims that police officers are outnumbered by their criminal counterparts and despite the political rhetoric of waging war on crime, police officers do considerably less "crime fighting" than one might imagine. When citizens reflect upon the role of the police, invariably they think in terms of their law enforcement capacity. Whether they are being depicted in a police series on television or in a current movie, police officers are portrayed almost solely as crime fighters. Citizens spend hours of leisure time watching cops engage in such activities as high-speed pursuits involving wanted felons, questioning persons who are suspected of having committed serious crimes, shooting it out with dangerous criminals, and involved in other law enforcement tasks.

Crime Fighting

Unfortunately, this image presented by the media is erroneous. It is a myth to believe that the police spend the majority of their time involved in crime fighting activity. In fact, the average cop on television probably sees more action in a half-hour than most officers witness in an entire career. As a general rule, most police work is quite mundane. Police spend a considerable part of their workload involved in such routine tasks as writing traffic citations, investigating automobile accidents, mediating disputes between neighbors and family members, directing traffic, and engaging in a variety of other service-related and order-maintaining activities. If television were to create a program that realistically depicted police work, it would soon go off the air due to poor ratings. Such a show would be quite boring and offer little in the way of "action" to viewers.

Since the 1960s, a variety of research techniques have been employed to study police workload (Greene and Klockars, 1991). Radio calls from dispatchers to patrol cars (Wilson, 1968; Bercal, 1970), telephone calls by citizens to the police (Cumming, Cumming and Edell, 1965), dispatch records (Reiss, 1971), observational data (Kelling, Pate, Dieckman and Brown, 1974), self-reports from police officers (O'Neill and Bloom, 1972) and telephone interviews of citizens (Mafstrofski, 1983) have all been utilized in an attempt to learn what the police actually do and how much time is spent on various activities. Despite the fact that these studies relied on different methodologies and were conducted in different communities and during different time periods, there is consensus among them that relatively little of an officer's day is taken up responding to crime-related activities. Although the proportions varied, as a rule of thumb, between 10 and 20 percent of the calls were of a law enforcement nature.

The findings from the various studies indicate that a substantial proportion of an officer's time does not involve any contact with the public. Police spend many hours engaged in preventive patrol, running errands, and performing a number of administrative tasks that consume a considerable part of their workday. In a recent study undertaken by Jack Greene and Karl Klockars (1991), the researchers excluded from their analysis time that was spent by the police in activities not involving direct contact with the citizenry. When officer workload is reconceptualized in this manner, the proportion of time that is classified as crime-related activity does increase. However, almost all this work involves taking crime reports from citizens. The authors conclude that the:

> findings in no way lend support to the headline news vision of police work as a violent running battle between police and criminals. It bears emphasis that our data show that the average police officer spent about one hour per week responding to reports of crimes in progress. When the officers arrive, they often find that what was described as a crime in progress was, in fact, not a crime or that the perpetrator is gone (Greene and Klockars, 1991: 283).

Police Shootings

Both television and movies frequently portray law enforcement officers as engaged in shoot-outs with dangerous criminals. Although this type of entertainment may produce high ratings for television programs and large profits for movie studios, how does this view of police work compare with reality? How often do police officers in real life fire their weapons at suspects? How many persons are shot and/or killed by the police each year in the United States?

Unfortunately, there are no national statistics published that address this issue. As a consequence, it is not a straightforward matter to determine how many people are killed and/or wounded by police bullets each year. Researchers have had to rely on data that have been collected for other purposes (*Vital Statistics of the United States*) and information that has voluntarily been supplied by police agencies to determine the annual number of police killings that occur.

Vital Statistics records the birth and death records that are collected and published by the United States Public Health Service. Because they contain a category that notes deaths due to legal intervention, they have been useful to researchers who study police killings of citizens. According to *Vital Statistics*, there was an average of 360 deaths due to legal intervention in the United States each year between 1970 and 1975. Because judicially ordered executions did not take place during this period, it can be assumed that almost all these persons died at the hands of police officers. Unfortunately, Lawrence W. Sherman and Robert Langworthy (1979) note that the *Vital Statistics* may underreport the number of police killings by as much as 51 percent. Therefore, there may have been as many as 735 killings by police each year during this period.

Sherman and Langworthy (1979) have concluded that data supplied by police departments is far more complete than the information on killings contained in the *Vital Statistics*. Unfortunately, there is no national survey that has relied on police records. The most comprehensive study to date was undertaken by Sherman and Ellen G. Cohn (1986) who utilized a variety of data sources, including information elicited from police departments, to examine the rate of police killings during a fifteen year (1970-84) period in the fifty largest cities of the United States. They report that in no year did the police in these cities kill more than 353 people (Sherman and Cohn, 1986:I).

Although these researchers report enormous variation in the rate

at which police officers kill citizens, it is clear that these are relatively rare events. Even though Jacksonville (Florida) ranked at the
top with respect to one measure of police homicide between 1980
and 1984, the average officer in that community would have to work
139 years before taking anyone's life. Honolulu, on the other hand,
ranked at the bottom during this same period. A police officer in
that community would kill a citizen, on average once every 7,692
years (Sherman and Cohn, 1986:I).

Not only are police killings rare events, the Sherman and Cohn
(1986) study also concludes that they are becoming even more infrequent. One of their major findings was that the number of persons
killed by big city police officers declined from 353 in 1971 to 172
in 1984. In effect, law enforcement personnel were killing about half
as many people in 1984 as they were in 1971. Despite a perception
on the part of many citizens and by the media that the streets are
becoming more dangerous, the number of citizens mortally
wounded by the police has clearly declined.

There are several explanations for this phenomena (Sherman and
Cohn, 1986:13). For one thing, almost all police departments that
serve large communities have adopted firearms policies that pro-
hibit the use of deadly force against certain fleeing felons (Fyfe and
Blumberg, 1985). Both James J. Fyfe (1978) and Sherman (1983)
have reported that a change to a more restrictive policy is followed
by a decline in the number of shootings by police officers. Second,
training has been improved and the level of discipline has been
tightened in many departments. Third, there has been an explosion
of civil litigation. The net effect of this has been a substantial
increase in the number of lawsuits that are filed as a result of police
shootings. Municipalities now have a strong financial incentive to
prevent unjustifiable incidents and thus avoid financial liability.

In order to gain an idea of how frequently police officers shoot
citizens, nonfatal incidents must also be examined. Unfortunately,
there is no national data that addresses this issue. However, Arnold
Binder and Lorie Fridell (1984) have surveyed the various studies
that have been conducted by researchers in individual departments.
Based on this review, they conclude that approximately 30 percent
of persons shot by the police will actually die (254). Based on this
ratio of woundings to fatalities, a police officer in Jacksonville (the
city with the highest rate of police homicide) would have to work
an average of forty-two years before shooting a citizen. In many
other communities, the time period would be appreciably longer.
Because a police career rarely lasts more than thirty-five years, the
majority of police officers will go their entire career and never shoot
anybody.

The Dangers of Police Work

One of the most pervasive myths about police work is that it is a dangerous occupation. Both film and television present portrayals of police officers being attacked and killed by criminals determined to commit crimes and escape punishment at any cost. This perception is reinforced by the occasional incident in which a police officer is gunned down. When such a tragic event occurs, the evening news will include footage of scenes taken at the deceased officer's funeral. This will vividly portray the hundreds of officers who have come from other departments to pay their last respects to the slain officer. Invariably, the story will include a commentary to the effect that police officers are on the frontline in the war against crime and that they face the possibility of death from a crazed assailant at any given moment.

Not only is policing portrayed as a dangerous occupation, but the message the public routinely receives is that it is becoming much more so. After all, our cities have become plagued with gangs, drugs, and automatic weapons. Police must deal with problems that did not even exist a decade ago, such as the epidemic of crack cocaine and the proliferation of high-powered weapons on the street. Obviously, being a cop today must be more dangerous than was the case in years past—or so we are told.

How accurate is this picture? Clearly, police officers are murdered by suspects. This is an undeniable fact, and each one of these killings is a terrible tragedy for the officer, the officer's survivors, the department, and the community. However, there are some questions that must be addressed: How pervasive is the danger that law enforcement officers face? Is policing really a dangerous occupation? Has it become more so in recent years?

Fortunately, these are relatively easy issues to resolve because the Uniform Crime Reports (UCR) publishes data each year with respect to the number of law enforcement officers who have been feloniously killed in the United States. It is believed that this is one of the most comprehensive and complete sections of the UCR (Konstantin, 1984:34). These data indicate that in the fifteen year period between 1974 and 1988, 1,398 police officers were feloniously killed in the United States (Flanagan and Maguire, 1990:401; Vaughn and Kappeler, 1986:4). Therefore, on the average, there were approximately 93 officers slain each year out of a law enforcement population that numbers over one-half million.

Not only are killings of police officers relatively rare events, the data indicate that they have declined dramatically in recent years. From a high of 132 in 1974, police killings declined to 78 by 1988.

In fact, when the period 1974-76 (Vaughn and Kappeler, 1986: Table 1) is compared to the years 1986-88, the average annual number of killings drops from 124 to 72.3 (Flanagan and Maguire, 1990:401). It is noteworthy that this risk associated with police work has declined despite the restrictions that have been placed on police use of firearms, the increase during this period in both the overall crime rate and the rate of violent crime, the proliferation of semi-automatic weapons on the streets of American cities, the war on drugs, and the increase in the level of gang-related violence that has occurred in many communities. During the period 1974-1988, the total number of crimes increased from 10,253,400 to 13,923,100; the number of violent crimes increased from 974,720 to 1,566,220; and the number of murders and non-negligent manslaughters remained relatively unchanged (Flanagan and Maguire, 1990:365). The level of danger to police is clearly not declining due to a decrease in the crime rate.

To some extent, these statistics on police killings mask the reduction in risk that has occurred because the number of law enforcement personnel has increased substantially during this period. Michael J. Hindelang, Michael R. Gottfredson, Christopher Dunn, and Nicolette Parisi (1977:71) report that there were 594,209 persons employed fulltime in law enforcement at all levels of government in 1974. By 1988, the number had risen to 728,018 (Flanagan and Maguire, 1990:15). Because there were 132 killings of police officers in 1974, the aggregate risk per officer was approximately one chance in 4,501 that year. With 78 deaths in 1988, each officer stood one chance in 9,333 of being slain. Obviously, this is an aggregate rate of risk for all law enforcement personnel. Some officers patrol neighborhoods or perform assignments that place them in somewhat greater danger. Overall, the risk to law enforcement personnel has declined by more than one-half in fourteen years.

Another way to examine the question of danger is to compare the fatality rate of police officers with that of persons working in other occupations and professions. Richard Holden (1991) has examined the mortality data published by the Bureau of Labor Statistics in an attempt to answer the question of whether policing is really more dangerous than other occupations. Comparative data for the years 1984-86 were reviewed. The analysis indicates that police officers consistently face a lower fatality rate than persons employed in mining, construction, transportation, and agriculture. However, the author cautions that a number of methodological problems make this comparison somewhat problematic. For example, the death rate for law enforcement personnel excludes officers who die as a result of traffic accidents unless they were in direct pursuit of a suspect. Therefore, this analysis must be considered somewhat tentative. Nonetheless, there is no support for the myth that policing is one of the most dangerous occupations.

The myth that policing is a dangerous occupation has a number of consequences for law enforcement. For one thing, this misperception is likely to result in an increased level of public support. Citizens who have an exaggerated sense of the danger that law enforcement personnel routinely confront are more likely to give the police the benefit of the doubt when it comes to various controversies involving the propriety of certain actions. Second, the public perception that the police are armed and ready to deal with danger twenty-four hours a day can be beneficial when it is time to engage in contract negotiations (Fyfe, 1982). Third, the belief that being a law enforcement officer is akin to the work of a soldier on the frontlines can have a deleterious affect on the officer's spouse (Niederhoffer and Niederhoffer, 1978). Finally, this pervasive sense that their mission is a dangerous one cannot help but affect the way that police officers deal with the public. One can only speculate about how many times officers use excessive force or are abrupt in their dealings with citizens because they perceive a world that is more dangerous than is actually the case.

Myth of Danger in Domestic Violence Incidents

There is perhaps no myth that is so widely engrained in police folklore as the belief that the domestic violence call is the most dangerous for an officer. William K. Muir (1977) reported that it was the "unanimous sentiment" of the officers he studied that more police are killed in these situations than in any other type of call. Family violence researchers have also emphasized the danger that lurks for police in domestic violence encounters (Straus, Gelles, and Steinmetz, 1980). However, the fact is that the risk of felonious death is far less in domestic violence situations than in many other types of assignments that the police handle.

This myth was seriously undermined by David Konstantin (1984) who analyzed the situational characteristics of all police killings that occurred in the United States between 1978 and 1980. He found that only 5.2 percent of these occurred in situations where officers had responded to domestic disturbances. This was substantially less than the proportion who died intervening in robbery situations, pursuing suspects, making traffic stops, investigating suspicious persons, or as a result of assaults (Konstantin, 1986:41).

Although this analysis suggests that domestic disturbance calls do not present a high level of risk, it is not definitive because it does not take into account the relative amounts of time that police officers spend performing various tasks. For example, domestic violence calls would be risky if they accounted for only one percent of total police calls for service but five percent of reported deaths. Fortunately, Joel Garner and Elizabeth Clemmer (1989) have utilized several existing measures of police activity to calculate the risk of death that officers face when they respond to a domestic violence complaint. These authors conclude that domestic violence consistently ranks below both robbery and burglary as a source of danger to police. In fact, the calculations resulting from one activity measure actually result in domestic violence ranking at the bottom in terms of officer fatality. Garner and Clemmer (1989) assert that "the available evidence strongly suggests that researchers and police managers abandon the notion that domestic disturbance calls result in a large number of police deaths" (527).

How did the myth develop that many police officers die responding to domestic violence calls? Konstantin (1984:43) offers a number of possible explanations. The most likely explanation is that police officials and researchers misinterpreted the data that were provided by the FBI in its annual publication, *Law Enforcement Officers Killed* (LEOK). Prior to 1982, all officer deaths resulting from disturbances were lumped into one category regardless of whether they resulted from domestic violence calls or other types of disturbances (Garner and Clemmer, 1989:517). Many persons mistakenly assumed that all these incidents involved domestic disturbances; in fact a substantial proportion were deaths that resulted from such calls as responding to bar fights, reports of a suspect with a weapon, and other types of disturbances that have nothing to do with family quarrels.

Konstantin gives other reasons why the level of danger in domestic violence calls may have been exaggerated. For one thing, responding to family quarrels can be a traumatic experience for a police officer. After all, it is the only situation where both the offender and the complainant may join forces against the officer. Second, it is possible that those who developed domestic crisis intervention training programs have overstated this danger in order to persuade police departments of the value of their programs. Finally, responding to family quarrels is likely to be perceived by police officers as "social work." Because these encounters take up so much of an officer's time, they may be viewed as demeaning to his/her image as a crime fighter. Therefore, in order to convince themselves that they are doing "real police work," the police may have exaggerated the danger from this type of assignment.

The myth that domestic violence calls represent a high level of danger results in a less effective response by police officers to these situations. Spokespersons for womens' rights organizations have often complained that the police do not take assaults perpetrated by husbands and boyfriends very seriously. Hopefully, as the police become educated to the true nature of the risk that this responsibility entails, they will feel free to develop alternative strategies for dealing with this problem in a more effective manner.

Myths of Police Stress

Stress is a neutral term but often carries with it a negative connotation. Stress can have both beneficial and adverse effects on people. Some people may perform and produce at their best when enough stress is present to encourage or motivate high levels of performance. People undergoing mild forms of stress may experience an increased sense of awareness or alertness and will thus be capable of better performance in the workplace. Sometimes excessive work-related stressors can be debilitating and hinder performance and productivity. People undergoing excessive stress may begin to falter in their jobs and personal lives. Massive amounts of stress have been linked to impairment of the immune system and can have deleterious physical consequences.

Stress in police work has been examined for over a decade. Currently little more is known about police stress than when researchers began studying it more than a decade ago. While it is generally recognized that police stress exists, there is little agreement regarding its cause, effect or extent (Mallory and Mays, 1984; Terry, 1983; Gaines and Van Tubergen, 1989). While it is plausible to assert that police stress exists, little scientific research has been conducted that proves the cause behind the stress law enforcement officers experience. Instead scholars have developed several perspectives on the extent and sources of police stress.

Some researchers view stress as a personal adjustment problem. They have defined stress in terms of its negative aspects as a personal-environmental fit "problem" (Lofquist and Davis, 1969). From this view of stress, police officers are seen as unable to cope with the demands made upon them by their profession. That is, certain police officers are not capable of performing under the strains of occupational demands. Stress affects officers differently, and since no two persons are the same, stress is thought to have differential effects on police officers. From this perspective, it is maintained that personal needs, values, abilities, and experiences all affect how individual police officers respond to the stress of their work environment.

An alternative and very different perspective views police stress as a structural problem that does not reside in any personal maladjustment but in the pathology of the police organization and the working environment. Scholars taking this perspective examine such factors as management style, role conflict, and other structural sources of stress. Scholars adopting this structural explanation feel that if officers are unable to perform, if they are hindered or having problems, the police organization and environment are at fault— not the individual officer.

Regardless of whether stress is a product of individual maladjustment or a structural deficiency in the police occupational environment, what are the effects of police stress and are they real? Do police officers experience higher levels of stress than bankers, lawyers or physicians? Are police suicides, drug abuse, divorce and mortality rates really side effects of the stress inherent in the police profession?

The Myth of Police Suicide

One of the most superficial, yet appealing, arguments for the high levels of stress in police work has been based on the suicide rate found among police officers. Suicide attempts by police officers are often linked, at least in perception, to the stress associated with police work (see Alpert and Dunham, 1988). Some have argued that "An informal consensus appears to have arisen to the effect that the suicide rate among police is appreciably greater than for other occupational groups" (Bedian, 1982 as cited in; Josephson and Reiser, 1990:227).

While relatively few studies have been conducted to examine the actual cause of police suicide, early studies have focused on comparisons between the rates of suicide among police officers and the general population. With few exceptions early studies concluded that police officers suffer a higher rate of suicide than the general public (Friedman, 1967; Labovitz and Hagedon, 1971; Lester, 1983). While the rate of suicide changes depending on the police population examined and the time periods covered by researchers, it has been a general contention that police officers experience suicide at higher rates than the general public. Urban police officers are said to experience the highest rate of suicide. Some studies have even suggested the rate of suicide among urban police might be six times higher than that experienced by the general public. Researchers studying the records of suicide in the city of Chicago found police officers were five times as likely to take their own lives as would ordinary citizens (Wagner and Brzeczek, 1983).

Additional research into police suicide has compared the rate of suicide across different occupations. In these studies, researchers have examined the suicide rates for numerous occupations and compared them to the police profession. One study of thirty-six occupations found that policing had the second highest rate of suicide (Labovitz and Hagedon, 1971). Nonetheless, Lester's (1983) research into police suicide found the suicide rate was also high among the self-employed and people in manufacturing occupations. Uncritical readings of these findings are often offered as direct evidence of the stress inherent in police work.

Even though early research into police suicide has generally indicated a high rate of suicide among police officers, this myth of policing is beginning to change as researchers collect additional data and take a more critical look at the problem. A 1990 study of police officer suicide in the Los Angeles Police Department found the suicide rate of police officers remained lower than the suicide rate for other adults in the same geographic area (Josephson and Reiser, 1990:227). These scholars felt that "research done at the Los Angeles Police Department (LAPD) and the data available in the literature fail to provide support for the belief of an inordinately high suicide rate among police in general" (see also Dash and Reiser, 1978). Other cautious researchers have offered alternative explanations other than stress for the seemingly high rate of police suicide. "First, police work is a male-dominated profession, and males have demonstrated a higher rate of successful suicide than females. Second, the use, availability and familiarity with firearms by police in their work provide them with a lethal weapon that affords the user little chance of surviving a serious suicide attempt" (Alpert and Dunham, 1988:146-47). There is also evidence that suggests at least some suicides by police officers may be spawned from the uncovering of acts of corruption or deviance rather than the inherent stress of police work. In several cases, most recently the New York City Police Department's probe of the "Buddy Boys," a corrupt police ring, officers have taken their lives during the investigation of corruption. While not all or even a majority of police suicides are a product of uncovering deviance and corruption, no research has been conducted regarding the relationship between corruption and suicide.

A review of the existing literature and arguments surrounding stress and police suicide indicates that conceptual and methodological problems associated with conducting this type of research makes it difficult to draw any firm conclusion. One can say with some confidence, however, that there is no available research that conclusively proves that the rate of suicide experienced by police officers is any greater than populations with similar background characteristics. Additionally, there is no conclusive evidence that work-related stress experienced by police officers is the cause of suicide. It is largely a myth that police kill themselves because of a level of stress greater than that experienced by members of other occupations.

Drug and Alcohol Abuse

Police officers are said to have high rates of alcoholism and drug abuse when compared to other occupations (Alpert and Dunham, 1988). Some have claimed that this is a product of police stress and a means by which police officers deal with the stress inherent in police work (Violanti, Marshall and Howe, 1985). Scholars studying the research on police alcohol use have determined that the literature "suggests that drinking problems among police officers are closely related to occupational stress and the perceived absence of alternative coping strategies that are effective in reducing stress" (Alpert and Dunham, 1988:145).

The first meaningful study of police misconduct specifically examining the use of alcohol by on-duty police officers was conducted by Albert Reiss in 1971. In researching infractions of departmental rules in three cities, Reiss found that drinking while on duty crossed all cities examined, and that the extent of on-duty use of alcohol ranged from 3.2 to 18.4 percent. A later study indicated that as many as 25 percent of police officers have serious problems with the use of alcohol (Kroes, 1976). Although these findings have been called into question (Lester, 1983), several studies of the use and abuse of alcohol and drugs support the finding that police use drugs and alcohol with much regularity.

Tom Barker (1983) found that of the forty-three officers responding to a self report survey, the "perceived" extent of drinking on the job was 8.05 percent. A 1988 study found that approximately 20 percent of police officers in a single agency used illegal drugs while on duty. Furthermore, these researchers found that the rate of on-duty alcohol use among veteran police officers reached nearly 20 percent (Kraska and Kappeler, 1988). Other researchers have drawn similar conclusions. More alarming, Van

Raalte (1979) found that 67 percent of the officers studied admitted drinking alcohol while on duty. John Violanti, James Marshall and Barbara Howe (1985) as well as Peter Kraska and Victor Kappeler (1988) offered explanations for the conflicting claims among researchers regarding the degree of police drug and alcohol use. They suggest that the study of police deviance is difficult and that there is the distinct possibility of underreporting of deviance by the police. As Violanti, et al has stated:

> Alcohol use among police is underestimated. Many officers, fearing departmental discipline, are unwilling to officially report their deviance. Police organizations appear ambivalent toward drinking problems, placing blame on the individual officer and not the police occupational structure (Kroes, 1976). Other departments may "hide" problem drinkers in positions where they will not adversely affect police operations (106).

Current research on police drug use was prompted by the adoption of employment drug-testing practices by police departments. This research has generally indicated a small proportion of drug use by police officers. In 1986, the New Jersey State Police tested all 2,300 members of its force for drug use. Only five officers or .2 percent of the agency tested positive (Burden, 1986). Similar results were found for the City of New York Police Department. The conflict between earlier observational and self-report studies and the drug-testing results are more than likely a product of one or two factors. First, much media attention has been given to the issue of police drug use, possibly making officers more careful and fearful of detection. Second, these drug-screening tests are often administered to probationary employees with advance warning. Officers would therefore have time to modify their behavior before taking a drug test. Since many traces of illegal drugs leave the body rapidly, little advanced warning is necessary for officers to modify their behavior.

While there is fairly strong evidence to support the extensive use of alcohol and drugs by police officers, there is less support of a direct causal relationship between drug use and police stress. An equally plausible explanation for the use of drugs and alcohol is that these substances are used for recreational purposes. In Kraska and Kappeler's (1988) study, they failed to uncover one police officer that reported current use of drugs who did not have a preemployment history of drug use. If police stress was a substantial cause of the abuse of these substances, one would expect to find officers without histories of drug use turning to these substances after experiencing the stresses of police work. Similarly, the different proportions of officers using drugs and alcohol might suggest that officers have recreational drugs of choice. Veteran officers may be more likely to use alcohol and younger officers more likely to use other illicit drugs. Very little, if any, research has been done comparing cross-cultural/generational samples of police officers and drug use. There is a distinct possibility that the differences between the levels of alcohol and drug use is a product of police subcultural acceptance of one drug over the other. Alternatively, officers may engage in these behaviors out of boredom or peer pressure as much as from any stress inherent in crime fighting.

The Myth of Police Mortality

One myth prevalent among law enforcement officers is that they experience greater mortality rates from natural causes than do other citizens. This myth of policing can be viewed as the culmination of stress-related myths of policing. When one links the dangers, the suicide rate, and the stress myths, it is a natural inference that police officers must experience a greater rate of work related mortality. This myth has been extended to the perception that police officers do not live long after retirement. This and like myths circulate within the law enforcement community. Myths associated with police mortality have been given credence by misreadings of research and unsupported statements in the police literature.

Police officers are said to have higher rates of mortality from heart disease and diabetes. Other studies have found that police officers run a greater risk of developing colon and liver cancers. Danielle Hitz (1973) reported a higher rate of cirrhosis of the liver due to alcohol use by police officers. While there are conflicting claims on the extent to which police officers suffer from higher mortality rates due to these ailments, a study of 2,376 police officers in Buffalo, New York, found that while the overall mortality rate among police officers for a variety of ailments was comparable to the general United States population, police officers showed a significantly higher rate of mortality from certain forms of cancer. Officers were particularly susceptible to cancer of the digestive organs (Violanti, Vena and Marshall, 1986). Stress, however, has never been demonstrated to cause cancer and other facts such as diet, smoking, and environmental factors can confound these findings.

Despite these mixed findings, Richard Raub (1988) has pointed out that statements such as "The average police officer dies within five years after retirement and reportedly has a life expectancy of twelve years less than that of other people" (Dittmar, 1986, as cited in Raub) and "Police officers do not retire well" (Schwartz and Schwartz, 1975, as cited in Raub) are not supported by the data. The appearance of these and similar statements as well as an uncritical reading of the research literature give credence to the already existing myth that police suffer an ill fate after retirement. While police stress has been linked to many problems including psychological, performance, and health issues (Terry, 1983; Kroes, 1976), Raub (1988) found that there was no empirical support for the myth that police officers have a shorter life expectancy after retirement than found in civilian populations. In his study of the life expectancies of retired officers from the Illinois, Kentucky, and Arizona state police agencies, he found that the length of time officers live after retirement matched mortality tables for general populations. This research also showed that officers who retired at older ages "enjoyed a longer life compared to those who are younger at retirement" (91-92). This study suggested that police retirees may even live longer lives after retirement than other populations.

Several explanations can be advanced for the disjuncture between the myth of police mortality and the existing research. First, uncritical readings of stress-related research may be passed on to police officers in the training academy with little concern for the limitations of the research studies. Second, inferences on mortality may be drawn that were not originally supported in existing research. Third, as some researchers have pointed out, some problems experienced by officers may be in part an effect of stress but may also be related to officer lifestyle and diet (Violanti, Vena and Marshall, 1986). There is little direct evidence that supports the myth that police experience higher rates of mortality because of the stress inherent in their work or that they experience shorter lives after retirement. If the stress and mortality myths were accurate, we would expect to find that officers who stayed in policing longer had shorter lives after retirement because of the toll exacted from crime fighters.

Police Divorces

Many authorities have commented on the high divorce rate that is believed to plague police marriages (Terry, III, 1981). Reports of this problem have come from a variety of sources. The media, police chaplains, departmental officials, the wives of police officers, and even some researchers have asserted that the stress inherent in law enforcement results in a very high level of divorce (Niederhoffer and Niederhoffer, 1978). Indeed, there are a number of features about police work that do place a strain on family life. For one thing, the schedule that many officers work may make it very difficult to have a normal social life. Because of rotating shifts, spouses must adjust to being left alone at night during certain periods of time. In addition, police officers may be required to work weekends and holidays. Second, the job presents many opportunities for marital infidelity. Spouses must take the officer's word that he/she really did have to work late or appear in court. Third, the trauma and pain that police witness as a routine part of their job can take an emotional toll on the officer and place an added strain on the relationship. Finally, police marriages are subject to all the same difficulties that trouble other couples (e.g., financial concerns, disagreements over child-rearing, etc.).

Because of the high level of interest in this topic, a great deal of empirical research has been conducted. However, the findings from various studies are contradictory. While some researchers report a high rate of police divorce (Durner, Kroeker, Miller and Reynolds, 1975), the majority conclude that the level of divorce is far lower than commonly assumed. Unfortunately, a number of methodological problems plague this body of research. The biggest drawback is that many studies do not distinguish between divorces that occurred prior to the time that the officer joined the department and those that occurred afterwards. Obviously, any stress inherent in law enforcement cannot account for a divorce that occurred before the individual joined the department.

It is noteworthy that the most comprehensive studies have concluded that police officers have a divorce rate that is no higher than the national average. James P. Lichtenberger (1968) examined data from the 1900 census and found that the rate of divorce for police was lower at that time than for most other occupations including doctors, lawyers, and college professors. Jack E. Whitehouse (1965) examined records from the 1960 census and observed that police and detectives had a divorce rate of 1.7 percent which compared favorably to the national average of 2.4 for males in the same age bracket. Nelson A. Watson and James W. Sterling (1969) undertook a massive study that brought responses from 246 police departments. They observed that not only was the police divorce rate lower than the national average for adult males, but that a far higher proportion of male officers were married. Finally, Arthur Niederhoffer and Elaine Niederhoffer (1978) came to a similar conclusion as a result of a questionnaire survey that elicited responses from 30 departments.

Despite all the anecdotal accounts and subjective reports detailing the horrors of police marriages, it is clear that these ideas are based on myth. The reality is that the overwhelming majority of police officers are family men who have stable marriages. As W. Clinton Terry, III (1981) reported after surveying the literature in this area, "the best evidence available supports the argument that police divorce rates are lower than the popular depiction of police family life would lead one to anticipate." In a similar vein, Niederhoffer and Niederhoffer (1978:170) conclude, "divorce, police style, may well be lower than divorce, American style."

Living the Crime Fighter Myth

Myths often become interpreted as reality for the people they affect. Behavior is often built around myth and perception rather than reality. Many of the myths of policing have contributed to the development of a group perspective among members of the police occupation. This cognitive group orientation and self-perception is often referred to as a culture. The term "culture" is used to describe differences between large social groups. Social groups differ in many aspects, and people from different cultures have varying beliefs, laws, morals, customs and other characteristics that set them apart from people of other cultures. These values and artifacts are unique to a given people and are transmitted from one generation to the next in a learning process. Cultural distinctions are easy to see when one compares, for example, the American and Japanese cultures. Clearly, Americans have different traditions, laws, language, customs, religions, and art forms than do the Japanese. These characteristics make American culture truly unique as compared to any other culture in the world.

There can also be cultural differences between people who form a single culture or social group. People who form a unique group within a given culture are called a subculture. The difference between a culture and a subculture is that members of a subculture, while sharing many values and beliefs of the larger dominant culture, have separate and distinct values. These differences make subcultural members unique as compared to the larger, more dominant culture. Clearly, police officers in America share our cultural heritage; they speak the same language; operate under the same laws; and share many values as do other Americans. There are certain myths and perceptions of the police subculture that make officers different from other members of society. Therefore, some scholars have maintained that the police are a unique occupational subculture.

The Dangerous World of Crime Fighting

Due in part to the police self-perception of danger and violence and the legal monopoly police have on the sanctioned use of violence (Westley, 1956; Bordua and Reiss, 1966; Reiss, 1971) and coercion (Westley, 1970; Bittner, 1970), police view themselves as a unique group separate from society. The police are, therefore, set apart from other members of society.

Because of their perception of police work—often based on myth—officers develop a unique worldview. Worldview is the manner in which a group sees the world and its own role and relationship to that world (Redfield, 1952). This means that various social groups, including the police, perceive the world, people, and situations differently from other social groups. By way of example, lawyers may view the world and events happening as a source of conflict and potential litigation. Physicians may view the world as a place of disease and illness calling for healing. The police worldview categorizes the world into insiders and outsiders. "The police as a result of combined features of their social situation, tend to develop ways of looking at the world distinctive to themselves, cognitive lenses through which to see situations and events" (Skolnick, 1966:42). The way the police see the world can be described as a "we-they" or "us-them" orientation. Police officers tend to see the world as being composed of cops and others. If a person is not a police officer, they tend to be considered an outsider to be viewed with suspicion.

This we-they worldview is created for a variety of reasons, including the danger myth. The myth of danger is reinforced in the formal socialization processes. Police officers undergo formal socialization when they enter the academy. One author noted that in the police academy:

> Group cohesiveness is encouraged by the instructors as well.
> The early roots of a separation between "the police" and "the
> public" is evident in many lectures and classroom discussions.
> In "war stories" and corridor anecdotes, it emerges as a full
> blown "us-them" mentality (Bahn, 1984:392).

Through these "war stories" in the course of field training and after graduation from the police academy officers re-learn and experience the myths of crime fighting, particularly the potential for danger. Danger in police work indisputably forms a great part of the American police officer's picture of the world. Police officers often see the world as a place of danger and potential injury. This allows officers to see citizens as potential sources of violence or even as enemies. These elements of the crime fighting myth do much to foster the we-they police worldview. Such a worldview allows police officers to see themselves as a close-knit distinct group and can even promote a view of citizens as "outsiders and enemies" (Westley, 1956; Sherman, 1982).

The Spirit of Crime Fighting

The concept of ethos encompasses the fundamental spirit of a culture. Ethos is a subculture's sentiments, beliefs, customs and practices. Ethos often includes the things valued most by a subculture or occupational group. When this term is applied to the police subculture, some general observations arise. First, the police value bravery. Bravery is a central component of the social character of policing. As such, it is related to the perceived and actual dangers of law enforcement. The potential to become the victim of a violent encounter, the need for support by fellow officers during such encounters, and the legitimate use of violence to accomplish the police mandate all contribute to a subculture that stresses the virtue of bravery. Also, the military trapping of policing, organizational policies such as "never back down," and informal peer pressure all contribute to instilling a sense of bravery in the police subculture. It is not unusual for police training officers to wait until a recruit has been presented with a dangerous situation before recommending the recruit be given full status on the department. Until new officers have been tested on the street, they are usually not fully accepted by their peers.

Learning Myths of Crime Fighting

Myths often contain postulates or statements of belief held by a group which reflect their basic orientations. Myths, in a less formal sense than academy training, reinforce expressions of general truth or principle as they are perceived by a group. Myths act as an oral vehicle for the transmission of culture from one generation to the next and tend to serve as a reinforcer of the subcultural worldview. Myths are advanced in the police academy, by field training officers, and during informal gatherings of police officers. Stories are told and retold regarding the dangers of policing and the bravery of crime fighters. Through exposure to myth, the new generations of police officers combine their experiences and perceptions of the world viewed through a police officer's eyes with these "truths" and develop a belief system which dictates acceptable and unacceptable behavior. These myths serve as unconscious reinforcers of the dangers and stress of police work and act as part of the socialization process for new crime fighters.

While all occupational groups undergo a socialization process and while socialization into a profession is not necessarily negative, when that socialization is based on myth it can have negative consequences. People may be attracted to police work because of the myths of excitement and danger. When the reality of day-to-day police work is experienced, new officers may become disillusioned with their chosen career. If the myths of policing are internalized by a majority of a police force, very aggressive practices can result that have negative effects not only on individual officers and their departments but also on the community they serve. Much of the alienation of the police from their community is a product of socializing based on myth and misperception.

Sources

Alpert, G. P. and Dunham, R. G. (1988). *Policing Urban America*. Prospect Heights, IL: Waveland Press, Inc.

Bahn, C. (1984). Police Socialization in the Eighties: Strains in the Forging of an Occupational Identity. *Journal of Police Science and Administration*, 12(4):390-94.

Barker, T. (1983). Rookie Police Officers' Perceptions of Police Occupational Deviance. *Police Studies*, 6:30-37.

Bedian, A. G. (1982). Suicide and Occupation: A Review. *Journal of Vocational Behavior*, 21:206-22.

Bennett, R. R. (1984). Becoming Blue: A Longitudinal Study of Police Recruit Occupational Socialization. *Journal of Police Science and Administration*, 12(1):47-57.

Bercal, T. (1970). Calls for Police Assistance. *American Behavioral Scientist*, 13:681-91.

Berg, B. L., Gertz, M. G. and True, E. J. (1984). Police-Community Relations and Alienation. *Police Chief*, 51(11):20-23.

Binder, A. and Fridell, L. (1984). Lethal Force as Police Response. *Criminal Justice Abstracts*, 16(2):250-80.

Bittner, E. (1970). *The Functions Of Police In Modern Society*. Chevy Chase, MD: National Clearinghouse for Mental Health.

Buder, L. (1985). Off-duty Abuse of Drugs Feared in Police Survey. *New York Times*, (July 5):1,4.

Burden, O. P. (1986). The Hidden Truths About Police Drug Use. *Law Enforcement News*, (March 10):5.

Cumming, E., Cumming, I. and Edell, L. (1965). Policeman as Philosopher, Friend and Guide. *Social Problems*, 12:14-49.

Dash, J. and Reiser, M. (1978). Suicide Among Police in Urban Law Enforcement Agencies. *Journal of Police Science and Administration*, 6(1):18-21.

Durner, J. A., Kroeker, M. A., Miller, C. R. and Reynolds, C. R. (1975). Divorce—Another Occupational Hazard. *Police Chief*, 62(11):48-53.

Flanagan, T. J. and Maguire, K. (1990). *Sourcebook of Criminal Justice Statistics—1989*. Albany, NY: The Hindelang Criminal Justice Research Center.

Friedman, P. (1967). Suicide Among Police. In Essays in Self-destruction E. Scheidman (ed.). New York: Science House.

Fyfe, J. J. (1982). In *Always Prepared: Police Off Duty Guns: Readings on Police Use of Deadly Force*, J. J. Fyfe (ed.). Washington, DC: Police Foundation.

———. (1979). Administrative Interventions on Police Shooting Discretion: An Empirical Examination. *Journal of Criminal Justice*, 7(4):309-23.

Fyfe, J. J. and Blumberg, M. (1985). Response to Griswold: A More Valid Test of the Justifiability of Police Actions. *American Journal of Police*, 4(2):110-32.

Gaines, L. K. and Van Tubergen, N. (1989). Job Stress in Police Work: An Exploratory Analysis into Structural Causes. *American Journal of Criminal Justice*, 13(3):197-214.

Garner, J. and Clemmer, E. (1986). Danger to Police in Domestic Disturbances—A New Look. In *Critical Issues in Policing: Contemporary Readings*, R. G. Dunham and G. Alpert (eds.). Prospect Heights, IL: Waveland Press, Inc.

Greene J. R. and Klockars, C. (1991). What Police Do. In *Thinking About Police: Contemporary Readings, Second edition*, C. B. Klockars and S. D. Mafstrofski (eds.). New York: McGraw-Hill, Inc.

Hernandez, J. (1989). *The Custer Syndrome*. Salem, WI: Sheffield Publishing Co.

Hindelang, M. J., Gottfredson, M. R., Dunn, C. S. and Parisi, N. (1977). *Sourcebook of Criminal Justice Statistics—1976*. Albany, NY: Criminal Justice Research Center.

Hitz, D. (1973). Drunken Sailors and Others: Drinking Problem in Specific Occupation. *Quarterly Journal of Studies on Alcohol*, 34:496-505.

Holden, R. (1991). Mortal Danger in Law Enforcement: A Statistical Comparison of Police Mortality with those of Other Occupations. A paper presented at the Academy of Criminal Justice Sciences, Nashville, TN (March 6).

Josephson, R. L. and Reiser, M. (1990). Officer Suicide in the Los Angeles Police Department: A Twelve-Year Follow-up. *Journal of Police Science and Administration*, 17(3):227-29.

Kelling, G. L., Pate, T., Dieckman, D. and Brown, C. E. (1974). *The Kansas City Preventive Patrol Experiment: A Summary Report*. Washington, DC: Police Foundation.

Konstantin, D. N. (1984). Homicides of American Law Enforcement Officers, 1978-80. *Justice Quarterly*, 1(1):29-45.

Kraska, P. B. and Kappeler, V. E. (1988). A Theoretical and Descriptive Study of Police On Duty Drug Use. *American Journal of Police*, 8(1):1-36.

Kroes, W. H. (1976). *Society's Victim, the Policeman: An Analysis of Job Stress in Policing*. Springfield, IL: Charles C. Thomas.

Labovitz, S. and Hagedorn, R. (1971). An Analysis of Job Suicide Rates Among Occupational Categories. *Sociological Inquiry*, 41(1).

Lester, D. (1983). Stress in Police Officers: An American Perspective. *The Police Journal*, 56(2):184-93.

Lichtenberger, J.P. (1968). *Divorce: A Study in Social Causation*. New York: AMS Press.

Lofquist, L. and Davis, R. (1969). *Adjustment of Work*. New York: Appleton-Century-Crofts.

Mallory, T. and Mays, G. (1984). The Police Stress Hypothesis: A Critical Evaluation. *Criminal Justice and Behavior*, 11(2):197-224.

Manning, P. K. (1971). The Police: Mandate, Strategies and Appearances. In *Managing The Police Organization*, L. K. Gaines and T. Ricks (eds.). St. Paul, MN: West Publishing Co.

Mafstrofski, S. (1983). The Police and Non-Crime Services. In *Evaluating Performance of Criminal Justice Agencies*, G. Whitaker and C. Phillips (eds.). Beverly Hills, CA: Sage.

Muir, W. K., Jr. (1977). *Police: Streetcorner Politicians*. Chicago: University of Chicago Press.

Niederhoffer, A. (1967). *Behind the Shield: The Police in Urban Society*. Garden City, NY: Doubleday.

Niederhoffer, A. and Niederhoffer, E. (1978). *The Police Family: From Station House to Ranch House*. Lexington, MA: Lexington Books.

O'Neill, M. and Bloom, C. J. (1972). The Field Officer: Is He Really Fighting Crime? *Police Chief*, 39 (February):30-32.

Putti, J., Aryee, S. and Kang, T. S. (1988). Personal Values of Recruits and Officers in a Law Enforcement Agency: An Exploratory Study. *Journal of Police Science and Administration*, 16(4):249-45.

Raub, R. A. (1988). Death of Police Officers After Retirement. *American Journal of Police*, 7(1):91-102.

Redfield, R. (1952). The Primitive World View. *Proceedings of the American Philosophical Society*, 96:30-36.

Reiss, A. J., Jr. (1971). *The Police and the Public*. New Haven, CT: Yale University Press.

Reiss, A. J. and Bordua, D. J. (1967). Environment and Organization: A Perspective on the Police. In *The Police: Six Sociological Essays*, D. J. Bordua (ed.). New York: John Wiley and Sons, Inc.

Rubinstein, J. (1973). *City Police*. New York: Farrar, Strauss and Giroux.

Sherman, L. W. (1982). Learning Police Ethics. *Criminal Justice Ethics*, 1(1):10-19.

Sherman, L. W. (1983). Reducing Police Gun Use: Critical Events, Administrative Policy, and Organizational Change. In *Control in the Police Organization*, M. Punch (ed.). Cambridge, MA: MIT Press.

Sherman L. W., Cohn, E. G. with Garten, P. R., Hamilton, E. E. and Rogan, D. P. (1986). *Citizens Killed by Big City Police — 1970-84*. Washington, DC: Crime Control Institute.

Sherman L. W. and Langworthy, R. H. (1979). Measuring Homicide by Police Officers. *Journal of Criminal Law and Criminology*, 70(4):546-60.

Skolnick, J. H. (1966:). *Justice Without Trial: Law Enforcement In a Democratic Society*. New York: John Wiley and Sons.

Stoddard, E. R. (1968). The Informal Code of Police Deviancy: A Group Approach to Blue-Collar Crime. *Journal of Criminal Law, Criminology and Police Science*, 59(2):201-13.

Straus, M. A., Gelles, R. J. and Steinmetz, S. K. (1980). *Behind Closed Doors: Violence in the American Family*. Garden City, NY: Anchor Books.

Terry, W. C. (1983). Police Stress as an Individual and Administrative Problem: Some Conceptual and Theoretical Difficulties. *Journal of Police Science and Administration*, 11(2):156-65.

_____ (1981). Police Stress: The Empirical Evidence. *Journal of Police Science and Administration*, 9(1):61-75.

Van Raalte, R. C. (1979). Alcohol as a Problem Among Officers. *Police Chief*, 44:38-40.

Vaughn, J. B. and Kappeler, V. E. (1986). *A Descriptive Study of Law Enforcement Officers Killed, 1974-1984*. Paper presented at the annual meeting of the Academy of Criminal Justice Sciences, Orlando, FL (March 18).

Violanti, J. M., Vena, J. E. and Marshall, J. R. (1986). Disease Risk and Mortality Among Police Officers: New Evidence and Contributing Factors. *Journal of Police Science and Administration*, 14(1):17-23.

Violanti, J. M., Marshall, J. R. and Howe, B. (1985). Stress, Coping, and Alcohol Use: The Police Connection. *Journal of Police Science and Administration*, 13(2):106-9.

Wagner, M. and Brzeczek, R. J. (1983). Alcoholism and Suicide: A Fatal Connection. *FBI Law Enforcement Bulletin*, (August):8-15.

Watson, N. A. and Sterling, J. W. (1969). *Police and their Opinions*. Gaithersburg, MD: International Association of Chiefs of Police.

Westley, W. A. (1970). *Violence And The Police: A Sociological Study Of Law Custom And Morality*. Cambridge, MA: MIT Press.

_____ (1956). Secrecy and the Police. *Social Forces*, 34(3):254-57.

Whitehouse, J. E. (1965). A Preliminary Inquiry into the Occupational Disadvantages of Law Enforcement Officers. *Police*, (May-June).

Wilson, J. Q. (1968). *Varieties of Police Behavior: The Management of Law and Order in Eight Communities*. Cambridge, MA: Harvard University Press.

chapter **8**

Drug War Cowboys
Myths of the Drug Crisis in America

There is probably no social problem that has so captured the imagination of the American public as the problem of drug abuse. Public opinion polls indicate that Americans think drugs are the number-one problem in the nation. In fact, over half of the public favors the use of the military in incursions into drug-producing countries (Benoit, 1989:33). This strong public reaction should surprise no one. We are bombarded daily by public service messages on television dramatically portraying the horrors of drug abuse. Television talk shows pander to the most sensational aspects of the drug problem, as Oprah, Geraldo, and Phil interview "crack" mothers, violent members of street gangs, and cocaine-dependent Yuppies whose conspicuous consumption has been imperiled by their expenditures on drugs. The rhetoric from politicians and government officials often borders on hysteria as they call for more prisons, more police, the abolition of constitutional protections, and even the death penalty for drug dealers. The problem of drugs has been elevated to a national crusade by leaders like President Ronald Reagan who said, "In this crusade, let us not forget who we are. Drug abuse is a repudiation of everything America is. The destructiveness and human wreckage mock our heritage" (Lyman and

Potter, 1991:23). President Bush leaves no doubt as to his administration's feeling on drugs: "Speak the truth: that drugs are evil,
that they ruin and end young lives . . . the drug dealers are
murderers and should be treated as such" (Lyman and Potter,
1991:62). In the streets of Washington, D.C., New York City,
Panama, and Colombia our leaders have called us to war: a war on
drugs.

There is no argument that drug abuse poses a significant problem
in America. The cost alone is staggering.

> It costs taxpayers $30 billion a year just to pay the criminal court
> costs for illicit drug trafficking. . . . hospital treatment for victims
> of drug-dealer wars costs an estimated $1 billion each year.
> American business must shoulder additional costs totaling an
> estimated $60 billion in lost productivity, absenteeism, work-
> place accidents and crime because of illegal drug use in the
> workplace. . . . All in all, drug and alcohol abuse costs the nation
> about $150 billion a year, according to the National Institute
> on Drug Abuse, more than double what it cost to fight the war
> in Vietnam at its height (Benoit, 1989:33).

The specter of babies being born drug dependent to drug-addicted
mothers is horrifying. The idea that inner-city youth are introduced
to drugs at an early age and are subsequently unable to perform
successfully in school or to obtain and hold jobs is a national
disaster. The massive violence associated with drug trafficking turf
wars (which is often random and claims innocent victims) is repugnant. The idea that citizens, particularly in our major cities, have
lost control of their neighborhoods to drug-dealing gangs is
unacceptable.

But the question facing the criminal justice system and society
as a whole is how do we best deal with these drug-related horrors?
For years a debate has raged in the medical, sociological, and law
enforcement communities over whether drug use and abuse was
a problem for the criminal justice system or for the public health
care system. Despite the rhetoric and sensationalism of today's anti-
drug campaigns, that question remains unresolved. As David Musto
(1973) tells us, this is not a new problem:

> American concern with narcotics is more than a medical or legal
> problem—it is in the fullest sense a political problem. The
> energy that has given impetus to drug control and prohibition
> came from profound tensions among socioeconomic groups,
> ethnic minorities, and generations—as well as the psychological
> attraction of certain drugs. The form of control has been shaped
> by the gradual evolution of federal police powers. The bad results

of drug use and the number of drug users have often been exaggerated for partisan advantage. Public demand for action against drug abuse has led to regulative decisions that lack a true regard for the reality of drug use. Regulations with foreign nations, often the sources of drugs, have been a theme in the domestic scene from the beginning of the American antinarcotic movement. Narcotics addiction has proven to be one of the most intractable medical inquiries ever faced by American clinicians and scientists (244).

It has, indeed, proved to be an intractable problem. It is a problem fueled by politics and the bureaucratic needs of law enforcement. The natural reaction for politicians to the drug problem is to pander to popular fear and frame the issue in the starkest, most unyielding terms. The "safe" political response to the issue of drugs is to call for more law and more order. The law enforcement bureaucracy responds to this by accepting the challenge. After all, there are very few issues on which public opinion and the rhetoric of decision-makers so closely coincide with opportunities for bureaucratic expansion. A "war on drugs" offers the opportunity for more money, more personnel, and most importantly, greater police power. It is a very attractive offer most police executives and others in the criminal justice system find impossible to refuse.

However, despite the public consensus, despite the speeches of presidents, and despite the dire warnings of the press and the law enforcement establishment, serious questions have been raised about the drug war. These questions are so serious that some public figures have broken ranks and have openly criticized the law enforcement approach to drug control (Lyman and Potter, 1991:322). Political leaders like former Secretary of State George Schultz and the mayor of Baltimore, Kurt Schmoke, have called for a discussion of precisely the opposite approach to drug control, drug legalization. They have been joined by conservative political theoreticians, like economist Milton Friedman and columnist William F. Buckley, as well as by liberals like Dr. Benjamin Spock. Most surprisingly, the legalization issue has been raised by some law enforcement officials, such as organized crime expert Ralph Salerno, former New York City police commissioner and Police Foundation head Patrick Murphy, San Jose police chief Joseph MacNamara, federal judge Rufus King and former Minneapolis police chief Anthony Bouza. The critics have posed a compelling question: Is the war on drugs having any positive impact on the problems associated with drug abuse? And if it is not, what are the alternatives?

This chapter will explore some of the issues related to this debate.

First, we will look at the question of drugs and related harm. What exactly do drugs do? What do we know about the potential of illicit drugs to kill and injure users? We will try to put the discussion of harm in context and separate the harms resulting from the abuse of drugs from the harms resulting from the illegality of drugs. Second, we will look at the connection between drugs and crime. One of the most effective tactics of today's drug warriors has been to create a mythical link between drugs and crimes against innocent citizens. This portrayal of drug users as "drug fiends" plays a key role in the popular conception of the drug problem. But is this view justified? Once again, we will try to put the issue of drugs and crime in context and to separate those dysfunctions caused by drugs from those dysfunctions caused by the illegality of drugs. Third, we will look at the drug war itself, the strategies employed, and their impact on the drug problem. Finally, we will consider the viability and importance of noncriminal justice approaches to the problem of drugs. Let us begin by taking a look at the major drugs of abuse.

Drugs and Harm

Central to the case for drug prohibition (and the prosecution of the drug war) is the idea that drugs are dangerous to users. The images presented in the media are stark and frightening. Fried eggs are used to simulate "your brain on drugs," addicts are shown cowering in corners in the throes of withdrawal, earnest actors portray cocaine users who have lost their houses, jobs, and spouses to this chemical seductress. No one will dispute that drugs, all drugs, are dangerous. People die of heroin overdoses and occasionally of cardiac and respiratory failure related to cocaine. People also die from lung cancer as a result of smoking tobacco and of a variety of diseases related to the consumption of alcohol, even though these drugs are quite legal. People can die and suffer injury from any drug, even aspirin and penicillin.

The question is not whether illegal drugs are dangerous, but whether they are dangerous enough to justify legal prohibition and the social outrage associated with their use. As with all other issues in the drug debate, the issue of harm has to be put in context and perspective. In order to do this, let us examine the three drugs which have elicited the strongest reaction from law makers and law enforcers: heroin, cocaine, and marijuana.

In the 1960s, during Richard Nixon's drug war, most public attention was focused on heroin. Heroin is a narcotic, a direct derivative of the opium poppy. Heroin users snort, smoke and inject the drug, although for the best "high" most users inject heroin into a vein ("mainlining"). Mainlining produces an immediate euphoric reaction (a "rush") followed by a period of sedation. The principal problem with heroin is that it is highly addictive. Repeated use of the drug creates a physical need for more of the drug. The drug also has a high tolerance level, which means that the more often it is used, the greater the quantity and frequency of use required to reach a "high." The net effect of this cycle of need and tolerance is addiction. Being a narcotic, heroin also suppresses both respiratory and cardiovascular activity, meaning that an overdose can produce respiratory arrest and shock — sometimes leading to death (Inciardi, 1986:52). However, if properly used, under supervised conditions, heroin is a relatively benign drug. As Inciardi points out, heroin is responsible for "little direct or permanent physiological damage" (Inciardi, 1986:52). The real dangers in the use of heroin are attributable to the potential for overdose and the fact that users on the street do not engage in standard practices of good hygiene, resulting in infection from hepatitis and, more recently, AIDS (Inciardi, 1986:65).

Today, the Reagan and Bush administrations, while still raising the specter of heroin, have shifted public concern to the use of cocaine. Cocaine is the most powerful natural stimulant available to man. It comes from the leaves of the South American coca plant. Like heroin, it produces a "rush" when used, but unlike heroin it is a stimulant which awakens and enlivens users. Most cocaine users snort cocaine hydrochloride (the white, crystalline powder) into their nasal passages. Snorting cocaine allows for rapid absorption of the drug into the bloodstream creating an intense but rather brief "high."

During the 1970s, it appeared that cocaine would become the new drug of choice for the wealthy. It was an expensive drug, selling for about $100 a gram on the street. Because of its expense, it had a limited market of upper middle-class and upper class users. Cocaine developed the reputation of being a glamour drug associated with sports figures and Hollywood. However, during 1985-1986 cocaine appeared in a new form, "crack," that made it accessible to everyone, even the poor. Crack is simply cocaine hydrochloride powder mixed with baking soda, ammonia, and water, dried and subsequently smoked. Crack sells for ten to fifteen dollars a "hit," making it far more affordable than cocaine hydrochloride. It was the advent of crack that heralded much of the concern about cocaine. In fact, research on the use of cocaine had indicated that it was a relatively safe drug. Surveys of medical examiners and coroners representing 30 percent of the population of the United

States and Canada had revealed only twenty-six cases of drug-induced deaths between 1971 and 1976 where cocaine had been the sole drug found in the body (McCaghy and Cernkovich, 1987:454). With the advent of crack and the subsequent increase in the smoking of cocaine, the numbers of cocaine-related deaths quadrupled. It is important to note that 92 percent of cocaine-related deaths result from smoking the drug, and only about 10 percent of all cocaine users smoke cocaine rather than snort cocaine (Goode, 1984:187-89). It would therefore appear that moderate use of cocaine is relatively safe, although heavy cocaine users, particularly those who smoke crack, exhibit a wide variety of symptoms such as nervousness, fatigue, irritability, and paranoia (Ray, 1983:301).

Before moving on to a discussion of marijuana, let us put the issue of drug-related deaths into context. If one were to listen to speeches of politicians and the warnings in anti-drug ads on television, it would appear that we are in the midst of a massive epidemic of illicit drug-related deaths. While any death is tragic and certainly should raise concern, there are two points to be made about drug-related deaths. First, they are relatively infrequent, despite popular impressions. Second, when they do occur, they are more directly attributable to drug laws than to the drugs themselves.

About 3,600 people die each year from the consumption of all illegal drugs put together (Nadelmann, 1989:943). This pales in comparison to the number of deaths on an annual basis from just two legal drugs, alcohol and tobacco. There are 200,000 alcohol-related deaths each year (Nadelmann, 1989:943). Add to that figure the estimated 320,000 people each year who die from illnesses related to the consumption of tobacco and you arrive at a figure 150 times larger than all the deaths related to illicit drug consumption. Yet the federal government has not declared a war on alcohol and tobacco, nor has it attempted to create the hysterical reaction to these legal drugs which has accompanied its campaign against heroin and cocaine.

While the numbers seem to belie the urgency of the "drug war," or at the very least suggest a degree of hypocrisy in that war, it is even more troubling to realize that most of the 3,600 or so drug-related deaths that occur each year occur not as a result of the drug used but as a result of drug laws. Take the case of heroin. As was pointed out earlier, heroin is a relatively benign drug. As Jeffrey Reiman tells us, "there is no evidence conclusively establishing a link between heroin and disease or tissue degeneration such as that which has been established for tobacco and alcohol" (Reiman, 1984:27). Why then do people die from using heroin? The answer is that the drug laws make inevitable the unregulated production, sale, and use of dangerous drugs. Consumers of heroin and other illicit drugs produced in clandestine laboratories under unregulated conditions are in constant danger of taking drugs which are mixed with other dangerous substances, mixed with other dangerous drugs, and have potencies far in excess of that which the user expects, leading directly to fatal overdoses and poisonings (Nadelmann, 1989:942). These are deaths directly attributable to the drug laws which force users to buy their supplies in an unregulated, unsafe market. Most drug overdoses result from the ingestion of adulterated drugs, not from user misuse or abuse. In addition, users engage in unsanitary practices related to drug use which result in further death and injury because of the clandestine nature of drug use necessitated by drug prohibition. Heroin addicts share needles, spreading disease and illness. One-quarter of all the AIDS cases in the United States can be directly attributed to the unsafe and unsanitary conditions in which illicit drugs are used (Nadelmann, 1989:942). Finally, the drug laws encourage misuse of illicit drugs. Consider the case of cocaine. Studies show that about 20 million Americans are cocaine users. Of that number, only about 3 percent are ever going to become problem cocaine abusers (National Institute on Drug Abuse, 1987). The real danger from cocaine is a direct result of the drug laws which encourage users to seek a more intense and cheaper high by smoking the drug rather than snorting it. The drug laws drive the price of cocaine up, and users innovate to compensate for the expense. They freebase and use crack for greater efficiency, and they are far more likely to suffer injury or death smoking the drug than snorting it.

So, it seems that the dangers of heroin and cocaine use, while real enough, are exaggerated by the government and exacerbated by the drug laws themselves. What about marijuana, the most commonly used illegal drug in the United States and the drug for which people are most frequently thrown into prison? Marijuana comes from the flowers and leaves of the *cannabis sativa* plant. The dried leaves and flowers are smoked, like tobacco, in cigarettes ("joints") or pipes. All the available evidence we have on marijuana indicates that it is not addictive, nor does a tolerance to the drug develop. In addition, there has never been a death resulting from marijuana consumption (Brecher, 1972:395; Goode, 1984:99-108). In fact, even the Drug Enforcement Administration (DEA) has trouble making marijuana look like a dangerous drug. In September 1988, Francis L. Young, the chief administrative law judge of the DEA reviewed all the medical and scientific evidence on marijuana and came to some startling conclusions.

- There has never been a single documented *cannabis*-related death.
- About 70 million Americans have used marijuana and there has never been a reported overdose, a striking contrast not just with alcohol but with aspirin.
- Marijuana, in its natural form, is one of the safest therapeutically active substances known to man.
- In strict medical terms, marijuana is far safer than many foods we commonly consume (Trebach, 1989).

The real danger to marijuana smokers comes from marijuana which has been tainted by government drug control programs, such as the spraying of paraquat and other herbicides on marijuana crops. While some problems are associated with marijuana use, such as injury to the mucous membranes and interrupted attention spans (Murray, 1986:23-55), it scarcely appears to deserve the attention it gets from law enforcement authorities, especially when considered alongside of tobacco, alcohol, and aspirin.

The data appear to tell us that the danger from the consumption of illicit drugs, while real, does not justify the panic reaction which the media and government have created. The dangers of illicit drugs appear to pale in comparison to the dangers from drugs which are tolerated, and even endorsed, in everyday life. While certainly not related to the issue of the harmfulness of drugs, it is appropriate that in discussing their effects we take note of the potentially positive contributions that illicit drugs could make if it were not for the legal prohibitions controlling them. The fact is that the drug laws, while making drugs more dangerous, also make it virtually impossible for us to make constructive use of these proscribed substances (Nadelmann, 1989; Trebach 1989). Marijuana, for example, has shown itself to be useful in treating disorders such as multiple sclerosis and glaucoma, and in relieving the side effects of chemotherapy for cancer patients. In fact, the Drug Enforcement Administration itself has argued for the medical legalization of marijuana. Heroin is a particularly useful and very safe pain reliever, as is cocaine, both of which are widely used outside of the United States for medical treatment. It appears that in yet another way, the drug laws make our drug problems even worse.

Drugs and Crime

One of the most compelling questions which has been raised in the debate on drug policy is whether drug use and drug addiction leads to an increase in crime in the United States. Those who favor drug prohibition point to several important research findings as indicators of a relationship between drugs and crime. For example, James Inciardi's study of narcotics users and non-narcotics users in Miami during the period between 1978 and 1981 showed that narcotic users "committed more crimes, engaged in a greater diversity of offenses, and in significantly larger proportions committed the more serious crimes of robbery and burglary" (Inciardi, 1986:129). Other findings have seemingly pointed to similar relationships between drugs and crime. For example, it appears that the degree of drug use is directly related to the degree of criminality. Drug addicts tend to commit substantially fewer crimes prior to the beginning of addiction and after the cessation of addiction than they do during addiction (Gropper, 1985). Among heroin users this effect is pronounced. Daily heroin users seem to commit twice the number of property crimes as regular users (those who use the drug three to five days a week) and five times as many property crimes as irregular (those who use the drug two days a week or less) heroin users. As the level of drug usage decreases, the involvement in crime decreases as well. In addition, research indicates that a history of drug abuse is one of the best predictors of involvement in serious offenses (Gropper, 1985).

These are seemingly damning data. However, in order to be understood and to be relevant to a discussion of drug control policy, they must be put into context. While there is an apparent relationship between the use of drugs and the amount of crime committed by users, it is a myth that drugs *cause* crime. Take the case of heroin. A majority of heroin users have been involved in criminal activity *prior* to their use of heroin (McGlothlin, Anglin and Wilson, 1978). In fact, heroin addicts engage in criminal activity "proportionally in excess of their numbers in the population before becoming involved with narcotics" (Goode, 1984:256). While it is easy for policymakers to make the emotional claim that drugs cause crime, a more accurate appraisal of the data is that "drugs do not cause criminality, but that addiction to narcotics like heroin clearly escalates criminal involvement" (Beirne and Messerschmidt, 1991:144).

There is a further irony in the drugs-crime connection, and that is the fact that the only drug for which a clear causal link with crime has been established is alcohol, a drug which is legal. We know that 54 percent of all inmates convicted of violent crimes used alcohol immediately prior to the commission of the crime (Bureau of Justice Statistics, 1987:398). In addition, we know that individuals convicted of murder, arson, involuntary manslaughter and rape are far more likely to have committed their crimes under the influence of alcohol than any other drug (Bureau of Justice Statistics, 1988:497).

So, while there is no evidence that drugs themselves cause crime, the same cannot be said for the drug laws. The fact is that the drug laws adversely affect the market for drugs and the conditions under which drugs are purchased and consumed. As a result, the drug laws create a great deal of serious crime with very real victims.

Illicit drug users, particularly those who have developed an addiction to a drug such as heroin, commit crimes such as robbery, burglary, prostitution, and drug dealing as a means of raising funds to support their drug habits. This criminal behavior results from laws prohibiting the sale and use of drugs, not from the drugs themselves. Because the illegality of drugs artificially and dramatically inflates their price, the cost of drug use quickly exceeds the income of the drug user and soon exhausts personal resources. A heroin user with a relatively moderate habit will spend about $7500 a year on heroin (McCaghy and Cernkovich, 1987:461). Individuals who come from poverty-wracked urban areas are simply not going to be able to pay for the necessities of life (food, clothing, shelter) and heroin. Compare the cost of illegal heroin with the cost of alcohol and tobacco, two legal drugs which are heavily taxed and regulated, and it becomes clear that legal drugs are far cheaper. It is the prohibitionary laws which inflate the price of illicit drugs forty to fifty times above market value. Drugs do not cause drug users to commit crime. It is the illegality of drugs—with the subsequent outrageous prices which can be demanded in the illicit market—that causes crime.

But the inflated price for drugs caused by prohibition is not the only criminogenic effect of the drug laws. Because drugs are illegal, purchasers are forced into a criminal underworld to buy drugs, thereby making them potential victims of crime and bringing them into contact with criminal actors with whom they would ordinarily never have contact (Kaplan, 1983:81-83). Crimes ancillary to drug use take place because of this relationship, a relationship entirely attributable to the illegality of drugs.

Finally, illegal markets, markets created by the criminal law, breed violence for many reasons. The profits realized from the sales of illegal drugs are so high that competition becomes intense and turf wars result. Illicit drug entrepreneurs have no recourse to legal institutions to resolve disputes over turf, quality of merchandise, and "brand" names. Because drugs are illegal, the law itself makes violence the only dispute resolution mechanism available to drug dealers. The victims of that violence are the poor and law-abiding citizens of urban America who have seen their streets turned into battle zones. The dramatic increases in urban murder rates in the past few years can be explained almost entirely by the rise in drug dealer killings of one another and the deaths of innocent bystanders in these turf battles (*Newsweek*, 1989:44).

Law Enforcement Strategies in the War on Drugs

In his book, *Deviant Behavior*, criminologist Charles McCaghy (1985) provides the most concise and direct evaluation of the war on drugs in the criminological literature:

> In baseball a player with three strikes is out. But after three dismal failures in trying to stop the use of alcohol, opiates, and marihuana, the United States government still stands at the plate determined to smash the hell out of the drug problem. Unlike ballplayers, who adjust to the peculiarities of various pitchers and who put past experience to use, United States legislators subscribe to a single-minded philosophy — if you don't hit it, you're not swinging hard enough (298).

Ever since Ronald Reagan proclaimed yet another war on drugs in 1980, the federal government has been swinging harder and striking out with greater regularity than ever before. The Reagan-Bush war on drugs is costing the federal government an average of ten billion dollars a year (National Drug Enforcement Policy Board, 1987). At the state and local levels, law enforcement agencies are expending more than 20 percent of their total budgets on drug enforcement (Nadelmann, 1989:940). Inmates who have been imprisoned on drug charges make up more than 33 percent of all federal prison inmates and 10 percent of all state inmates (Bureau of Justice Statistics, 1988:490, 494, 518). From 1980 to 1988, the prison population in the United States rose 90.2 percent. The United States imprisons four times as many people as does West Germany and the United Kingdom, seven times as many as Sweden, and eight times as many as the Netherlands. Between 1980 and 1987, drug arrests in the United States increased 61 percent (Trebach, 1989). Of all the felony arrests made in the United States, 23 percent are for individuals arrested on drug charges (National Institute on Drug Abuse, 1987). Of these 750,000 felony arrests, more than 75 percent are not for drug trafficking, not for selling drugs to innocent school children, but for possession of drugs, most commonly marijuana, the most innocuous of all the legal and illegal drugs. Even so, all of these felony convictions account for only a little more than 1 percent of the Americans who use drugs.

Despite all of this law enforcement activity, all of these arrests and incarcerations, little has changed. During the ten years of the Reagan-Bush drug war, the price of a kilo of cocaine has dropped 80 percent and there is ten times as much cocaine on the streets today as there was when the drug war started (Benoit, 1989:33). During the same period, the purity of cocaine on the streets has quintupled, and the profits from the sale of cocaine have climbed to an estimated $50 billion a year (Benoit, 1989:33). Precisely the same effects have been noted with regard to heroin. In addition, about 25 percent of the American public, or 50 to 60 million people, still use an illegal drug at least once a year. There are about 18 to 35 million regular marijuana users in the United States, five to ten million cocaine users, and five million heroin users (Trebach and Engelsman, 1989:40).

Why has there been so little progress made after such a huge expenditure of money and after so many arrests and incarcerations? As McCaghy (1985:298) suggested, it is because present drug enforcement policies do not work and can not be made to work, even with dramatic increases in resources and personnel. The government's strategy in the war on drugs hinges on three basic policies: eradication, interdiction and street-level drug enforcement.

Let us first consider interdiction as a strategy. Interdiction assumes that with sufficient resources drugs can be stopped from entering the United States by controlling the borders. As the numbers reported above indicate, interdiction has failed with regard to both heroin and cocaine. The only minor success that the interdiction campaign can claim is with marijuana, a bulky commodity which is difficult to transport. Yet the net effect of that success has become an even bigger problem. Marijuana smugglers and growers in other countries have simply moved to cocaine and heroin as substitutes for marijuana, meaning even more of those drugs are being imported to the United States, and marijuana production in the United States has increased dramatically in the last ten years. A Rand Corporation evaluation study of interdiction determined that "even massively stepped-up drug interdiction efforts are not likely to greatly affect the availability of cocaine and heroin in the United States" (Reuter, Crawford and Cace, 1988).

Efforts directed at crop eradication in producing countries have failed miserably. The reasons for this should be obvious. First of all, drugs like heroin, cocaine, and marijuana can be grown and processed in a wide variety of locations, making crop eradication programs impossible to implement. Even if a particular locale is targeted and eradication programs are successfully carried out there, growers in other locations will merely make up for the deficit in supply. If heroin supplies in the Golden Crescent (Afghanistan,

Iran, Pakistan) are targeted, opium growers in the Golden Triangle (Thailand, Burma, Laos) or in Mexico will simply grow more and supply the demand. These three regions have had no problem in supplying the demand for heroin for the last century, although the relative importance of each fluctuates with enforcement efforts. The case of cocaine is even more instructive. In theory, cocaine should be the easiest of the illicit crops to subject to an eradication strategy. It grows only in South America and principally in Peru and Bolivia (with Colombia, Ecuador, and Brazil making small contributions to the supply). At the moment, the world's entire cocaine supply is grown on 700 square miles of arable land. Even so it would still be prohibitively costly to eradicate the crop. But the fact is that cocaine, even though it can only be grown in certain areas of South America, can be grown on 2,500,000 square miles of arable land (Nadelmann, 1989:945). Eradication as a control strategy is doomed to failure by Mother Nature herself.

In addition, crop eradication programs in producer countries are very difficult to arrange and carry out. In those countries there is well-organized political opposition to these programs. Obviously, crop eradication cannot be carried out without the support and active participation of the country involved. The production of cocaine and opium brings in billions of dollars in hard currency to impoverished countries and puts money in the pockets of millions of cultivators, processors, and smugglers. These governments, therefore, are extremely reluctant to give their approval to eradication efforts, and even when they do, they are often unable to provide the logistical support necessary for success. Peru is an example of another problem. The prime cocaine-growing areas are not under government control but rather under the influence of the Sendero Luminoso guerrilla group. The government of Peru, even if it wished to support an eradication program, is in no position to do so. The same could be said of opium-growing areas in the Golden Triangle, most of which are ruled by renegade warlords beyond the reach and control of the government (Lyman and Potter, 1991).

A word needs to be said about domestic crop eradication programs as well. Efforts to eradicate the marijuana crop in the United States have not only failed but have made the marijuana industry stronger and more dangerous than ever before (Potter, Gaines and Holbrook, 1990). In Kentucky, where the state participates in a federally-funded program to find and burn the marijuana crop, the net effect of the eradication program has been to spread marijuana cultivation throughout the state, to increase the quantity of marijuana being produced, and to increase the quality of the marijuana being produced. In addition, the eradication program has taken what was essentially a "Mom and Pop" industry a few years ago and turned it into a highly organized criminal cartel which is not only dangerous but also enjoys a high degree of community support in the marijuana-belt counties.

Street-level drug enforcement efforts in the United States have also shown little hope of success in the drug war. Intensive street-level law enforcement efforts are very expensive. Although they result in the arrests of thousands of low-level drug dealers and users, they have little impact on the other elements involved in illicit drug supply. While some of these enforcement efforts have been able to claim "temporary and transitory success," they have not impacted at all on the availability of illegal drugs (Chaiken, 1988). In fact, many illegal drug prices have fallen, purity has increased, the supply has increased, and use levels have increased in jurisdictions where intensive street-level enforcement has been tried. In addition, crimes ancillary to drug trafficking have increased in almost every case where saturation enforcement strategies have been utilized.

The classic case study of draconian law enforcement efforts being employed against drug use and drug trafficking is New York's experience with the infamous "Rockefeller Drug Law." In 1973, New York law was amended as part of an all-out drug war in that state. Individuals caught selling drugs were subjected to mandatory prison terms of fifteen to twenty-five years. In 1977, the New York Bar Association appointed a commission to evaluate New York's "drug war." They found that the state had spent $32 million in implementing the laws, but the net effect of the three years of intensive enforcement was negligible. There was no reduction in drug-related crime or in heroin usage, and there were ample supplies of drugs still on the streets. The commission declared the law an expensive failure (Association of the Bar of the City of New York, 1978). In fact, the history of the drug laws is clear. Drug use actually increases during periods in which criminal penalties are harshest and enforcement most vigorous.

As if it were not enough that these drug war strategies have failed, they have also created a number of serious problems that would not exist if it were not for the intensive enforcement efforts against drugs.

First, intensive drug enforcement efforts lead to corruption of law enforcement and other criminal justice personnel. The immense amounts of money generated by the drug trade makes it possible to offer substantial inducements to enforcement personnel to overlook activities by specific traffickers and groups. Political and police corruption in America is certainly nothing new. Official corruption related to liquor and gambling laws has been well documented in virtually every American city during the early years of the century when alcohol prohibition was in effect. The same type of prohibition-style corruption is rampant today in drug enforcement. For example, in 1988, over seventy-five Miami police officers were under investigation for involvement in criminal activities including drug dealing, robbery, theft and murder. One investigation in particular revealed several officers who had ambushed drug dealers bringing cocaine into Miami. This investigation revealed that officers loaded the cocaine into marked police vehicles. Duffel bags full of cocaine were reportedly "stacked to the ceilings of the patrol car." Three of the suspects, in an effort to escape, jumped into the river and drowned (Lyman and Potter, 1991:140). The Miami case is not atypical. According to a report in the *New York Times*, more than one hundred drug corruption cases involving law enforcement officers are prosecuted in federal and state courts each year (Shenon, 1988:A12). Piers Beirne and James Messerschmidt (1991:247) report other examples of police corruption:

> In several rural Georgia areas certain sheriffs accepted bribes of $50,000 each to allow drug smugglers to land planes on stretches of abandoned highway.
>
> A member of the Justice Department's Organized Crime Strike Force provided drug dealers with the identities of government informants for $210,000.
>
> An FBI agent accumulated over $850,000 in money, real estate, and other property for not only allowing drug dealers to sell cocaine, but selling it himself.
>
> A customs agent was paid $50,000 for each marijuana-packed automobile he allowed to cross from Mexico into the United States without inspection.

While we usually think of corruption in relation to police officers on the street and local prosecutors, the drug war has managed to offer incentives for corruption that reach to the very highest levels of the United States government. It is indeed ironic that the very agencies of government who are beating the drums loudest in the war on drugs have also established an infamous record of accepting assistance from and providing logistical support to some of the largest drug-trafficking syndicates in the world. Consider the following examples (Chambliss and Block, 1981; Lernoux, 1984; McCoy, 1972; Mills, 1986).

- For more than three decades the United States government has directly supported the opium-growing warlords of the Golden Triangle in Southeast Asia. Not only does the government provide them with military assistance and arms under the guise of fighting communism, but it has also protected corrupt governments, such as that of Thailand, which nurture the heroin industry.

- During the Vietnam war and for some time thereafter, CIA-funded Laotian tribesmen were used to refine opium poppies into heroin. A CIA front company, Air America, was used to transport the heroin out of Southeast Asia.

- The CIA has helped to establish money-laundering facilities for the Southeast Asian heroin connection. The Nugan Hand Bank, established in Australia in 1973, laundered funds for both the CIA and the Southeast Asian heroin traffickers.

- CIA associates in the Caribbean, including the paymaster for the ill-fated Bay of Pigs invasion, played key roles in the operations of Castle Bank, a Florida money laundry for organized crime's drug money.

- Another Florida bank with strong intelligence-community connections, the Bank of Perrine, has been used by the Colombian cartels to launder money from their burgeoning cocaine business.

- The CIA and organized crime played a key role in establishing and operating the World Finance Corporation, a Florida-based company involved in laundering drug money and supporting terrorist activities in the early 1970s.

- Mexican heroin magnate Alberto Sicilia-Falcon not only claimed to have been a CIA agent operating on orders from Washington but also had access to classified CIA documents and had a chief enforcer with CIA ties.

- The world's largest opium merchant, Chang Chi-fu, operated as a CIA "client." Another heroin czar, Li Wen-huan, was given direct financial and logistical assistance by the CIA. A third major heroin trafficker, Lu Hus-shui, was protected from a Drug Enforcement Administration investigation on orders from the CIA.

- The CIA effectively blocked a major DEA investigation of drug trafficking and money laundering by Manuel Noriega in Panama. The State Department blocked an investigation targeting the government of the Bahamas after evidence revealed that the government and drug traffickers were making a deal to use the islands as a safe haven for both drugs and money.

These cases represent only the tip of the iceberg. In other cases still under investigation, suspicious trails have been found linking United States government agencies to drug trafficking by the Contras in Nicaragua and by the governments of Guatemala and Chile.

Closely related to the spread of drug-related corruption has been the added impetus the drug war has given to organized crime. The fact is that the drug laws and intensified enforcement strategies related to the drug war have strengthened organized crime and created a whole new generation of prohibition-conceived organized crime groups (Lyman and Potter, 1991). Drug enforcement is by its very nature highly selective and discriminatory. It targets only those easiest to catch and most visible to the police. Those dealers who are arrested are the least important, smallest operators. The net effect of drug enforcement is to weed out the inefficient and slothful drug dealers, giving organized crime an exclusive monopoly in drug trafficking. The mob now makes the most of its monopoly, raking in profits of $78 billion a year from drugs, and conducting their business with virtual immunity. Compare that figure with organized crime's profits of about $200 million in the bootlegging of tobacco, a legal drug, and it is easy to understand why organized crime is such a strong supporter of drug prohibition (Nadelmann, 1989:941). The only reason organized crime can realize such enormous profits in the drug market is the fact that drugs are illegal. The actual cost of growing and producing illegal drugs is modest, but the criminal surcharge that organized crime can add to the cost of drugs, because it competes with no legitimate suppliers, is staggering. The drug laws, in effect, act like a government-sponsored subsidy to organized crime, a subsidy worth billions of dollars a year.

Not only have the strategies designed to control drug use and drug trafficking been unsuccessful, but the very act of vigorously enforcing the drug laws has created social problems far more serious than any caused by drug use alone. Let us be clear on this point. Drug control policy has not failed for lack of resources, funding, legal powers, or adequate manpower. It has failed because the problem is not amenable to a criminal justice solution. As the Pennsylvania Crime Commission concluded in its 1987 report on organized crime:

> It should be understood that, short of creating a police state, there is no evidence to suggest that vast expansion of investigative efforts would lead to the eradication of illegal drugs.

In the past decade, expenditures on drug enforcement have tripled; the number of Americans in prison has doubled. Paying for the construction and maintenance of prisons now represents the fastest growing item in state budgets. Yet, despite this dramatic increase in punitiveness, most aspects of the drug problem are getting worse.

Making Peace in the War on Drugs

The list of failures of our present drug control initiatives could go on endlessly. We could talk about the inconsistency in the drug laws. The two most dangerous drugs in America—tobacco and alcohol—are freely available, while less dangerous drugs lead to felony convictions. We could talk about the racist nature of drug enforcement. We could talk about the threats to our basic constitutional rights created by questionable police tactics emanating from the difficulties of drug enforcement. We could talk about the disrespect for the law, in general, bred by drug enforcement. However, the facts are straightforward and relatively simple. Law enforcement efforts directed at the drug problem have failed and will continue to fail.

We have allowed the drug problem to be framed by political leaders and law enforcement officials as strictly a criminal justice system problem. As we have seen, the problem of drugs is far more complex than this simple approach. While it is beyond the purview of this present discussion to fully explore the alternatives to a criminal justice approach to drugs, we can take the time to raise a few issues.

First, there appears to be a much greater chance of success in reducing the incidence of drug use through drug education and drug treatment programs than through the use of the criminal law. Everything we know about rehabilitation and education programs demonstrates that they are exponentially more effective than law enforcement strategies in reducing drug use.

- *Drug Rehabilitation.* Despite the fact that available research points to great successes in drug rehabilitation and drug counseling, the problem is that these programs are simply not available where they are needed (particularly the inner city) nor are they available in sufficient number. Currently, there are more than 100,000 persons on waiting lists for drug treatment in the United States, (National Commission on AIDS, 1991:1). Available evidence, although sparse, would seem to indicate that the diversion of resources from enforcement to control through educational and medical strategies would result in a net decline in drug use (Trebach, 1989:4-10).

- *Drug Education.* Using drug education to deglamorize drugs might be the single most important component of any national drug control strategy. Deglamorization programs combine drug education in schools with useful and realistic portrayals of the problems of drugs in media advertising in an attempt to convince would-be drug users to exercise extreme caution in making their choices. All the available evidence suggests that drug education is the most effective means of drug control. However, such a strategy would require a massive diversion of funds from law enforcement into educational programs in order to be successful. Present drug education efforts are woefully underfunded (Lyman and Potter, 1991:347).

Second, it is time to revive an idea which showed great promise in dealing with the problems of drug addiction/drug maintenance (Trebach, 1989). Drug maintenance is not a new idea. In the period between 1919 and 1923, after the passage of the Harrison Narcotics Act, there were at least forty clinics operating in the United States which distributed morphine and heroin to thousands of opiate addicts. Later experiments with drug maintenance included a New York City experiment with methadone maintenance in the 1960s. Methadone is a heroin substitute which does not cure addiction, but which does allow addicts to function quite normally in society despite their addiction. The fact is, despite the criticisms of how methadone maintenance programs were administered and the moral objection that methadone merely panders to addiction, methadone maintenance is the most successful approach to American drug control in the history of American drug policy. Drug maintenance experiments have also shown great success in the Liverpool-Mersey area of England, where health professionals have worked with both the police and educators to develop a series of interrelated projects designed to free addicts from both their addiction and the social environment of drug users. The Liverpool-Mersey experiment includes the dispensing of drugs to addicts as part of a regular program of drug maintenance; a needle-exchange program; detoxification counseling; and the provision of general health care to drug abusers (Trebach, 1989).

Finally, it is time to open the debate on the alternative to current law enforcement efforts against drugs. It is time to begin to talk about the legalization of drugs. This is a topic which must be approached with great caution, as Arnold Trebach (1989:4-5) has urged:

> While I do not recommend it at this point in history, I have become convinced in recent years that our societies would be safer and healthier if all of the illegal drugs were fully removed from the control of the criminal law tomorrow morning at the start of business. If that happened, I would be very worried about the possibility of future harm, but less worried than I am now about the reality of present harm being inflicted every day by our current laws and policies.

As difficult as it may be to raise the issue of legalization in the present environment of drug war hysteria, there are some possible benefits which should be subjected to further research and debate.

• Repealing drug prohibition will save us at least $10 billion a year in enforcement costs which could be used to supplement the present inadequate funding for more promising approaches such as education and rehabilitation.

• Repealing the drug laws could result in a reduction of crime, particularly in the inner city where the quality of life might well improve; homicide, burglary and robbery rates would fall.

• We would certainly see some diminution in the dangerous trend toward large-scale, systematic political and law enforcement corruption, which threatens our whole system of criminal justice.

• Organized crime groups, particularly those newer groups dependent on the drug trade which have not yet had the time to expand their enterprises into more traditional areas of vice, would be dealt a severe and potentially terminal setback.

• Certainly the quality of life for hundreds of thousands of drug abusers and millions of drug users would improve significantly if legal controls were removed (Nadelmann, 1989).

Admittedly, legalization is a dangerous policy alternative. No one knows how such a system would operate. No one knows if there would be a subsequent increase in drug use. Certainly we do not want to create a situation in which heroin and cocaine are as prevalent and freely used as tobacco and alcohol. There are, however, some encouraging indicators which should at least stimulate the debate.

In the eleven states which decriminalized marijuana during the 1970s, there was no significant increase in the level of marijuana usage over levels noted prior to decriminalization (Nadelmann, 1989:943). This would seem to mitigate against concerns that the removal of legal prohibitions would lead to an epidemic of drug use, particularly if educational programs were in place and functioning.

In addition, the experience with drug decriminalization in the Netherlands has been very encouraging. In the Netherlands, the decriminalization of marijuana led to actual declines in the consumption of marijuana from 10 percent of the population in 1976 to 2 percent in 1985. Overall marijuana consumption in the Netherlands is considerably less than in the United States where marijuana possession is still illegal. Fully a third fewer people use marijuana in the Netherlands than use marijuana in the United States. Finally, the decriminalization of cocaine has shown an even more disparate pattern of use. In the Netherlands, decriminalized cocaine is used by 1200 percent fewer people than in the United States (Trebach and Engelsman, 1989:44-45). While there are clear differences in the two societies, particularly in the provision of quality health care and social services, the experience of the Netherlands in successfully handling its drug problems is worthy of further study and discussion.

While none of these alternatives promises to solve all aspects of the problem and many of them are highly controversial, they do represent new and innovative ideas. The simple fact is that the many myths which have been fostered about drug use and drug users make constructive policy choices difficult. A realistic drug policy requires that we look beyond these myths. While there may be moral objections to drug policy reform, questions about how best to proceed, and disagreements over the dangers of new initiatives, there are no questions about the law enforcement approach to drug control. It is a failure. A failure which makes a very bad situation much worse. It would be much more dangerous to continue on the present course, knowing the disasters which confront us, than to reconsider the parameters of drug control in America.

Sources

Association of the Bar of the City of New York (1978). *The Nation's Toughest Drug Law: Evaluating the New York Experience.* New York: Association of the Bar of the City of New York.

Beirne, Piers and James Messerschmidt (1991). *Criminology.* New York: Harcourt Brace Jovanovich.

Benoit, Ellen (1989). The Case for Legalization. *Financial World.* (October 3):32-35.

Brecher, Edward M. (1972). *Licit and Illicit Drugs.* Boston: Little, Brown.

Bureau of Justice Statistics (1987). *Sourcebook of Criminal Justice Statistics, 1986.* Washington, DC: United States Department of Justice.

Bureau of Justice Statistics (1988). *Sourcebook of Criminal Justice Statistics, 1987.* Washington, DC: United States Department of Justice.

Chaiken, Marcia R. (1988). *Street-Level Drug Enforcement: Examining the Issues.* Washington, DC: United States Department of Justice.

Chambliss, William and Alan Block (1981). *Organizing Crime.* New York: Elsevier.

Goode, Erich (1984). *Drugs in American Society.* New York: Alfred A. Knopf.

Gropper, Bernard A. (1985). Probing the Links Between Drugs and Crime. *National Institute of Justice: Research in Brief.* Washington, DC: United States Government Printing Office.

Inciardi, James (1986). *The War on Drugs: Heroin, Cocaine, Crime, and Public Policy.* Palo Alto, CA: Mayfield.

Kaplan, John (1983). *The Hardest Drug: Heroin and Public Policy.* Chicago: University of Chicago Press.

Lernoux, Penny (1984). *In Banks We Trust.* New York: Doubleday.

Lyman, Michael and Gary W. Potter (1991). *Drugs in Society.* Cincinnati, OH: Anderson.

McCaghy, Charles H. (1985). *Deviant Behavior.* New York: Macmillan.

McCaghy, Charles H. and Stephen A. Cernkovich (1987). *Crime in American Society.* New York: Macmillan.

McCoy, Alfred (1972). *The Politics of Heroin in Southeast Asia.* New York: Harper & Row.

McGlothlin, William H., M. Douglas Anglin, and Bruce D. Wilson (1978). Narcotic Addiction and Crime. *Criminology,* 16 (November):293-315.

Mills, James (1986). *The Underground Empire.* New York: Doubleday.

Murray, John (1986). Marijuana's Effects on Human Cognitive Functions, Psychomotor Functions, and Personality. *Journal of General Psychology* 113(1):23-55.

Musto, David (1973). *The American Disease: Origins of Narcotic Control.* New Haven, CT: Yale University Press.

Nadelmann, Ethan A. (1989). Drug Prohibition in the United States: Costs, Consequences, and Alternatives. *Science* 245 (September):939-47.

National Commission of AIDS (1991). *Report: The Twin Epidemics of Substance Use and HIV.* Washington, DC: Government Printing Office, July.

National Drug Enforcement Policy Board (1987). *National and International Drug Law Enforcement Strategy.* Washington, DC: Department of Justice.

National Institute on Drug Abuse (1987). *Data from the 1985 National Household Survey on Drug Abuse.* Rockville, MD: National Institute on Drug Abuse.

Newsweek (1989). A Tide of Drug Killing. (January 16):44.

Pennsylvania Crime Commission (1987). *Annual Report.* Conshocken, PA: Commonwealth of Pennsylvania.

Potter, Gary W., Larry Gaines and Beth Holbrook (1990). Blowing Smoke: Marijuana Eradication in Kentucky. *American Journal of Police* 9.

Ray, Oakley (1983). *Drugs, Society and Human Behavior.* St. Louis: C.V. Mosby.

Reiman, Jeffrey (1984). *The Rich Get Richer and the Poor Get Prison.* New York: John Wiley.

Reuter, Peter, G. Crawford and J. Cace (1988). *Sealing the Borders: the Effects of Increased Military Participation in Drug Interdiction.* Santa Barbara, CA: The Rand Corporation.

Shenon, Philip (1988). Enemy Within: Drug Money Is Corrupting the Enforcers. *New York Times*, (Apr. 11):A1, A12.

Trebach, Arnold (1989). Drug Policies for the Democracies. Statement before the Public Hearing on Drug Control, Interior Committee of the Deutscher Bundestag, The Parliament of the Federal Republic of Germany (March 13).

Trebach, Arnold and Eddy Engelsman (1989). Why Not Decriminalize? *NPQ*, (Summer):40-45.

chapter 9

The Transmission of HIV
Exploring Some Misconceptions Related to Criminal Justice*

Many people working in the criminal justice system have beliefs about the transmission of AIDS that are unfounded. Despite the vigorous educational campaigns that have been mounted by public health officials over the last decade, a substantial number of individuals are still misinformed with respect to this ailment (Blendon and Donelan, 1988). Anxiety concerning AIDS has led to such actions as police officers wearing gloves at gay rights demonstrations (Blumberg, 1989:210), court personnel utilizing protective clothing in the presence of HIV-infected defendants (Wallace, 1990), and prison guards refusing to transport seropositive inmates (Hammett, 1988:106).

This chapter examines five common misconceptions regarding the transmission of the Human Immunodeficiency Virus (HIV) that must be corrected if the criminal justice system is going to respond to the AIDS crisis in an appropriate manner. Too often, decision making in this area has been hindered by needless anxiety, faulty assumptions, and misinformation. Because it is necessary to

---

*This chapter originally appeared in Volume 4, No. 4 of *Criminal Justice Police Review* (December 1990).

possess accurate scientific knowledge before sound policies can be implemented, this chapter explores the epidemiology and dynamics of HIV transmission in an attempt to correct a number of misconceptions that have often dominated the policy debate in this area.

The following beliefs are challenged:

1) Persons who work in the criminal justice system face a significant risk of HIV infection as a result of the assaultive behavior of seropositive offenders ("seropositive" refers to individuals whose blood test indicates that they have been exposed to the human immunodeficiency virus).

2) The transmission of HIV by female prostitutes to their male customers is an important source of viral infection in the United States.

3) Female rape victims face a significant risk of being infected with the AIDS virus.

4) HIV is being transmitted on a regular basis in the nation's prisons.

5) Intravenous drug users (IVDUs) will not alter their "high-risk" behavior.

Occupational Transmission and Criminal Justice

A common misconception regarding HIV transmission is the belief that persons who interact with offenders as part of their occupational duties are at risk of infection. Despite this concern, several national surveys indicate that not a single police officer, prison guard or any other person working in the criminal justice system has become infected as a result of his or her employment (Hammett, 1988:15).

An examination of the dynamics of HIV transmission indicates that this finding should not be surprising. In this regard, a study undertaken by the Centers for Disease Control (CDC) is instructive. There has been a great deal of concern regarding the case of Dr. David Acer, the Florida dentist who apparently infected five of his patients with HIV. Because this is the first report of a health care worker infecting a patient, the CDC calculated the risk that infected surgeons and dentists present. It was estimated that the likelihood HIV will be transmitted from an infected surgeon to a patient as a result of a single procedure ranged from between 1 in 41,667 to 1 in 416,667. For an infected dentist, the risk ranged from 1 in 263,158 to 1 in 2,631,579 (Altman, 1991:A10). Clearly, this risk is quite negligible despite the fact that surgeons perform invasive procedures and dentists routinely come in contact with blood from their patients.

The risk to persons working in the criminal justice system is even smaller. After all, police and correctional officers do not perform invasive procedures. Almost all interactions between offenders and criminal justice agency personnel involve the kinds of nonintimate casual contact that present no risk of viral transmission.

However, justice system personnel often express anxiety that certain types of assaultive behavior on the part of offenders falls outside the definition of casual contact and therefore may place them at risk. Specifically, there is anxiety regarding three types of assaults: 1) being spit upon or bitten by a seropositive assailant; 2) being hit by urine or feces thrown by an infected inmate and; 3) being stabbed with a needle that is contaminated with the blood of a seropositive offender. The inherent risks of HIV transmission in each of these scenarios are examined below.

Spitting and Biting Incidents

The Human Immunodeficiency Virus has been isolated in the saliva of some infected persons. Nonetheless, there is strong evidence indicating that transmission of the virus through spitting is highly improbable. Laboratory tests have revealed that HIV is present in the saliva of very few infected persons (Ho, Byington, Schooley, Flynn, Rota and Hirsch, 1985). When the virus is present, it is in such minute quantity that transmission to another person would be extremely difficult. It has been estimated that one quart of saliva would have to enter the bloodstream of an individual for infection to occur (Hammett, 1988:16). HIV does not pass through intact skin. Unless a seropositive person spit directly upon an open sore, transmission could not occur even if the virus were present in sufficient quantity (which it is not) in saliva. Finally, studies of individuals living in households where persons with AIDS reside have reported no cases of viral transmission as a result of casual nonintimate interaction. This is in spite of the fact that many of these family members shared plates, silverware, toothbrushes, and other items likely to have become contaminated with saliva from the infected individual (Friedland, Saltzman, Rogers, Kahl, Lesser, Mayers and Klein, 1986).

. Biting incidents are another source of anxiety for persons working in the criminal justice system. Because HIV is a blood-borne disease, it might appear that a bite poses a serious risk of infection. However, the medical evidence suggests that this is not so. Recently, a study was reported in which HIV antibody tests were administered to thirty health care workers who had been bitten by a single AIDS patient. None of these individuals were infected with the virus (Hammett, 1988:16). This outcome is not surprising, given the fact that it is the assailant who generally comes in contact with blood as a result of a bite and not the victim. The only theoretical risk of infection under these circumstances would occur if the offender had blood in his/her mouth at the time of the assault.

To date, there are no documented cases of HIV transmission as a result of either a bite or a spitting incident (Gostin, 1989a:1023; Lifson, 1988:1353-54). In fact, the risks associated with saliva are so minimal that the Centers for Disease Control no longer recommend that universal body fluid precautions (i.e., that all such fluid be treated as if it were infectious) be followed when contact with saliva is anticipated (Centers for Disease Control, 1988). Nonetheless, the courts occasionally treat these incidents as extremely serious matters. Recently, a prison inmate in New Jersey was given a sentence of twenty-five years for biting a correctional officer (Sullivan, 1990:25). This kind of response by the justice system sends the wrong message to both the public and to persons who must interact with seropositive offenders; it incorrectly implies that assaults of this nature present a serious risk of viral transmission. Offenders who assault correctional officers should be punished. However, it should be made clear that this action is being taken in response to the offender's behavior and not because there is a danger of HIV transmission.

Assaults with Bodily Waste

Jails and prisons are institutions that house a substantial number of violent and sociopathic individuals. Thus, it is not surprising that correctional officers have occasionally been assaulted by inmates who throw bags containing body waste. Despite the repugnant nature of this conduct, institutional personnel can take comfort from the fact that HIV transmission under these circumstances is extremely unlikely. The AIDS virus is not present in the feces of infected persons and is present in urine in such low concentrations as to make transmission quite improbable (Hammett, 1989a:3). For these reasons, the CDC no longer recommend that persons take "universal precautions" when contact with these body fluids is anticipated (Centers for Disease Control, 1988).

Needle Sticks

Another source of concern among persons working in the criminal justice system is that they will suffer accidental or intentional wounds from needles that are contaminated with the blood of seropositive individuals. Unlike other types of assaults, needle sticks do present a small risk of HIV infection. Studies of health care workers who have accidentally pricked themselves with needles that were used on seropositive patients indicate that the risk of viral transmission under these circumstances is approximately 0.4 percent (Peterman and Petersen, 1990:401). In other words, there will be one seroconversion (a positive HIV antibody status for an individual who was not previously infected) for every 250 needle sticks that involve exposure to contaminated blood. For this reason, criminal justice agencies must institute operational procedures that minimize the likelihood that this type of injury will occur. Offenders who intentionally assault others with needles should be subject to legal sanctions. In addition, employees who receive such injuries should be counseled regarding the low probability that viral transmission will actually occur and instructed on the proper method by which to apply first aid to the wound.

Female Prostitution

Many female prostitutes in the United States have become infected with HIV. To date, the evidence indicates that this has occurred almost exclusively as a result of intravenous drug use (IVDU) and not from sexual contact with customers (Cohen, Alexander and Wofsy, 1988). However, because the AIDS virus is transmitted primarily through sexual activity, concern has been expressed that these individuals could become a conduit for viral transmission into the general population. Often, this anxiety is exacerbated by media stories about infected prostitutes who remain sexually active (*New York Times*, 1985) and by enforcement policies that are based on the assumption that prostitutes are transmitting the virus to clients (Cohen et al., 1988). A number of states have enacted statutes that mandate HIV testing for persons charged with or convicted of prostitution (Gostin, 1989b:1626). Other jurisdictions have reclassified prostitution as a felony in situations in which the offender has previously tested seropositive. In a recent case, a Las Vegas prostitute was sentenced to twenty years imprisonment under such a statute (Gostin, 1990:1963).

Despite the severe punishments that are occasionally inflicted on infected prostitutes, there is little evidence to indicate that female prostitutes are actually transmitting HIV to their male clients. There are over 63,000 female arrests for prostitution each year in the United States (Flanagan and Jamieson, 1988: Table 4.6). The average female prostitute sees approximately 1,500 male customers per year (Bergman, 1988:782-83). Despite the fact that the AIDS virus has been present in the United States since at least 1978, not a single case to date has been definitively traced to a specific prostitute (Cohen et al., 1988:18). If sexual contact with female prostitutes were an important source of HIV transmission, there should have been hundreds (if not thousands) of AIDS cases reported by now among males who had patronized the services of these sex workers (Bergman, 1988:783).

The following question naturally arises: if HIV is a sexually transmitted disease, why are female prostitutes not infecting their male clients in substantial numbers? Several factors probably help to explain this apparent anomaly. First, the likelihood of viral transmission as a result of a single heterosexual encounter involving vaginal intercourse is quite low (Hearst and Hulley, 1988). Second, many prostitutes have been educated about safer sex and are using condoms to prevent infection (Rosenberg and Weiner, 1988:422). Third, studies have indicated that oral sex [which presents a low risk of viral transmission (Lyman, Ascher and Levy, 1986:1703)] is the most common sexual activity requested of female prostitutes and that anal sex [which presents a high risk (Winkelstein, et al., 1987:324)] is not commonly performed (Rosenberg and Weiner, 1988:42). Finally, the AIDS virus may be transmitted with less efficiency from females to males than in the opposite direction (Friedland and Klein, 1987:1129).

There are other reasons to be confident that female prostitutes are not a significant source of viral transmission in the United States. Early reports which suggested that contact with female prostitutes was a risk factor for AIDS infection among military personnel (Redfield et al., 1985:2094-96) have turned out to be false. Many servicemen who initially claimed contact with a female prostitute as their only risk factor eventually admitted to having engaged in traditional "high-risk" behaviors (same-sex contact or intravenous drug use) upon being reinterviewed by civilian public health authorities (Potterat, Phillips and Muth, 1987:1727). It is not surprising that these military personnel would initially claim contact with a female prostitute as a risk factor and deny having engaged in either homosexual behavior or intravenous drug use. After all, the former is not punishable and the latter are serious breaches of military discipline.

Epidemiological data also lend credence to the belief that female prostitutes are not transmitting HIV to their male clients in substantial numbers. As of May 1990, there have been 121,282 documented adolescent/adult AIDS cases among males in the United States (Centers for Disease Control, 1990:10). Ninety-two percent of these have occurred among persons who engaged in homosexual activity and/or intravenous drug use (Centers for Disease Control, 1990:10). The Centers for Disease Control have undertaken further analysis of the small proportion of cases among males that initially were reported without any identifiable risk factor. Only 76 of these involved men who claimed that sexual contact with a prostitute was their only risk factor (Centers for Disease Control, 1990:16).

Finally, if prostitutes were transmitting AIDS to their male customers (many of whom are married), there would already be reported cases in which the female partners of these men and/or their newborn infants had become infected. This has not occurred. To date, the overwhelming majority of cases involving heterosexual transmission has occurred among females who are the steady sex partners of IVDUs (Centers for Disease Control, 1990:10; Haverkos and Edelman, 1988). Likewise, the overwhelming majority of pediatric cases are linked to mothers who either report a history of intravenous drug use or are the sexual partners of IVDUs (Moss, 1987:389). It is often suggested that transmission patterns cannot be discerned based on reported cases of AIDS. Because the median incubation period for AIDS is 9.8 years (Bacchetti and Moss, 1989), critics contend that cases of "full-blown" AIDS represent infections that took place many years ago and that the epidemiology of the disease may have changed. However, this is somewhat misleading because the median represents the midpoint, and half the cases will have an incubation period of less than 9.8 years. In fact, it has been reported that 15 percent of infected persons will progress to full-blown AIDS within 36 months of seroconversion (Cooper and Jeffers, 1988:525). Therefore, a strong case could be made that by now we would have seen many more cases of AIDS associated with female prostitution if this were a significant factor in the transmission of the virus.

Female Rape Survivors

Females who are sexually assaulted may be at risk for a number of sexually transmitted diseases (Glaser, Hammerschlag, and McCormack, 1989). Because HIV is also transmitted through sexual contact, it is plausible to assume that these females face a serious risk of HIV infection as well. However, a close examination of data regarding both the epidemiology and dynamics of HIV transmission in the United States suggests that this is not the case.

In order to accurately assess the risk of HIV transmission for female rape survivors, it is necessary to answer three questions.

1) What types of sexual assaults are committed by rapists?

2) What are the risks of HIV infection associated with various forms of sexual activity?

3) What proportion of rape assailants are infected with HIV?

The most recent analysis of sexual assaults directed against females indicates that almost all survivors experience forced vaginal intercourse (Holmstrom and Burgess, 1980). Fortunately, the risk of viral transmission that is likely to result from a single assault of this nature is quite minimal. Hearst and Hulley (1988:2429) have calculated that the likelihood of a female seroconverting as a result of a single act of unprotected heterosexual intercourse with an infected male to be about 1 in 500. Whether the act is consensual or coerced should not affect the aggregate statistical analysis that is undertaken below.

Females who are sexually assaulted are sometimes the victims of either oral and/or anal sodomy as well. Although oral sex has been linked to the transmission of HIV (Rozenbaum, Gharakhanian, Cardon, Duval, and Coulaud, 1988), the risks associated with this practice are believed to be minimal (Lyman et al., 1986). Anal sex, as noted above, is quite risky (Winkelstein et al., 1987). In fact, Kingsley, Rinaldo, Lyter, Valdiserri, Belle, and Ho (1990:230) report that more than 90 percent of new infections among gay males are attributable to anal intercourse. However, only a small proportion of assaults directed at females (5 percent) involve this type of "high-risk" behavior (Holmstrom and Burgess (1980:431-32).

As previously noted, the number of rape survivors who can be expected to seroconvert is a function not only of the risks inherent in a single assault, but also of the proportion of offenders who are seropositive. Because some states have begun to require HIV testing for persons charged with or convicted of rape (Gostin, 1989b), data should soon become available regarding the prevalence of HIV among these offenders. In the interim, the critical question is: which group of persons who have been tested for HIV is most likely to approximate the rate of infection found among rapists who assault females?

In 1985, a blood test to detect antibodies to the AIDS virus became available. This discovery provided the opportunity to conduct widespread testing of various populations in order to determine their rate of seroprevalence. Hospital patients, blood donors, patients at clinics that treat sexually transmitted diseases (STDs), newborn infants, applicants for the armed forces, and others have all been tested for HIV (Centers for Disease Control, 1989a). Researchers have used these data in an attempt to learn the extent to which the AIDS virus has affected various populations within the United States.

For several reasons, it would appear that the most appropriate epidemiological data for the purpose at hand are the results of HIV antibody screening that has been carried out among all prospective recruits for the armed forces since October 1985. In the United States, gay males and IV drug users account for almost 90 percent of the AIDS cases (Centers for Disease Control, 1990:10). However, it is unlikely that gay males are, to any large extent, participants in sexual assaults directed at females. IVDUs are also unlikely to engage in this type of behavior. Generally, alcohol is far more likely to be a precipitating factor in the crime of rape than is drug addiction. Because the military attempts to exclude members of both these "risk groups" from its ranks, the process of self-selection probably results in relatively few gay males and IV drug users being included in these epidemiological data.

The military data are appropriate for other reasons as well. Because applicants for the armed services are largely male, at an age where they are likely to be sexually active, and disproportionately drawn from minority backgrounds, they share some of the same demographic and behavioral characteristics as do apprehended rape offenders who are also often young males and disproportionately members of minority groups.

An examination of the results of HIV testing among prospective male military recruits indicate that 1.5 out of 1,000 (0.15 percent) are infected with HIV (Centers for Disease Control, 1989a:10). There were 45,640 completed rape victimizations in the United States during 1986 (Flanagan and Jamieson, 1988: Table 3.1). If it is assumed that 0.15 percent of these offenses are committed by offenders who are seropositive (the same rate found among military recruits), then 68 of these assailants have the capacity to infect their female victims with HIV through forced vaginal intercourse. However, because the risk of infection from a single heterosexual assault is so slight (0.02 percent), less than one case of AIDS infection per annum in the United States among female rape survivors should be expected.

However, it has already been noted that for the small proportion of victims who are anally sodomized, the odds of infection are somewhat greater. The medical literature reports that the receptive partner in anal-genital intercourse has a substantial risk of exposure to the AIDS virus (Friedland and Klein, 1987). For this reason, females who are assaulted in this manner are likely to be seriously concerned about the possibility that they have contracted a deadly disease. Although it is certainly true that the risk of infection is greater under these circumstances, the odds are still against it.

Confidence in this conclusion is buttressed because more than one decade has passed since the AIDS virus first appeared, and not a single case has been reported in the United States in which a female rape victim became infected as a result of a sexual assault. In telephone conversations with both the National Institute of Justice (NIJ) AIDS Clearinghouse on January 5, 1989 and the Centers for Disease Control (CDC) on January 12, 1989, staff persons indicated that no cases of AIDS among female rape victims had come to their attention. Although neither agency has compiled data that specifically address this issue, the spokesperson at CDC noted that the agency had undertaken an analysis of cases in which females with no known risk factor (i.e., no history of IV drug use, no record of receiving a possibly contaminated blood transfusion, and no identifiable sex partner in a "high-risk" group) had become infected with AIDS. The agency did not find any of these cases attributable to sexual assault. This is despite the fact that thousands of cases of forcible rape occurred each year during this period.

HIV Transmission within Correctional Institutions

Another common misconception about HIV transmission is the belief that our correctional institutions have become breeding grounds for the spread of the virus. After all, prisons and jails contain a substantial number of inmates who have a history of intravenous drug use (Vlahov and Polk, 1988) and there is evidence that indicates a substantial proportion of prisoners engage in homosexual behavior during incarceration (Nacci and Kane, 1983; Wooden and Parker, 1982). In an attempt to prevent institutional transmission from occurring, a number of jurisdictions have adopted policies that are quite controversial such as isolating seropositive inmates from the general prison population (Whitman, 1990). Despite these fears regarding AIDS, the evidence to date suggests that little HIV transmission is occurring within the nation's prison system.

In order to determine whether viral transmission is occurring to a significant degree in correctional institutions, two sources of data are reviewed. The first examines the proportion of AIDS cases that have been diagnosed in persons who have been continuously incarcerated for many years. One might attribute any seropositive outcomes among this group to homosexual activity or IVDU that occurred within the institution. However, because the incubation period for AIDS is quite lengthy, the possibility still exists that these cases represent instances of viral transmission that occurred prior to incarceration. The second source examines studies that have tested the same cohort of inmates both upon entry to the institution and at a later date for antibodies to HIV. These data provide a much better picture about the frequency of institutional transmission.

Analysis of the prison records of inmates diagnosed with AIDS, in both New York and Florida, indicates that very few cases have occurred among persons who have been incarcerated for a substantial period of time. New York reports no cases of AIDS among inmates who have been continuously incarcerated for more than seven years and only five cases among those incarcerated between five and seven years (Hammett, 1988:31). Likewise, Florida officials report that 98 percent of their institutional AIDS cases involve inmates who have been continuously incarcerated for less than two years (Hammett, 1988:31). These data suggest that almost all prisoners with AIDS in these two states became infected prior to incarceration.

The findings from three serological studies that have utilized a longitudinal approach also suggest that HIV transmission within the institution is not a common occurrence. The first study screened 542 inmates incarcerated at a military prison operated by the United States Army. These inmates were initially tested between 1982 and 1984 and retested during July 1985. None had seroconverted (Kelley, Redfield, Ward, Burke and Miller, 1986:2189). The second study examined 393 inmates who were seronegative upon entry into the Maryland state prison system. Upon follow-up (one to two years later), two of these individuals had seroconverted which was interpreted by the researchers as "the strongest evidence to date that transmission of HIV-1 occurs in prison" (Brewer, Vlahov, Taylor, Hall, Munoz and Polk, 1988:363).

The final longitudinal study examined inmates in the Nevada state prison system. Horsburgh, Jarvis, McArthur, Ignacio and Stock (1990) report that two prisoners who were initially seronegative had converted by the time they were again tested upon leaving the system (209). For this reason, the researchers conclude that HIV transmission among inmates within the Nevada prison system is rare.

Both the Maryland and the Nevada studies suggest that HIV transmission may be occurring at a relatively low rate. However, it should be noted that some persons infected with HIV do not produce antibodies. Consequently, they do not test positive for as long as thirty-six months (Imagawa, Lee, Wolinsky, Sano, Morales, Kwok, Sninsky, Nishanian, Giorgi, Fahey, Dudley, Visscher, and Detels, 1989). For this reason, the authors of the Nevada study are not able to rule out the possibility that the two inmates who sero-converted were actually already infected at the time they were initially tested. The Maryland researchers are more confident that institutional transmission has been documented because the two inmates in their sample who seroconverted had been detained for 69 and 146 days, respectively, prior to initial testing. Persons exposed to the AIDS virus usually seroconvert within six to twelve weeks after exposure (Petricciani and Epstein, 1988:236). However, because the latency period that precedes the development of anti-bodies to HIV is occasionally much longer, institutional transmission in these cases cannot be clearly established.

Although preliminary studies suggest that institutional transmission of HIV is not a common event, more research is clearly needed on this question. It is well known that there are substantial differences between jurisdictions with regard to the rate of seroprevalence among inmates (Hammett, 1989b:15) and it is quite likely that there are also differences between facilities with respect to the prevalence of "high-risk" behaviors that occur. Fortunately, the CDC has initiated a longitudinal study of 2,500 inmates in Illinois that will eventually provide more complete data on the question of viral transmission within the prison (Hammett, 1989b:17).

Risk Reduction Among Intravenous Drug Users

The final misconception to be addressed in this chapter is the "general impression that IVDUs are incapable of (or disinterested in) changing their behavior" (Becker and Joseph, 1988:403) in order to protect themselves from the AIDS virus. The ability and willing-ness of IVDUs to reduce their level of risk is a very important question from the standpoint of public health. One-third of new AIDS cases in the United States are now associated with IVDU (Centers for Disease Control, 1989b:165). In addition, the majority of cases that involve either heterosexual (Haverkos and Edelman, 1988) or perinatal transmission (Moss, 1987) are also linked to IVDU. Although educational campaigns designed to eliminate "high-risk" behavior have been very effective in reducing the level of new AIDS cases among gay men, many persons remain skeptical of whether such efforts can succeed among IVDUs.

Programs to educate IVDUs about AIDS are more difficult to implement than similar campaigns that have reached out to gay men. For one thing, the gay community already had a well developed organizational structure in place prior to the AIDS crisis (Friedman et al., 1987). Intravenous drug users, on the other hand, lack this organizational structure and are usually socially isolated. Second, many homosexual males are well educated and come from middle-class backgrounds. This contrasts with IVDUs who generally have little education and are often drawn from the ranks of the economically disadvantaged. Third, gay men are often deeply involved in a network of social relationships. IVDUs lack these ties and often have fragile relationships with family members and friends. Because they are involved in an activity that violates the law, IVDUs are generally suspicious of public officials and agencies. Finally, many IVDUs already confront a number of potential threats to their physical well-being (e.g., the possibility of an overdose, contracting hepatitis, potential violence on the part of persons with whom they interact, etc.). For these reasons, many are skeptical that widespread behavioral change among this group is possible. James Inciardi (1990:191-92) notes the difficulty that is likely to accompany efforts designed to educate IVDUs about a danger they may face five or more years down the road when, in many cases, they are already risking disease and death on a daily basis.

Despite these obstacles to behavioral change, a review of various studies suggests that many IVDUs have already taken steps to reduce their risk of HIV infection (Des Jarlais and Friedman, 1987:403-4). These measures have included such practices as: no longer sharing injection equipment, reducing the number of persons with whom they share needles, only using sterile needles, cleaning injection equipment prior to use, or reducing their level of drug use.

In addition to these self-reported behavioral changes among IVDUs, interviews with drug sellers indicate an increased demand for sterile needles on the part of users as well. Don Des Jarlais and William Hopkins (1985) note that dealers in New York sometimes use the offer of sterile needles as a means of attracting prospective buyers, either through 2-for-1 sales or by including free needles with the purchase of $25 and $50 bags of heroin. Other dealers engage in less scrupulous practices such as repackaging used needles and selling them as new (Des Jarlais, Friedman and Hopkins, 1985).

In spite of the encouraging findings from almost all the studies that have been undertaken, it is clear that much remains to be accomplished. For one thing, many IVDUs still engage in practices that are quite risky. A substantial proportion continues to engage in behavior that places both themselves and others at risk of HIV infection. Many addicts continue to share "dirty" needles (Selwyn, 1987:102). Others utilize ineffective means for avoiding infection [e.g., using water to clean injection equipment (Hopkins, 1988:24)]. Some continue to share needles but only with close associates. Although this practice is probably less risky than indiscriminate needle sharing, it still carries a substantial risk of HIV infection. Finally, there is growing evidence that fewer precautions are being taken to avoid sexual transmission than is the case with respect to injection practices (Des Jarlais and Friedman, 1988). Many IVDUs continue to engage in such unsafe activities as having multiple partners, failing to use condoms, or engaging in anal intercourse (Harris, Langrod, Hebert, Lowinson, Zang and Wynder, 1990:124-25). Clearly, much remains to be done with respect to altering behavior among members of this "high-risk" group.

Conclusion

In the preceding discussion, it has been observed that: 1) persons who work in the criminal justice system face a minimal risk of HIV infection (in many cases that risk approaches zero) from assaultive seropositve offenders; 2) female prostitutes rarely transmit the AIDS virus to their male customers; 3) the risk of HIV infection is minimal for almost all female rape victims; 4) there is evidence that the rate of viral transmission in the prison system is quite low; and 5) many IVDUs have responded to the threat of AIDS and modified their "high-risk" behavior.

A clearer understanding of these facts can lead to more informed policy decisions. For example, if the actual risks associated with a bite or spitting incident were more widely understood, courts may become less willing to impose lengthy prison sentences in these cases just because the offender is infected with HIV. Likewise, persons who are the victims of such assaults might become less concerned with learning the HIV antibody status of the offender. The same holds true for rape victims. Recently, a prosecutor in New York City recommended a more lenient sentence for a convicted rapist because the latter agreed to take an HIV antibody test and share the results with the victim (Salholz et al, 1990). Had there been a better appreciation of the low risk of viral transmission that such assaults generally entail, the prosecutor may have been less willing to consent to this agreement.

Accurate information could be a deterrent to misguided public policy in other areas as well. For example, prison administrators often encounter strong political pressures to segregate seropositive inmates. Perhaps recognition of the fact that institutional transmission is not a common occurrence will lessen these pressures and lead to more enlightened policies. The same holds true with respect to prostitution. Once it is understood that female prostitutes are not a major source of viral transmission, the futility of dealing with the AIDS crisis by cracking down on these individuals should be quite evident. Finally, efforts to curb the spread of HIV among IVDUs could receive a real boost when it is acknowledged that this is not a group composed solely of self-destructive, incorrigible individuals who care nothing about their health.

Sources

Altman, Lawrence K. (1991). United States Experts Try to Estimate AIDS Infections by Doctors. *New York Times*, (February 7): A10.

Bacchetti P. and A. R. Moss (1989). The Incubation Period of AIDS in San Francisco. *Nature*, 338:251-53.

Becker, M. H. and J. G. Joseph (1988). AIDS and Behavior Change to Reduce Risk: A Review. *American Journal of Public Health*, 78(4):394-410.

Bergman, B. (1988). AIDS, Prostitution, and the Use of Historical Stereotypes to Legislate Sexuality. *The John Marshall Law Review*, 21:777-830.

Blendon, R. J. and K. Donelan (1988). Discrimination Against People with AIDS: The Public's Perspective. *The New England Journal of Medicine*, 319(15):1022-26.

Blumberg, M. (1989). The AIDS Epidemic and the Police. In Roger G. Dunham and Geoffrey Alpert (eds.). *Critical Issues in Policing: Contemporary Readings*, 205-15. Prospect Heights, IL: Waveland Press, Inc.

Brewer, T., D. V. Fordham, E. Taylor, D. Hall, A. Munoz and B. F. Polk (1988). Transmission of HIV Within a Statewide Prison System. *AIDS*, 2(5):363-66.

Centers for Disease Control (1990). *HIV/AIDS Surveillance Report*. Atlanta, GA: United States Department of Health and Human Services, (June).

_____ (1989a). AIDS and Human Immunodeficiency Virus Infection in the United States:1988 Update. *Morbidity and Mortality Weekly Report*, 38(4): (May 12).

Centers for Disease Control (1989b). Update: Acquired Immunodeficiency Syndrome Associated with Intravenous Drug Use—United States, 1988. *Morbidity and Mortality Weekly Report*, 38(10):165-70.

_____ (1988). Update: Universal Precautions for Prevention of Transmission of Human Immunodeficiency Virus, Hepatitis B Virus, and Other Bloodborne Pathogens in Health-Care Settings. *Morbidity and Mortality Weekly Report*, 37(2): (June 24).

Cohen, J., P. Alexander and C. Wofsy (1988). Prostitution and AIDS: Public Policy Issues. *AIDS & Public Policy Journal*, 3(2):16-22.

Cooper, G, S. and D. J. Jeffers (1988). The Clinical Progression of HIV-1 Infection: A Review of 32 Follow-up Studies. *Journal of General Internal Medicine*, 3(6):525-31.

Des Jarlais, Don C. and Samuel R. Friedman (1988). The Psychology of Preventing AIDS Among Intravenous Drug Users. *American Psychologist*, 43(11):865-70.

_____ (1987). HIV Infection Among Intravenous Drug Users: Epidemiology and Risk Reduction. *AIDS*, 1(2):67-76.

Des Jarlais, D. C., S. R. Friedman and W. Hopkins (1985). Risk Reduction for the Acquired Immunodeficiency Syndrome Among Intravenous Drug Users. *Annals of Internal Medicine*, 103(5):755-59.

Des Jarlais, D. C. and W. Hopkins (1985). Free Needles for Intravenous Drug Users at Risk for AIDS: Current Developments in New York City. *New England Journal of Medicine*, 313(23):1476.

Flanagan, Timothy J. and Katherine M. Jamieson (1988). *Sourcebook of Criminal Justice Statistics 1987*. Albany, NY: The Hindelang Criminal Justice Research Center.

Friedland, Gerald H., Brian R. Saltzman, Martha F. Rogers, Patricia A. Kahl, Martin L. Lesser, Marguerite M. Mayers and Robert S. Klein (1986). Lack of Transmission of HTLV-111/LAV Infection to Household Contacts of Patients with AIDS or AIDS-Related Complex with Oral Candidiasis. *The New England Journal of Medicine*, 314(6):344-49.

Friedland, Gerald H. and Robert S. Klein (1987). Transmission of the Human Immunodeficiency Virus. *The New England Journal of Medicine*, 317(18):1125-35.

Friedman, Samuel R., Don C. Des Jarlais, Jo L. Sotheran, Jonathan Garber, Henry Cohen and Donald Smith (1987). AIDS and Self-Organization Among Intravenous Drug Users. *The International Journal of the Addictions*, 22(3):201-19.

Glaser, Jordan B., Margaret R. Hammerschlag and William M. McCormack (1989). Epidemiology of Sexually Transmitted Diseases in Rape Victims. *Review of Infectious Diseases*, 11(2):246-54.

Gostin, Lawrence O. (1990). The AIDS Litigation Project—A National Review of Court and Human Rights Commission Decisions, Part 1: The Social Impact of AIDS. *Journal of the American Medical Association*, 263(14):1961-70.

_____ (1989a). The Politics of AIDS: Compulsory State Powers, Public Health, and Civil Liberties. *Ohio State Law Journal*, 49(4):1017-58.

Gostin, Lawrence O. (1989b). Public Health Strategies for Confronting AIDS: Legislative and Regulatory Policy in the United States. *Journal of the American Medical Association*, 261(11):1621-30.

Groth, A. Nicholas and Ann Wolbert Burgess (1977). Sexual Dysfunction During Rape. *The New England Journal of Medicine*, 297(14):764-66.

Hammett, Theodore M. (1989a). *AIDS and HIV Training and Education in Criminal Justice Agencies*. Washington, DC: National Institute of Justice, (August).

_____. (1989b). *1988 Update: AIDS in Correctional Facilities*. Washington, DC: National Institute of Justice, (June).

_____. (1988). *AIDS in Correctional Facilities: Issues and Options*, Third Edition. Washington, DC: National Institute of Justice, (April).

Harris, Randall E., John Langrod, James R. Hebert, Joyce Lowinson, Edith Zang and Ernst L. Wynder (1990). Changes in AIDS Risk Behavior Among Intravenous Drug Abusers in New York City. *New York State Journal of Medicine*, (March):123-26.

Haverkos, Harry W. and Robert Edelman (1988). The Epidemiology of Acquired Immunodeficiency Syndrome Among Heterosexuals. *Journal of the American Medical Association*, 260 (13):1922-29.

Hearst, Norman and Stephen B. Hulley (1988). Preventing the Heterosexual Spread of AIDS: Are We Giving Our Patients the Best Advice? *Journal of the American Medical Association*, 259 (16):2428-32.

Ho, David D., Roy E. Byington, Robert T. Schooley, Theresa Flynn, Teresa R. Rota and Martin S. Hirsch (1985). Infrequency of Isolation of HTLV-111 Virus from Saliva in AIDS. *The New England Journal of Medicine*, 313 (25):1606.

Holmstrom, Lynda Lytle and Ann Wolbert Burgess (1980). Sexual Behavior of Assailants During Reported Rapes. *Archives of Sexual Behavior*, 9 (5):427-39.

Hopkins, William (1988). Needle Sharing and Street Behavior in Response to AIDS in New York City. In *Needle Sharing Among Intravenous Drug Abusers: National and International Perspectives*, Robert J. Battjes and Roy W. Pickens (eds.). Rockville, MD: National Institute on Drug Abuse.

Horsburgh, C. Robert, Joseph Q. Jarvis, Trudy McArthur, Terri Ignacio and Patricia Stock (1990). Seroconversion to Human Immunodeficiency Virus in Prison Inmates. *American Journal of Public Health*, 80 (2):209-10.

Imagawa, David T., Moon H. Lee, Steven Wolinsky, Kouichi Sano, Fatima Morales, Shirley Kwok, John J. Sninsky, Parunag G. Nishanian, Janis Giorgi, John L. Fahey, Jan Dudley, Barbara R. Visscher and Roger Detels (1989). Human Immunodeficiency Virus Type 1 Infection in Homosexual Men Who Remain Seronegative for Prolonged Periods. *The New England Journal of Medicine*, 320 (22):1458-62.

Inciardi, James A. (1990). HIV, AIDS and Intravenous Drug Use: Some Considerations. *Journal of Drug Issues*, 20(2):181-94.

Kelley, Patrick. W., Robert R. Redfield, David L. Ward, Donald S. Burke and Richard N. Miller (1986). Prevalence and Incidence of HTLV-111 in a Prison. (letter). *Journal of the American Medical Association*, 256 (16):2198-99.

Kingsley, Lawrence A., Charles R. Rinaldo, David W. Lyter, Ronald O. Valdiserri, Steven H. Belle and Monto Ho (1990). Sexual Transmission Efficiency of Hepatitis B Virus and Human Immunodeficiency Virus Among Homosexual Men. *Journal of the American Medical Association*, 264(2):230-34.

Lifson, Alan R. (1988). Do Alternate Modes for Transmission of Human Immunodeficiency Virus Exist?: A Review. *Journal of the American Medical Association*, 259 (9):1353-56.

Lyman, David, Michael Ascher and Jay A. Levy (1986). Minimal Risk of Transmission of AIDS-Associated Retrovirus Infection by Oral-Genital Contact. *Journal of the American Medical Association*, 255 (13):1703.

Moss, A. R. (1987). AIDS and Intravenous Drug Use: The Real Heterosexual Epidemic. *British Medical Journal*, 294 (6):389-90.

Murphy, S., V. Kitchen, J. R. W. Harris and S. M. Forster (1989). Rape and Subsequent Seroconversion to HIV. *British Medical Journal*, 299(16):718.

Nacci, Peter L. and Thomas R. Kane (1983). The Incidence of Sex and Sexual Aggression in Federal Prisons. *Federal Probation*, 47(4):31-36.

New York Times (1985). Prostitute Seized In Chicago Is Said To Have Spread AIDS, A21, col. 6 (December 26).

Peterman, Thomas A. and Lyle R. Petersen (1990). Stalking the HIV Epidemic: Which Tracks to Follow and How Far. *American Journal of Public Health*, 80(4):401-2.

Petricciani, John C. and Jay S. Epstein (1988). The Effects of the AIDS Epidemic on the Safety of the Nation's Blood Supply. *Public Health Reports*, 103(3):236-41.

Potterat, John J., Lyanne Phillips and John B. Muth (1987). Lying to Military Physicians About Risk Factors for HIV Infections. *Journal of the American Medical Association*, 257 (13):1727.

Redfield, Robert R., Phillip D. Markham, Syed Zaki Salahuddin, D. Craig Wright, M. G. Sarngadharan and Robert C. Gallo (1985). Heterosexually Acquired HTLV-111/LAV Disease (AIDS-Related Complex and AIDS): Epidemiologic Evidence for Female-to-Male Transmission. *Journal of the American Medical Association*, 254 (15):2094-96.

Rosenberg, Michael J. and Jodie M. Weiner (1988). Prostitutes and AIDS: A Health Department Priority? *American Journal of Public Health*, 78(4):418-23.

Rozenbaum, W., S. Gharakhanian, B. Cardon, E. Duval and J. P. Coulaud (1988). HIV Transmission By Oral Sex. *The Lancet*, I (8589):1395.

Salholz, Eloise, Karen Springen, Nonny De La Pena and Deborah Witherspoon (1990). A Frightening Aftermath. *Newsweek*, (July 23):53.

Selwyn, Peter A. (1987). Sterile Needles and the Epidemic of Acquired Immunodeficiency Syndrome: Issues for Drug Abuse Treatment and Public Health. *Advances in Alcohol and Substance Abuse*, 7(2):99-105.

Sullivan, Joseph F. (1990). AIDS-Infected Prisoner Receives 25 Years for Biting a Jail Guard. *New York Times*, (May 19):25.

Vlahov, David and B. Frank Polk (1988). Intravenous Drug Use and Human Immunodeficiency Virus (HIV) Infection in Prison. *AIDS Public Policy Journal*, 3 (2):42-46.

Wallace, Donald H. (1990). AIDS in the Courtroom. In *AIDS:The Impact on the Criminal Justice System*, Mark Blumberg (ed.), 61-69. Columbus, OH: Merrill Publishing Co.

Whitman, David (1990). Inside An AIDS Colony. *U.S. News and World Report*, (January 29):20-26.

Winkelstein, Warren, David Lyman, Nancy Padian, Robert Grant, Michael Samuel, James A. Wiley, Robert E. Anderson, William Lang, John Riggs and Jay A. Levy (1987). Sexual Practices and the Risk of Infection by the Human Immunodeficiency Virus: The San Francisco Men's Health Study. *Journal of the American Medical Association*, 257(3):321-25.

Wooden, Wayne S. and Jay Parker (1982). *Men Behind Bars: Sexual Exploitation in Prison*. New York: Plenum Press.

chapter **10**

The Myth of a Lenient Criminal Justice System in the United States

The evidence is overwhelming that the United States has the highest rate of violent crime among western industrial societies. According to the Bureau of Justice Statistics, "crimes of violence (homicide, rape and robbery) are four to nine times more frequent in the United States than they are in Europe; crimes of theft are also more frequent (burglary, theft, and auto theft), but not to the same degree" (Kalish, 1988: 1). The homicide rate offers a good illustration of the differences that exist with respect to violent crime between the United States and other western democracies. In 1984, there were 7.9 homicides in the United States per 100,000 people. This contrasts with a rate of 2.7 for Canada, 1.1 for England and Wales, 2.1 for Italy, 1.7 for New Zealand and 1.4 for Sweden (Kalish, 1988: 3). In other words, if the United States had the same homicide rate as Canada, there would not have been 18,690 murders in 1984 (Flanagan and McGarrell, 1986: 365) but 6,388 instead. Likewise, if the rate had been 1.1 as in England and Wales, the total number of killings reported that year would have been 2,602. The same pattern is true with respect to other violent crimes (Kalish, 1988).

Why does the United States have such a high rate of violent crime compared to other Western societies? One explanation often advanced is that the courts are too lenient with offenders. Various politicians, many police officers, and a majority of the citizenry all decry the fact that criminals do not receive the severe punishments they deserve. If judges would impose tougher sentences, then we would be able to reduce the crime rate, or so it is often suggested. According to a 1989 Gallup survey, 83 percent of the respondents ascribe to the view that their local courts do not deal harshly enough with criminals (Maguire and Flanagan, 1991: 191).

This belief — that our system of criminal justice is soft on crime — is not confined to laypersons. Some criminologists share this sentiment. Ernest Van Den Haag (1992: 50) has asserted that "nonpunishment is the major 'social' cause of crime. And nonpunishment will remain our practice, until we have courts that are not too busy to punish criminals and prisons in which they can serve their time." This view of the criminal justice system, however, is a myth. There is no evidence that offenders are treated leniently in the United States. In fact, a strong case can be made that the opposite is true: our society is quite punitive in its treatment of criminals.

This chapter examines both cross-national and longitudinal data with respect to punishment. In the first section, correctional practices in the United States are compared with those of other Western democracies. The analysis utilizes two indicators of leniency: incarceration rates and practices with respect to the use of capital punishment. In both cases, it is clear that the United States is not more lenient than other comparable societies.

The second section of this chapter lends further support to the mythical nature of the belief that the justice system is lenient. This conclusion is based on an examination of the data regarding various correctional populations. Included in this analysis are statistics with respect to the number of jail inmates, sentenced federal and state prisoners, probationers and parolees. When the underlying trend is examined in each of these populations, it is difficult to make the case that our system of justice has become lenient in recent years.

International Comparison

Incarceration Rates

In an attempt to determine whether the high rates of violent crime in the United States are the result of lenient criminal justice practices, it is necessary to examine correctional policies that are currently followed in other Western nations. Because these societies share our democratic political tradition and have economies that are quite similar to ours, a strong case exists for comparing correctional practices in the United States to those of Canada, Great Britain, Australia, and the other industrialized nations of Western Europe.

Table 1 examines the incarceration rate for various Western democracies. It is clear from inspection of these data that the United States incarceration rate is far higher than that of any other Western nation. In 1988, the United States imprisoned 388 persons for every 100,000 residents in the population. This is a rate four times greater than that of Turkey, more than 4.5 times the rate of France and West Germany, almost seven times greater than Sweden, and almost ten times the rate of the Netherlands. The United Kingdom has the highest incarceration rate among the nations of Western Europe, but it is still almost four times lower than in the United States.

When we examine Western nations that lie outside Europe, the picture does not change. Canada, our neighbor to the north and a society that is remarkably similar to the United States, has an incarceration rate of around 110 persons for every 100,000 residents in the population (Council of Europe, 1990: 4). Australia and New Zealand, two other nations with which we share not only a common language but also the same legal tradition, incarcerate only 72 and 100, respectively (Mauer, 1991: Table 3).

The United States not only has a higher rate of incarceration than any other Western society, there is also some evidence that the United States may be the world leader in this area (Mauer, 1991). In a recent study, it was reported that the United States has overtaken both the former Soviet Union and South Africa in terms of prison incarceration. Formerly, those societies had the highest known rates in the world. Although comparisons with other societies (especially authoritarian nations) are always problematic, recent changes in such nations give reason to believe that these data may be fairly reliable. The review of cross-national incarceration rates indicates clearly that, at least in terms of prison use, the United States is not lenient with offenders.

Table 1

Incarceration Rates for the United States and Western Europe in 1988

Nation	Rate*
United States	388.0
Austria	77.0
Belgium	65.4
Denmark	68.0
France	81.1
West Germany	84.9
Greece	44.0
Ireland	55.0
Italy	60.4
Netherlands	40.0
Norway	48.4
Portugal	83.0
Spain	75.8
Sweden	56.0
Switzerland	73.1
Turkey	95.6
United Kingdom	97.4

*Per 100,000 population.

Sources: *Prison Information Bulletin*, Council of Europe.

Prisoners in 1988, U.S. Department of Justice, Bureau of Justice Statistics, Washington, D.C.

Census of Local Jails 1988, U.S. Department of Justice, Bureau of Justice Statistics, Washington, D.C.

Capital Punishment

When we inquire whether the United States is lenient with convicted criminals, it is also helpful to look at practices with respect to the death penalty. Here "the pattern is so simple, it is stunning. Every Western industrial nation has stopped executing criminals, except the United States" (Zimring and Hawkins, 1986: 3). Canada, Great Britain, Australia, New Zealand, and all the nations of Western Europe have halted this practice. In the United States, however, capital punishment statutes remain on the books in 37 states and over 100 executions have taken place since 1977.

The abolition of capital punishment is not a recent development in many societies. The last execution for a civil crime took place as far back as 1860 in the Netherlands, 1863 in Belgium, and 1892 in Denmark. Norway has not imposed the death penalty for a civil offense since 1875 and Italy since 1876 (Zimring and Hawkins, 1986: 10). Of course, in other cases, abolition is of more recent origin. Great Britain did not have its last execution until 1964. Canada did not abolish the death penalty for civilian offenses until 1976. Spain and France were among the last Western European societies to do away with capital punishment, in 1978 and 1981 respectively.

Most jurisdictions in the United States have not followed suit. Although no executions took place between 1968 and 1976, the trend in recent years has been in the opposite direction. Not only are the number of persons sentenced to death increasing, but executions are becoming increasingly more frequent. It appears that the United States is not ready to join the rest of the Western world which has seen fit to abolish capital punishment.

The United States is not merely the only western society that retains the death penalty, it is one of the few societies in the world that permits the execution of persons for crimes committed as juveniles. More than three-quarters of the nations have set 18 as the minimum age for execution (Streib, 1987: 30). This policy has won the support of the United Nations as well as the Geneva Convention which prohibits, even in wartime, the execution of civilians for crimes committed under the age of 18. Although it is not common for juveniles to be put to death in the United States, this sentence is permitted under the statutes that have been enacted in approximately half the states. Clearly, with respect to capital punishment, there is no evidence that the United States is lenient with offenders.

Why is the United States far more punitive in its treatment of offenders than other Western democracies? Part of the explanation obviously lies in the fact that the United States has a substantially higher crime rate than most other societies (Bureau of Justice Statistics, 1987). James P. Lynch (1988) in fact has argued that when overall crime rates are considered, United States courts do not incarcerate a greater proportion of offenders. However, rising crime rates do not explain the tremendous increase in correctional populations that have occurred in recent years. Nor does the myth of leniency with offenders explain the high crime rate. The United States is the only Western democracy that still uses the death penalty and is among a small minority of nations where juveniles can be executed for crimes. Despite a system of justice that is far more harsh in its treatment of offenders, the United States continues to have far higher rates of violent crime than any other Western nation.

The Trend Toward Greater Punitiveness in the United States

As indicated above, not only is the American system of justice more punitive than systems in other democracies, but there is also strong evidence that the United States has become even more severe in its treatment of offenders in recent years. It should be noted that the trend toward increased incarceration is not a universal phenomenon. Both Denmark (Brydensholt, 1992) and England (Mauer, 1992) have developed policies that are designed to reduce the number of prison inmates. The United States is moving in the opposite direction. In this section, four sources of data are examined which highlight the trend toward more persons under the control of the criminal justice system. These include statistics regarding the number of offenders incarcerated in prison, incarcerated in jail, under supervision in the community on probation and parole, and under judicial sentence of death.

Prison Incarceration

Table 2 indicates that the number of sentenced prisoners in state and federal institutions more than tripled during the eighteen-year period between 1972 and 1990. In 1972, there were 196,092 prison inmates in the United States. During this period, the number increased by 543,525 to an all-time record of 739,617. Data that go back to 1925 are available regarding the number of sentenced prisoners (see Maguire and Flanagan, 1991: 604). They indicate that such an increase is unprecedented in American history.

In order to determine whether population changes account for this increase, Table 2 presents data regarding the rate of prison incarceration per 100,000 residents during this period. Between 1972 and 1990, this rate increased more than threefold—from 93 to 293. Although the United States population increased somewhat during these years, the population increase accounted for a very small proportion of the growth in prison incarceration. In addition, there has been a decline in the number of persons in the most "crime prone" age group of 15-24 (Steffensmeier and Harer: 1991). The rise in the number of inmates has been so dramatic that

Table 2

**Number and Rate of Sentenced Prisoners in State
and Federal Institutions on December 31**

Year	Total	Rate*
1972	196,092	93
1974	218,466	102
1976	262,833	120
1978	294,396	132
1980	315,974	138
1982	394,374	170
1984	443,398	188
1986	522,084	216
1988	603,732	244
1990	739,763	293

*Rate per 100,000 population.

Sources: *Sourcebook of Criminal Justice Statistics-1990*, The Hindelang Criminal Justice Research Center, Albany, NY.

Prisoners in 1990, U.S. Department of Justice, Bureau of Justice Statistics, Washington, D.C.

overcrowding has become the major problem in American prisons. In many states, the situation is so critical that courts have ruled that this condition constitutes "cruel and unusual punishment" and is in violation of the constitution. As a consequence, correctional administrators have been ordered to reduce the number of persons in these institutions. By the end of 1990, the problem had become so serious that "21 jurisdictions reported a total of 18,380 state prisoners held in local jails or other facilities because of overcrowding in State facilities" (Cohen, 1991: 5). Given this level of overcrowding, it would be very difficult to argue that the prison environment has become less harsh than in previous years.

Jail Incarceration

Generally speaking, prisons hold inmates who have been convicted of a felony and have been sentenced to serve more than one year in custody. Jails, on the other hand, house persons who are awaiting trial or have been convicted of a misdemeanor. However, Table 3 indicates that the situation with respect to both prisons and jails is quite similar. In 1978, the average daily population of local jails was 157,930. By 1990, there had been an increase of approximately one-quarter million to 408,075. In a span of twelve years, the jail population has more than doubled. The Bureau of Justice Statistics reports that local expenditures for jails "totaled slightly more than $4.5 billion during the year ending June 1988." This sum (not adjusted for inflation) was 67 percent greater than 1983 expenditures (1990: 9).

The increase in the number of jail inmates cannot be explained by population growth in the United States. In 1978, there were 76 inmates in local jails per 100,000 residents (Bureau of Justice Statistics, 1984: 1). This proportion increased to 98 by 1983 (Bureau of Justice Statistics, 1984: 1) and grew to 144 per 100,000 by 1988 (Bureau of Justice Statistics, 1990: 1). In a decade, the rate of jail incarceration almost doubled. Had the total population of the United States remained unchanged during this period, there would have been almost twice as many people in the nation's jails in 1988

Table 3

Average Daily Population of Jail Inmates

Year	Average Daily Population
1978	157,930
1983	227,541
1984	230,641
1985	265,010
1986	265,517
1987	290,300
1988	336,017
1989	386,845
1990	408,075

Sources: *Jail Inmates, 1990*, U.S. Department of Justice, Bureau of Justice Statistics, Washington, D.C.

Jail Inmates, 1989, U.S. Department of Justice, Bureau of Justice Statistics, Washington, D.C.

Jail Inmates, 1987, U.S. Department of Justice, Bureau of Justice Statistics, Washington, D.C.

compared to 1978. In short, demographics cannot account for the rising tide of jail inmates.

As the number of jail inmates has skyrocketed, many jails are facing some of the same problems with respect to overcrowding as prisons. In 1990, 28 percent of the jurisdictions in the United States were under court order to limit population in at least one jail under their control (Stephan and Jankowski, 1991: 1). In addition, over 150 jail jurisdictions were operating under court directive to improve one of a number of specific conditions of confinement (Stephan and Jankowski, 1991: 3). Clearly, it cannot be argued that jail is a more pleasant environment than in previous years.

The enormity of the rise in institutional populations is even more striking when the numbers of inmates in both jails and prisons are combined. In 1978, there were a total of 452,326 persons in America's penal institutions. Twelve years later, this number had surpassed the million mark, growing to a grand total of 1,147,692 persons. The combined rate of prison and jail incarceration also skyrocketed during this period, from 208 per 100,000 in 1978 to 388 in 1988. Based on these statistics, the view that the United States has become lenient with criminal offenders is clearly a myth.

Probation and Parole Populations

Not only have institutional populations increased dramatically in recent times, the number of persons under community supervision has risen quite rapidly as well. Table 4 indicates that in 1980, there were 1,118,097 adult probationers and 220,438 adult parolees in the United States. Ten years later, these populations had risen to 2,670,234 and 531,407 respectively. Not only has the number of probationers and parolees more than doubled in a single decade; the total now exceeds one percent of the United States population.

If jail and prison populations had declined during this period, a strong argument could be made that the greater number of probationers and parolees was indicative of a trend toward greater reliance on community alternatives to institutionalization. However, this is not the case. The data indicate that not only are more individuals being placed in institutions but that this is occurring at a pace which is unprecedented in American history.

In order to get an even better picture of the changes that have taken place in the criminal justice system in recent years, it is helpful to examine the data with respect to the total number of persons under correctional supervision. This includes not only inmates in the nation's jails and prisons but also persons who have

Table 4

Number of Adults On Probation and Parole in the United States, 1989-1990*

Year	Probation	Parole
1980	1,118,097	220,438
1982	1,357,264	224,604
1984	1,711,190	268,515
1986	2,114,621	325,638
1988	2,356,483	407,977
1990	2,670,234	531,407

*All counts reflect the total at the end of the year.

Sources: *Probation and Parole 1990*, U.S. Department of Justice, Bureau of Justice Statistics, Washington, D.C.

Probation and Parole 1984, U.S. Department of Justice, Bureau of Justice Statistics, Washington, D.C.

Probation and Parole 1983, U.S. Department of Justice, Bureau of Justice Statistics, Washington, D.C.

Probation and Parole 1981, U.S. Department of Justice, Bureau of Justice Statistics, Washington, D.C.

been placed under probation or parole supervision. According to the National Council on Crime and Delinquency (Austin, 1990: 3), there were 1,832,350 individuals under the control of the correctional system in 1980. Ten years later, this total had increased to an estimated 4,350,000 persons, approximately 2.4 percent of the adult population (Jankowski, 1991: 5). In a single decade, the number of persons in this category more than doubled. As a consequence, the Bureau of Justice Statistics (Jankowski, 1991: 1) reports that one out of every forty-three adults in the United States was under some form of correctional supervision by 1990.

The data reported indicate that the United States punishes a substantial number of its citizens, a proportion far greater than any other Western democracy. For young black males, the situation is even more bleak. In a recent study, Mauer (1990: 3) noted that "almost one in four (23 percent) Black men in the age group 20-29 is either in prison, jail, on probation, or parole on any given day." In fact, "the number of young Black men under the control of the criminal justice system—609,690—is greater than the total number of Black men of all ages enrolled in college—436,000 as of 1986." Furthermore, black males in the United States have a rate of incarceration that is four times greater than that of black males in South Africa (Mauer, 1991: 3). It would be quite difficult to make a case that this pattern is indicative of a criminal justice system that is soft on crime.

Persons Under Sentence of Death

Two decades ago, the United States Supreme Court ruled in *Furman v. Georgia* (1972) that the death penalty was unconstitutional because of the selective and arbitrary manner in which it was being applied. As a consequence, all the statutes authorizing capital punishment were stricken from the books. The United States seemed ready to join the other Western democracies which had halted the practice of executing citizens for crimes committed in peacetime.

The Supreme Court in its 1972 Furman decision did not, however, address the question of whether executions in themselves were cruel and unusual punishment. Instead, the court merely stated that the manner in which the death penalty had previously been administered violated the constitution. The door was therefore left open for states to draft new statutes with respect to capital punishment. Within four years, approximately thirty-five states had done so. By the time the United States Supreme Court finally addressed the question of whether executions were constitutional (1976), the composition of the court had changed in a more conservative direction. In addition, public opinion had also shifted, with many more Americans voicing support for the death penalty. Thus, it was not very surprising when the Supreme Court ruled that capital punishment in and of itself does not violate the constitution.

Between 1968 and 1976, no one was executed in the United States. However, in *Gregg v. Georgia* (1976), the United States Supreme Court ruled that the death penalty may be imposed as long as certain procedural standards are followed. As a consequence, executions resumed in 1977. At first, the pace was quite slow. The late 1970s saw only a handful of individuals put to death. As time passed, the numbers increased substantially. By the mid-1980s, executions had become relatively routine events which generated little public attention and little media publicity in most cases. Between 1977 and 1989, 120 prisoners were executed in the United States (Maguire and Flanagan, 1991: 684). By 1990, there were, on average, two executions per month (Bureau of Justice Statistics, 1992: 2).

The number of persons actually executed is only part of this picture. Following the *Gregg* decision, the number of convicts under sentence of death also increased rather substantially. Table 5 indicates that there were only 423 persons on death row in 1977, the year after the United States Supreme Court gave its constitutional approval to the continued use of the death penalty. Six years later, there were almost three times as many persons under sentence of death (1,209). By 1989, the total had grown to 2,250. Because defendants were being sentenced to death at a pace which outstripped the ability of the courts to dispose of the various appeals, the number of individuals on death row was more than five times greater in 1989 than had been the case in 1977.

The Crime Rate in the United States

What factors account for the more punitive criminal justice practices that have evolved in recent years? It has already been noted that population changes do not account for the increased number of individuals under correctional supervision. Another possibility is that these changes in the jail, prison, probation, and parole populations merely reflect changes in the crime rate that

Table 5

Persons Under Sentence of Death on December 31, 1973-1989

Year	Number
1973	134
1975	488
1977	423
1979	593
1981	856
1983	1209
1985	1591
1987	1984
1989	2250

Source: *Sourcebook of Criminal Justice Statistics-1990*, The Hindelang
Criminal Justice Research Center, Albany, NY.

have occurred during this period. If there was a dramatic rise in crime, we would expect more offenders to be incarcerated and/or released into the community under the supervision of the courts.

According to the Uniform Crime Reports (UCR), there was a small (4 percent) decrease in the reported crime rate between 1980 and 1988. The National Crime Survey (NCS) data indicate a 17 percent decline during the same period (Mauer, 1992: 7); however, most of this reduction can be explained by the fact that the age distribution of the United States population changed somewhat during the 1980s and that there were fewer individuals in the most "crime prone" age group (Steffensmeier and Harer, 1991). The net result is that the age-adjusted crime rate changed relatively little during this time.

Despite the fact that the crime rate remained relatively stable, the number of adults arrested rose somewhat (39 percent—from 6.1 to 8.5 million). However, this increase was dwarfed by the dramatic rise in various correctional populations during the 1980s. Between 1980 and 1988, the number of jail inmates rose 110 percent, the number of prisoners rose 90 percent, the number of probationers increased by 111 percent, and the number of parolees increased 85 percent (Austin, 1990: Table 1). Clearly, these data suggest that the huge rise in the number of persons under correctional supervision in the United States has not been in response to an increased crime rate.

If increased crime rates do not explain the dramatic rises in various correctional populations that have occurred in recent years, what factors do account for this trend? There are several explanations. The "war on drugs" has contributed to a substantial part of the increase (Austin and McVey, 1991). In the federal prison system, the number of persons serving time for drug offenses has more than doubled since 1981 and now accounts for 53 percent of the inmate population (Mauer, 1992: 7). The Bureau of Justice Statistics (1988a: 1) notes that a greater proportion of drug violators are being incarcerated than in previous years and that sentence lengths for this crime have increased. On the state and local level, the impact of the war on drugs is also evident. In recent years, the proportion of offenders sentenced to prison for drug violations has increased dramatically (Austin and McVey, 1989: 4). In addition, the increased emphasis on drug testing has contributed to a higher failure rate among parolees. The United States Department of Justice reports that there was "a 284 percent increase in the number of parole violators returned to prison between 1977 and 1987" (Austin and McVey, 1989: 5). The fact that more than 40 percent of the rise in the jail population between 1983 and 1988 was the result of an increase in the number of inmates accused or convicted of drug offenses should not be overlooked (Bureau of Justice Statistics, 1991: 8).

Secondly, sentencing practices have become more punitive as many states and the federal government have enacted mandatory sentence statutes that apply to various offenses (Mauer, 1992). These laws *require* judges to sentence offenders to a period of incarceration, often for a specified period of time. There is no possibility of the defendant receiving probation or a suspended prison sentence. Forty-six states now have mandatory sentence statutes (Bureau of Justice Statistics, 1988: 91). An analysis by the United States Sentencing Commission concluded that mandatory sentences have been a contributing factor in the dramatic rise of the federal prison population (Mauer, 1992: 10).

Finally, a conservative ideology has developed which asserts that society can solve its crime problem by taking a hard-line approach (Marenin, 1991). One result of this philosophical shift has been a narrowing of defendants' rights. Although the impact of such changes in criminal procedure are mostly symbolic (Gordon, 1990), this attitude has encouraged politicians to offer the public other simplistic "get tough" measures for dealing with offenders instead of rational policies that seek to alleviate the root causes of crime and violence. In fact, Richard Thornburgh, the former attorney general of the United States, opened a recent "crime summit" by telling law enforcement officials to leave consideration of the causes of crime to ivory-tower types (Fyfe, 1991). Increasingly, candidates for political office appear unwilling to propose solutions that could make a difference. Instead, policymakers continue to call for more prisons, longer sentences, and the death penalty for more offenses. It is not surprising that these policies resurged during a decade that also witnessed declining public interest in the problems of the disadvantaged and greater income disparity between rich and poor (Phillips, 1990).

If the get-tough approach had significantly reduced the level of crime and violence in America, a strong case could be made that it was worth the human and financial costs. However, what is striking is how little impact these policies have had on the crime problem. Despite a prison population that more than doubled during the previous decade, crime rates have not changed appreciably. In fact, the late 1980s witnessed a rise in the number of reported violent crimes. Not only is this approach to crime control ineffective, it is also expensive. State and local government spending on correctional institutions totaled over fifteen billion dollars in 1988 (Maguire and Flanagan, 1991: 7). In fact, during the 1980s, spending by state governments for corrections was increasing at a substantial pace while expenditures for other needs, such as education and hospitals, lagged behind (Austin, 1990: 5). Not only is the money spent on jails and prisons producing little in the way of tangible results, it is also diverting funds from programs that could have a positive impact on the lives of citizens. As Elliott Currie (1985) has written, the time has come to view the get-tough approach to crime as a conservative social experiment which failed:

> It is difficult to think of any social experiment in recent years whose central ideas have been so thoroughly and consistently carried out. The number of people we have put behind bars, for ever-longer terms, is unprecedented in American history. And unlike most such experiments which are usually undertaken with minimal funding and on a limited scale, this one has been both massively financed and carried out on a grand scale in nearly every state of the union. If it has failed to work in the way its promoters expected, they have fewer excuses than most applied social theorists (12).

Conclusion

Despite the data, the myth persists that we are lenient with offenders. Public opinion data indicate that the proportion of Americans who believe the courts do not deal harshly enough with criminals is identical to the number who expressed this sentiment in 1980 (Maguire and Flanagan, 1991). How can one account for this disparity between the attitudes of citizens and the reality of our justice system?

To some extent, this public perception is shaped by the fact that some offenders are treated more leniently than is appropriate. Because citizens receive much of their information regarding the operation of the criminal justice system from accounts that are presented in the media, anecdotes that discuss how a serious offender escaped punishment probably play an important role in shaping perceptions about the system. Unfortunately, citizens often do not appreciate the fact that such accounts receive so much press attention precisely because they are atypical. Thus, events that are relatively rare (for example, a murder suspect who escapes punishment as a result of a legal technicality) come to be viewed as everyday occurrences. According to several studies, the reality of the situation is that most serious offenders are not treated leniently by the courts (Walker, 1989).

Another reason that may account for the false perception that the system is lenient is the unacceptably high level of crime and violence in our society. Citizens, especially those residing in urban areas, hear and read reports in the media of murders, robberies, and rapes which seem to occur on a continuing basis. Despite the increased probability during the 1980s that a convicted offender would go to prison (Cohen, 1991), there are still a large number of crimes that do not result in an arrest. For this reason, citizens see society as inundated with crime and assume that the criminal justice system must not be doing its job. Often, the complaint is that "the courts must be soft, why else would there be so much crime?" Unfortunately, what most citizens fail to appreciate is that this is a problem which the criminal justice system cannot solve by itself and that harsh sentences do not necessarily deter crime. Without basic social reforms, there is little that the police, the courts, and the corrections system can do.

The most harmful consequence for society of the leniency myth is that it continues to divert public attention and resources away from policies that could really make a difference in the fight against crime. As Marenin (1991:17) has noted, "conservatism politicized and ideologized a difficult social problem and made it harder to seek solutions which might work but which cannot be reduced to a thirty-second commercial." As a consequence, decision makers have been forced to pursue policies which focus on increasing the severity of criminal penalties and locking up more offenders. Programs which could have a real impact on crime (such as restricting the availability of high-powered firearms, expanding access to drug treatment, or increasing economic opportunity for members of the underclass) are dismissed as too "soft." However, these measures are likely to be far more effective and less costly in the long run than a continuation of the present "get tough" approach.

Sources

Austin, J. (1990). *America's Growing Correctional-Industrial Complex.* National Council on Crime and Delinquency, San Francisco, CA (December).

Austin, J. and McVey, A. D. (1989). *The 1989 NCCD Prison Population Forecast: The Impact of the War on Drugs.* National Council on Crime and Delinquency, San Francisco, CA (December).

Brydensholt, H. H. (1992). "Crime Policy in Denmark: How We Managed to Reduce the Prison Population." In *Prisons Around the World*, M. K. Carlie and K. I. Minor (eds.). Dubuque, IA: Wm. C. Brown Publishers.

Bureau of Justice Statistics (1992). *National Update.* Vol. 1, No. 3. Washington, DC (January).

_____ (1991). *National Update.* Vol. 1, No. 1. Washington, DC (July).

_____ (1990). *Census of Local Jails 1988.* Washington, DC (February).

_____ (1988a). *Drug Law Violators, 1980-86.* Washington, DC (June).

_____ (1988b). *Report to the Nation on Crime and Justice, Second Edition.* Washington, DC (March).

_____ (1987). *Imprisonment in Four Countries.* Special Report (February).

_____ (1984). *The 1983 Jail Census.* Washington, DC (November).

Cohen, R. L. (1991). *Prisoners in 1990.* Bureau of Justice Statistics, Washington, DC (May).

Currie, E. (1985). *Confronting Crime: An American Challenge.* New York: Pantheon Books.

Flanagan, T. J. and McGarrell, E. F. (1986). *Sourcebook of Criminal Justice Statistics-1985.* Albany, NY: The Hindelang Criminal Justice Research Center.

Fyfe, J. J. (1991). "Why Won't Crime Stop? Because We Cling to Our Favorite Social Myths." *Washington Post*, (March 17): D1.

Gordon, D. R. (1990). *The Justice Juggernaut.* New Brunswick, NJ: Rutgers University Press.

Kalish, C. B. (1988). *International Crime Rates.* Bureau of Justice Statistics, Washington, DC (May).

Lynch, J. P. (1988). "A Comparison of Prison Use in England, Canada, West Germany, and the United States: A Limited Test of the Punitive Hypothesis." The Journal of Criminal Law and Criminology. Vol. 79, No. 1.

Maguire, K. and Flanagan, T. J. (1991). *Sourcebook of Criminal Justice Statistics-1990.* Albany, NY: The Hindelang Criminal Justice Research Center.

Marenin, O. (1991). "Making A Tough Job Tougher: The Legacy of Conservatism." *ACJS Today.* Vol. 10, No. 2 (September/October).

Mauer, M. (1992). *Americans Behind Bars: One Year Later.* The Sentencing Project, Washington, DC (February).

_____ (1991). *Americans Behind Bars: A Comparison of International Rates of Incarceration.* The Sentencing Project, Washington, DC (January).

_____ (1990). *Young Black Men and the Criminal Justice System: A Growing National Problem.* The Sentencing Project, Washington, DC (February).

Steffensmeier D. and Harer, M. D. (1991). "Did Crime Rise or Fall During the Reagan Presidency?: The Effects of an 'Aging' United States Population on the Nation's Crime Rate." *Journal of Research in Crime and Delinquency.* Vol. 28, No. 3 (August).

Stephan, J. and Jankowski, L. W. (1991). *Jail Inmates, 1990.* Bureau of Justice Statistics, Washington, DC (June).

Streib, V. (1987). *Death Penalty for Juveniles.* Bloomington, IN: Indiana University Press.

Van Den Haag, E. (1992). "When Felons Go Free: Worse than a Crime." *National Review* (January 20).

Walker, S. (1989). *Sense and Nonsense about Crime: A Policy Guide, Second Edition.* Pacific Grove, CA: Brooks/Cole.

Zimring, F. E. and Hawkins, G. (1986). *Capital Punishment and the American Agenda.* Cambridge, MA: Cambridge University Press.

Cases

Furman v. Georgia, 408 U.S. 238 (1972).
Gregg v. Georgia, 428 U.S. 158 (1976).

chapter 11

Debunking the Death Penalty
Myths of Crime Control and Capital Punishment

Capital punishment is an issue that has generated intense public interest over the centuries. Criminologists have written volumes on this subject, appellate courts have devoted considerable time to deciding death penalty cases, and politicians have used it as an effective campaign issue. Capital punishment has even played a role in presidential elections. For example, it is widely believed that the response of Michael Dukakis during the second presidential debate to a question posed regarding the death penalty contributed to his landslide defeat by George Bush in the 1988 election. The Democratic nominee had been asked by a journalist if he would favor this sanction if his wife were raped and murdered. He replied that he would not.

As the Democrats learned to their chagrin, the question of capital punishment has taken on a large symbolic meaning in recent years. Increasingly, crime and many other policy questions are discussed in a simplistic manner that focuses more on symbols than on solutions to complex social problems. Politicians have found that it is easier to reaffirm their support for the death penalty during a political campaign by using a thirty-second sound bite than to offer a meaningful program that seriously addresses the crime problem in America. As a consequence, support for capital punishment has become a litmus test of how tough one is willing to be on crime. At the same time, policymakers and citizens place an importance on this sanction that is disproportionate to its actual role in the criminal justice system.

Although the question of capital punishment is often debated more passionately than any other public policy question in the area of corrections, there is good reason to believe that the public is not well informed on this subject. Various opinion polls suggest that sizeable segments of the public believe that the death penalty acts as a deterrent to murder or that it is necessary to protect society (Jamieson and Flanagan, 1989:230). Citizens also sometimes question whether society should be forced to bear the cost of incarcerating convicted murderers for life, thereby implying that it would be less expensive to execute these individuals. In addition, it is routinely asserted that any vigorous attack on our tremendous crime problem must include capital punishment if it is to be successful. Yet all these beliefs are based on myth. There is no empirical support in the research literature on capital punishment for any of these positions.

This chapter debunks a number of common myths regarding the death penalty. These include: 1) the myth that the death penalty is a more effective deterrent to murder than life imprisonment; 2) the myth that the death penalty is less expensive to impose than life imprisonment; 3) the myth that the death penalty is necessary to protect society from convicted killers who are likely to repeat their offense; and 4) the myth that capital punishment is necessary in order to fight crime.

The Myth of General Deterrence

In a Gallup Poll taken in 1986, 67 percent of Americans expressed the view that the death penalty is a deterrent to murder (Jamieson and Flanagan, 1989:229). This belief is probably due to the strong confidence that most Americans place in the ability of punishment to alter behavior. It is often reasoned that if parents are able to modify their children's actions with very mild sanctions, then the threat of execution (a very serious penalty) should deter people from committing murder (a very serious crime). However, a review of the literature indicates that this confidence in the efficacy of capital punishment is misguided. The overwhelming majority of studies report finding no deterrent effect. Below, the methodology and the findings from the various research reports are examined.

Probably no other question has received as much attention as the issue of whether the death penalty is a more effective deterrent to murder than a lengthy prison sentence. From a scientific perspective, the ideal way to address this question would be to use a lottery drawing to assign persons at birth to either life imprisonment or the death sentence should they eventually be convicted of capital murder (Zeisel, 1977). It would then be possible to ascertain whether persons who were at risk of receiving the death penalty were less likely to commit those types of murder that could land one on death row. For moral and legal reasons that require little explanation, this kind of experiment is unthinkable in a democratic society. As a consequence, scholars have been forced to rely on research designs that utilize "naturally grown" data in an attempt to approximate this impossible experiment.

Exploring the question of whether the death penalty is a better deterrent, researchers have employed a variety of strategies. This chapter examines eight approaches that have been utilized to address this issue: 1) a comparative analysis of homicide rates in contiguous states where one jurisdiction exercises captial punishment and another does not; 2) an examination of the change in the homicide rate after the death penalty has been abolished or reinstated in a particular state; 3) the impact of an execution on the homicide rate in a specific jurisdiction where the sentence was recently carried out; 4) a comparative examination of the rate at which police officers are murdered in states that do and do not have capital punishment; 5) an examination of whether prison inmates are more likely to kill in states that have abolished capital punishment; 6) an analysis of the same question regarding the behavior of murderers who are eventually released on parole; 7) the impact of the death penalty on the level of noncapital felonies that are committed; and 8) various statistical models that have attempted to determine whether the death penalty is a more effective deterrent to murder than imprisonment.

Contiguous States

Some of the earliest work on the question of deterrence involved a comparative examination of the homicide rates in contiguous states where one jurisdiction had abolished capital punishment and the other(s) retained this penalty. The rationale underlying the use of contiguous states is that they are likely to be similar in other ways that could affect their homicide rate. If these jurisdictions share various economic, demographic, and social characteristics, any difference observed with respect to their murder rate should be attributable to the fact that they differ in the imposition of the death penalty. The classic studies utilizing this approach were conducted by Thorsten Sellin (1980). He compared Kansas (an abolitionist state) with Missouri and Colorado (retentionist states) as well as Maine (an abolitionist state) with the retentionist states of Massachusetts and New Hampshire. Sellin observed that the homicide rates in the abolitionist states were not higher (in some cases they were actually lower) than those reported in the retentionist states. Based on a number of comparisons of this type, Sellin (1980) was able to conclude that there is no evidence of a greater deterrent effect when a jurisdiction retains the death penalty.

Abolition/Retention of the Death Penalty

Another approach that was used by Sellin (1980) to study this issue was to examine jurisdictions that have either abolished or reinstated the death penalty. During the nineteenth and twentieth centuries, a number of states changed their statutes regarding this sanction. The early studies only looked at the before and after homicide rate in jurisdictions that had revised their death penalty statute. However, later studies also examined the trend in contiguous states that had not made a change (Zeisel, 1977). This research found no evidence of an increased deterrent effect in jurisdictions that retained or reintroduced the death penalty. In general, the homicide rate closely followed the trend in contiguous states (Sellin, 1980). Whether capital punishment was abolished or reinstated did not seem to matter.

Impact of an Execution

The third approach employed is to examine the impact of an execution on the murder rate in the specific jurisdiction where the sentence was recently carried out. The first such study of this type was conducted by Robert Dann (1935) during a period when executions were quite common in the United States. He examined the impact of five executions in Philadelphia which had not been followed by another execution for a sixty-day period. The rationale underlying this approach was that if capital punishment indeed deterred murder, all the publicity that surrounded an execution should cause the homicide rate to decline in the days and weeks subsequent to the execution. However, Dann observed that the murder rate actually increased somewhat in the sixty-day period that followed this punishment.

In California, a similar study was conducted by William Graves (1956). He examined the homicide records of Los Angeles, San Francisco, and Alameda counties in order to determine whether there were fewer murders in the days following an execution than was the case in the days leading up to this event. As a comparative measure, he examined the same days of the week for those periods in which an execution did not occur. Graves (1956) reported that compared with weeks when no death sentences were carried out, the number of murders actually increased the day prior to an execution and on the day of the execution. However, they declined in the two-day period that followed the execution. The result was that the slight deterrent effect was almost entirely cancelled out by the earlier brutalization effect. This finding led Graves (1956) to speculate that persons contemplating homicide may be "stimulated by the state's taking of life to act sooner" (137). What Graves did not note because of the manner in which his data had been classified was "that homicides were higher in the weeks after than in the weeks before executions" (Bowers, Pierce and McDevitt, 1984:284).

More recently, Steven Stack (1987) has conducted an analysis of publicized executions that took place in the United States between 1950 and 1980. This researcher does report a small deterrent impact for those executions which received national publicity. However, the number of executions in this category is quite small. No deterrent impact was observed in the overwhelming number of cases that did not generate national publicity. The author notes that "as executions become more common, the amount of press coverage tends to decline" (538). As a consequence, the death penalty soon loses even the marginal deterrent impact that was observed in this study.

Killings of Police Officers

Under our legal system, not all homicides are eligible for the death penalty. As a general rule, in order to be convicted of first degree murder, one must either act with premeditation or take a life during the commission of a felony. For this reason, killers of police officers would appear to be excellent candidates for this sanction in jurisdictions that retain capital punishment. Unlike many homicides that are so-called "passion crimes," these killings generally meet the necessary legal criteria to qualify as capital offenses. In addition, the apprehension rate is very high. Persons who murder police officers can expect to be both arrested and convicted. Therefore, if the death penalty is a more effective deterrent than incarceration, criminals should be less likely to kill police officers in those states that have retained this penalty.

There have been several studies that have addressed this question (Sellin, 1967; Cardarelli, 1968; Sellin, 1980; Bailey, 1982; Bailey and Peterson, 1987). Despite the fact that these were conducted by different researchers, who utilized different methodologies and examined various time periods, the results have been remarkably similar. The homicide rate among law enforcement officers is no higher in states that have abandoned capital punishment. The job of a police officer is not made more hazardous by the abolition of the death penalty.

Homicides Committed by Prisoners

Another approach employed to assess the deterrent impact of the death penalty is to compare the homicidal behavior of prisoners incarcerated in retentionist and abolitionist jurisdictions. In a study undertaken by Sellin (1980:113), it was reported that over 90 percent of these killings occurred in states that retained capital punishment. Furthermore, Wolfson (1982) has concluded that "the percentage of imprisoned murderers who recidivate is approximately the same in retentionist and abolitionist jurisdictions" (167). She criticizes as seriously flawed an assumption of the deterrence argument that these individuals can be deterred by the same legal threat that was ineffective in preventing them from killing before they arrived in prison.

Homicides Committed by Parolees

In the United States, a substantial proportion of inmates serving a life sentence are eventually released on parole. Because even in retentionist jurisdictions, the overwhelming majority of persons convicted of homicide receive a prison sentence, many persons convicted of murder will eventually be released from custody. Therefore, researchers have asked whether these parolees are less likely to kill again in jurisdictions that retain the death penalty.

Although the data to address this issue are scarce, the tentative conclusion reached by Hugh Adam Bedau (1982) who examined this question is quite encouraging for society. For one thing, he observed that murderers rarely kill again. "Both with regard to the commission of felonies generally and the crime of homicide, no other class of offenders has such a low rate of recidivism" (180). In addition, the post-release conduct of murderers in abolitionist states was actually somewhat better than the conduct of those released in jurisdictions that still retained capital punishment. We will return to this issue later in the chapter.

Deterrence of Noncapital Felonies

Almost all research has focused on the impact that the death penalty has on the murder rate. The only exception is a study conducted by William Bailey (1991) who attempted to ascertain whether executions deter persons from committing noncapital felonies. Drawing upon arguments offered by Johannes Andenaes (1974), Marlene Lehtinen (1977), Ernest van den Haag (1978), and Walter Berns (1979), Bailey suggests three conceivable ways that the death sentence acts as a deterrent for other types of offenses. The first is that as a form of punishment the death penalty serves to educate people regarding the importance of obeying the law. The second is that the death penalty deters those crimes where a killing is not intended but could result nonetheless. Armed robbery is an example of this type of offense because there is always the possibility that the victim will resist and thus be killed (whether intentionally or inadvertently). Finally, the third hypothesis is that the death penalty conserves scarce criminal justice resources which could be used to investigate and prosecute other types of crime if capital punishment had the effect of actually lowering the homicide rate.

The analysis undertaken by Bailey (1991) offers no support to the deterrence argument. Despite the fact that this study measured the death penalty in a number of ways (e.g., the number of executions during the year, the ratio of the number of executions to the number of homicides reported during the same year, etc.), there was no observed relationship between the use of capital punishment and the index felony rate. The author notes that "this pattern holds for the traditional targeted offense of murder, the person crimes (sic) of negligent manslaughter, rape, assault, and robbery, as well as the property crimes of burglary, grand larceny, and vehicle theft. In other words, there is no evidence . . . that residents of death penalty jurisdictions are afforded an added measure of protection against serious crimes by executions" (35).

Multiple Regression Analysis

All the previous methodologies refute the myth that the death penalty is a more effective deterrent than incarceration for the crime of murder. Therefore, it was quite a shock when Isaac Ehrlich (1975) reported that his statistical model indicated that each execution saved the lives of seven to eight innocent victims. He had used a then complex statistical technique known as multiple regression analysis to examine the impact of various factors on the homicide rate in the United States between 1933 and 1969. Multiple regression is a procedure that allows researchers to examine many variables simultaneously in order to determine the independent impact that each has on the murder rate. Theoretically at least, it should be possible to separate the impact on the homicide rate of the death penalty from other factors that also may contribute to homicide (such as the unemployment rate, the age distribution of the population, the proportion of citizens who own handguns, etc.). In practice, however, multiple regression models may give conflicting results depending on what variables are included in the analysis, how they are measured, and what period of observation is employed (Shin, 1978:11).

Ehrlich's study received widespread notice both in the popular media and among policymakers. Not surprisingly, it was the only study on deterrence cited by the Solicitor General (Robert Bork) in a brief before the United States Supreme Court that purported to show that executions deter homicide (Ellsworth, 1988). The work of Ehrlich also stimulated a great deal of research by other scholars who employed the same methodology. There were many attempts to replicate his findings. Invariably, these were unsuccessful because subsequent analysis revealed a number of critical flaws in the design of the Ehrlich study. Unfortunately, it is only possible to provide a brief overview in this chapter of these methodological shortcomings. Persons who wish to examine this issue in greater detail should consult addtional sources (Bowers and Pierce, 1975; Passell and Taylor, 1976; Zeisel, 1977; Klein, Forst and Filatov, 1978; Wilson, 1983; and Bowers, 1988).

Peter Passell and John Taylor (1976) have recognized one serious problem with Ehrlich's analysis. They report that when the 1960s are omitted from Ehrlich's data, the deterrent effect disappears. The 1960s were a period when executions were becoming relatively uncommon in the United States. Therefore, one is left to ponder the implausible conclusion that executions were not a deterrent during the 1930s and the 1940s when they were relatively routine but that they served as a deterrent during the entire time span studied by Ehrlich.

Another major criticism is that Ehrlich conducted a national analysis which did not distinguish between jurisdictions that did and those that did not execute citizens (Zeisel, 1977). Others have noted that the study failed to incorporate important variables in the data analysis (Wilson, 1983). Most importantly, the overwhelming majority of scholars who have utilized this methodology (and even the same data) have not reached the same conclusion (Passell and Taylor, 1976). Although a few studies have reported evidence of deterrence (Yunker, 1976; Layson, 1985), the overwhelming evidence on this issue points in the opposite direction (Bowers, 1988).

None of the studies that examine the deterrence question can reach the level of design that would be provided by our impossible experiment discussed earlier. Much of the research in this area contains shortcomings that have been noted by various authors (Wilson, 1983). First, the use of contiguous states may mask important differences between jurisdictions that can impact their homicide rate. Second, researchers may classify a state as retentionist because the death penalty remains on the books, even though no executions have been carried out in many years. Third, many studies utilize the total homicide rate to measure deterrence. However, not all homicides are capital crimes. A more appropriate measure would include only homicides which qualify for the death penalty. Unfortunately, these data generally do not exist.

Despite these shortcomings, what is striking is that studies utilizing a wide array of different methodologies have almost always come to the same conclusion: the belief that capital punishment is a more effective deterrent to murder than imprisonment is a myth. In fact, there are a number of research reports that suggest the death penalty may actually have a brutalizing impact on individuals (Bowers, 1988). In other words, the state does not deter homicide but in fact does the opposite when it executes a criminal. It sets a bad example and thereby its citizens also commit murder. If this turns out to be correct, the use of capital punishment may actually be counterproductive to the goals that many supporters believe it can accomplish.

Why is the death penalty not a more effective deterrent? First, the majority of homicides occur between people who are acquainted with each other. Most of these are killings that do not involve any kind of rational calculation. Instead, the offender commits the crime in a moment of rage or passion without giving any thought whatsoever to the future consequences of this behavior. Second, in those cases that do involve premeditation, the offender generally does not expect to be apprehended. Regardless of the potential ·sanction, it cannot serve as a deterrent if the perpetrator does not believe that it will be applied. Finally, the death penalty does not deter more effectively than life imprisonment because these are both very harsh sentences. Douglas Heckathorn (1985) notes that no difference can be expected with respect to the general deterrent impact of two sanctions if both are perceived as severe, even if one is somewhat harsher than the other. In other words, an upper threshold is reached with respect to severity beyond which no additional deterrence occurs. For most persons, there is little meaningful difference between being put to death and spending a good part of the rest of their lives in prison. Both are very unattractive options.

The Cost of the Death Penalty

It is commonly believed that it is cheaper to execute a criminal than to maintain him/her in prison for life. In fact, the authors have often been asked by students, "why should society pay to keep convicted killers housed, clothed and fed for the rest of their lives when they could be executed?" Implicit in this question is the belief that the death penalty can reduce the financial burden on the corrections system. However, this is not the case.

Intuitively, one would think that executions should be cheaper than supporting an offender in the penitentiary for many years. Indeed, a system of justice that executed suspected murderers on the spot would in fact be less expensive than maintaining those individuals in prison for life. However, this is not the way that capital punishment is carried out in a democratic society. Because our justice system places a very high premium on protecting the lives of innocent persons, an extensive number of procedural burdens must be met before a defendant can be executed. These protections are extremely costly but they are necessary to insure that only guilty persons actually receive the death penalty. Although there is some question as to whether these safeguards are always effective in accomplishing this goal, their presence insures that any system of capital punishment devised by our society will be much more expensive than life imprisonment.

There are several factors that contribute to the high cost of capital punishment. For one thing, capital cases almost always go to trial. The overwhelming majority of other serious felony cases in the United States are resolved through guilty pleas (Bureau of Justice

Statistics, 1987). Many of the latter are the result of plea bargaining. However, this is not possible in a capital case. Because the prosecutor is asking for the death penalty, the state has nothing to offer that can induce the defendant to enter a guilty plea. Very few defendants are likely to consent to a death sentence. In a few unique cases, defendants have requested that a death sentence be carried out. These requests, however, are seldom made before adjudication. Therefore, a criminal trial becomes inevitable.

Obviously, trials take considerably more time and are more expensive than simply accepting a guilty plea from the defendant at arraignment. However, capital trials are even more time consuming and involve far greater expense than do noncapital cases. The Supreme Court has stated on several occasions that death as a punishment is qualitatively different and that defendants in such cases are entitled to a higher standard of due process. This makes every aspect of a capital trial more complex and more time consuming for the parties involved.

When the state seeks to impose the death penalty, the costs begin to accumulate even before the case is heard by the court. In a noncapital trial, prosecutors and defense attorneys routinely scrutinize prospective jurors in an attempt to gain maximum advantage at trial. However, in capital cases, the *voir dire* process becomes considerably more time consuming and requires that a greater number of prospective jurors be interviewed. To some extent, this results from the fact that the United States Supreme Court allows prosecutors in capital cases to exclude opponents of capital punishment from serving as jurors if they are unable to vote for a death sentence (*Wainwright v. Witt*, 1985). As a consequence, each prospective juror must be questioned at length regarding their views on capital punishment.

There are other reasons as well why the *voir dire* process takes longer in a capital case. Each side may be allowed a greater number of peremptory challenges than in a noncapital trial. More importantly, because there is a high degree of public interest in a capital case, a great amount of pretrial publicity may have been generated. Therefore, the defense attorney may be required to spend a substantial period of time questioning prospective jurors to insure that they have not formed an opinion prejudicial to the defendant. The cumulative effect of all these factors is that the *voir dire* process takes 5.3 times longer than in noncapital trials (Spangenberg and Walsh, 1989:52).

The extensive *voir dire* is not the only additional cost in a capital trial. Several other factors also come into play. Not only are defendants likely to raise a greater number of pretrial motions in these cases, these motions also tend to be more lengthy, more complex and to involve issues unique to cases where the death sentence is a potential outcome (Spangeberg and Walsh, 1989:50). In addition, there is generally greater use of expert witnesses in capital cases. If the defendant raises the insanity defense (which is more likely in a capital case), psychiatric testimony will be presented by experts on behalf of both the defense and the prosecution. Because many defendants are indigent, the state will be obligated to pay the psychiatric witnesses from both sides, unlike noncapital cases. In 1982, it was estimated that such testimony costs as much as $150 per hour (New York State Defenders Association, Inc., 1982:15).

There is one final cost that must be considered when analyzing the trial stage of a capital case. In almost every jurisdiction in the United States, capital trials are bifurcated. This means that the issue of sentence (execution or imprisonment) is determined in a separate hearing that follows the verdict. In essence, there are two phases to the trial: conviction and punishment. Both of these allow for the introduction of evidence and the presentation of witnesses before the jury. As a consequence, both the prosecutor and the defense attorney may be forced to incur some of the same expenses twice. In the process, court time is also utilized in a manner that would not occur in noncapital trials.

The trial is not the only added financial burden in a capital case. There is also an appeals process that is more drawn out than in other criminal cases. Obviously, if the state is seeking the death penalty, the courts seek assurance that a grievous error has not been committed. For this reason, most states with capital punishment provide for an automatic review of death sentences by a state appellate court. In addition, there are other appeals by the defendant to both state and federal courts. This tends to be a very long and drawn-out process. Because appellate courts often give somewhat greater scrutiny to death penalty cases than to other appeals, prejudicial errors are more likely to be uncovered (Nakell, 1982:243). The result is that capital cases result not just in more trials but in more retrials as well.

The appeals process adds greatly to the cost of processing capital defendants. Both judges and prosecutors are forced to spend a considerable amount of time (both in court and out) dealing with issues that are raised by the defendant. This is a burden on defense attorneys as well. Robert Spangeberg and Elizabeth Walsh (1989:52) note that on average, a capital appeal requires between five hundred and one thousand hours of defense attorney time. In some cases, the entire defense cost is paid by the state.

The final cost consideration is that capital defendants require special accommodations within the correctional system. They are not treated like other inmates. Instead, they are placed in a maximum security setting in jail upon arrest. This is followed by a move to death row after their sentence is handed down. The level of security on death row is far more elaborate than in other sections of the prison. This entails substantially greater cost in terms of staff time than would be needed to house other inmates. In addition, the stay is not brief. For persons executed during 1989, the average time spent under a sentence of death was seven years and eleven months (Bureau of Justice Statistics, 1990:9).

When all these extra costs are considered, it is not surprising that a number of empirical studies have found that a criminal justice system that includes the death penalty is more expensive than one without this sanction. For example, the New York State Defender Association concluded in 1982 that it would cost over $1.8 million to process a capital case. On the other hand, the cost over a forty-year period for housing a prisoner in that jurisdiction was estimated to be $602,000 (New York State Defender's Association, Inc., 1982:23). In essence, the cost of one execution is equivalent to incarcerating three inmates for life.

Similar findings have been reported for other states as well (Tabak and Lane, 1989: 136). In Florida, each execution cost that jurisdiction over $3 million, or approximately six times the amount that would be spent to incarcerate these individuals for life. The cost of executing one person in New Jersey was estimated to be approximately $7.3 million. In California, it has been reported that the taxpayers could save $90 million per year by abolishing the death penalty (Tabak and Lane, 1989:136). Finally, in Kansas, the enormous costs associated with capital cases was one factor in the legislature's decision not to reinstate the death penalty (Spangenberg and Walsh, 1989:57).

Having observed that capital punishment is more expensive than life imprisonment, the question arises: how much weight should financial considerations play in the debate over the death penalty? Proponents of the death penalty would argue that if justice demands this sanction for certain offenders, cost should not be a factor in the decision-making process. However, this rationale overlooks the fact that only a finite amount of resources are available to the criminal justice system. Therefore, the proper context in which to consider cost is to compare the benefits of capital punishment versus other policy options. For example, is society better protected by executing a small number of persons, or could these dollars be utilized more effectively by permanently incarcerating three times as many offenders? Perhaps it would be wiser to allocate this money for more police officers. These are the kinds of public policy alternatives that could be addressed once it is understood that the death penalty is more expensive than life imprisonment.

Incapacitation

Another myth surrounding the death penalty is the belief that this punishment is necessary to protect both society and prison inmates from persons who are likely to kill again. Indeed, correctional administrators often express concern that if convicted capital offenders are not put to death, they will cause mayhem in the institution and place the lives of other inmates in jeopardy. Whether this concern is warranted is a question that has received some attention in the research literature.

Clearly, persons who receive the death penalty cannot commit future murders. However, the question that must be addressed is whether capital punishment performs this incapacitative function more effectively than life imprisonment. In other words, what is the marginal benefit of the death penalty in terms of protecting society from persons who have already demonstrated that they have the capacity to take human life? This is a question that has been examined from a number of perspectives.

Persons serving time for murder may have the opportunity to kill again under one of two circumstances: they may commit another homicide while in prison or in the community if released on parole. The most massive study of recidivism by parolees who had been convicted of murder was undertaken by Sellin (1980). He reported on the post-release behavior of 6,835 male convicts serving sentences for willful homicide who were released on parole from state institutions between 1969 and 1973. This study concluded that in the three-year period following their release, 310 (4.5 percent) of these individuals were returned to prison for committing a new crime. However, only 21 (0.31 percent of the total group) returned because they had committed another willful homicide (Sellin, 1980:114). In fact, these individuals were less likely to commit murder while on parole than persons who originally had been sentenced for armed robbery, forcible rape or aggravated assault (Sellin, 1980:116).

Unfortunately, the Sellin study is not an examination of the behavior of persons who had been sentenced for capital murder. Many of the individuals in his study had been convicted of second degree murder or voluntary manslaughter. Thus, it may not be possible to infer from this research how persons convicted of capital murder would behave if released from prison. However, an event occurred in 1972 that made such analysis possible. The United States Supreme Court ruled in *Furman v. Georgia* that the death penalty as it had been administered up to that time was cruel and unusual punishment in violation of the Eighth and Fourteenth Amendments to the constitution. As a consequence, all persons who were awaiting execution in the United States had their sentences commuted to life imprisonment.

At the time of the *Furman* decision, there were over 600 inmates on death row. This ruling by the Court therefore provided an opportunity to conduct a natural experiment. Researchers have been able to follow up on the activities of these commuted inmates and observe how they behave when released into the general prison population. In addition, because many of these prisoners have eventually been placed on parole, it has been possible to examine their behavior upon release into the community.

To date, several researchers have tracked the behavior of inmates whose sentences were commuted as a result of the *Furman* decision. James Marquart and Jonathan Sorensen (1988) looked at 47 persons in Texas who were taken off death row by this decision. They compared these convicts to a control group of 156 inmates who had been sentenced to life imprisonment for either murder or rape (the same offenses for which the *Furman* inmates had been sentenced to death). Comparisons were drawn between the behavior of these inmates both in prison and upon release on parole.

The study reported that despite the fact that both groups spent an average of approximately one decade in prison, 75 percent of the *Furman*-commuted inmates and 70 percent of the comparison group did not commit a serious violation of institutional rules (Marquart and Sorensen, 1988:685). Most significantly, no inmate in either group was implicated in a prison homicide. The authors conclude that "the *Furman* inmates, as compared with the life sentence cohort, were not unusually disruptive or rebellious, nor did they pose a disproportionate threat to other inmates and staff, as had been previously predicted by clinicians and administrators" (Marquart and Sorensen, 1988:686).

These researchers also analyzed the parole behavior of inmates who had been released into the community. Overall, only fourteen percent of the *Furman*-commuted inmates committed a new felony upon release. Although this is a somewhat higher figure than the percentage for the life sentence cohort (6 percent), the authors attribute this finding to the somewhat longer period that the former group had spent in the community (Marquart and Sorensen,

1988:687). There was little actual difference upon release between
the behavior of convicts who had originally been sentenced to death
and those who had been given life imprisonment. Furthermore, only
one of the parolees who had spent time on death row committed
another homicide after being released from the institution. Clearly,
fears that these individuals would be a menace to society if released
turned out to be unfounded.

Gerraro Vito, Pat Koester and Deborah Wilson (1991) have
undertaken additional analysis of *Furman*-commuted inmates.
Although their focus is similar to that of Marquart and Sorensen,
the cohort they examined includes all persons still living in 1987
who were removed from death row in twenty-six states by the
Furman decision in 1972 (N = 457). These authors report that 177
of these inmates were eventually paroled and that eight (4.5 percent)
committed another violent crime upon release. This included three
parolees who committed a new murder. Consequently, the repeat
homicide rate for this group was 1.6 percent (Vito, Koester and
Wilson, 1991:95). Based on these findings, the authors conclude
"that societal protection from convicted capital murderers is not
greatly enhanced by the death penalty" (96).

The various studies suggest that a few convicted murderers do
kill again. Sellin (1980) observed that murderers on parole are less
likely to kill than convicts paroled after being convicted of other
violent offenses. Marquart and Sorensen (1988) noted that persons
who originally were placed on death row in Texas were no more
dangerous either in prison or upon release into the community than
inmates sentenced to life imprisonment. In fact, many of the
convicts who had their sentence commuted by *Furman* became
model prisoners. In a similar vein, Vito, Koester and Wilson (1991)
found that only a tiny number of *Furman*-commuted inmates
across the nation committed another homicide upon release.

Therefore, it must be concluded that the death penalty offers little
additional protection to society over that which can be achieved
through life imprisonment. It is a myth to believe that the safety
of citizens, inmates or prison staff depends in any way on the
imposition of capital punishment.

Fighting Crime

Another myth regarding the death penalty is that it is an effective
tool in the battle against crime. It is true that the United States is
plagued with an inordinate amount of violent crime compared to
other Western nations. However, whether or not we continue to

execute offenders is irrelevant in society's attempt to control crime. Despite the rhetoric that is often generated by candidates for public office, much of the discussion regarding capital punishment that takes place in political campaigns is a diversion from the real issues that must be confronted if we are to reduce the level of crime in America.

The United States Supreme Court ruled in *Coker v. Georgia* (1977) that the death penalty may not be imposed for the crime of raping an adult woman. Although the court did not explicitly rule out the use of capital punishment for other offenses that do not include the death of the victim, the rationale of this decision would seem to preclude this possibility. The holding was that rape is a very serious crime, but it does not involve the taking of a human life. Consequently, to execute an offender for the rape of an adult woman would constitute cruel and unusual punishment in violation of the Eighth Amendment. This decision would seem to rule out the use of capital punishment for other serious crimes that did not cause death, such as armed robbery and air piracy.

As a result of the *Coker* decision, the death penalty is a possibility only in cases where the defendant is charged with murder. In fact, in those jurisdictions that retain this sanction, it is authorized only for certain types of murder. Not only must the crime meet the requisite legal criteria to be classified as capital murder, the prosecutor must also demonstrate to the jury that certain aggravating circumstances were present. As a consequence, only a small proportion of persons charged with murder can be sentenced to death. Even fewer are actually sentenced and executed.

In order to understand how infrequently capital punishment is actually carried out, it is necessary to present a few facts. Between 1977 (the date when executions resumed in the United States after a ten-year hiatus) and 1988, there were 245,350 murders reported to the police (Flanagan and Maguire, 1990:365). The Bureau of Justice Statistics (1990:6) notes that there were 2,250 persons under sentence of death in 34 states at the end of 1989. However, during the same period (1977 and 1988), only 104 executions were actually carried out. This translates into approximately one execution for every 2,360 murders committed during this time frame. Clearly, the death penalty is a rare event and cannot be considered a serious crime control strategy.

Capital punishment is applied in only a tiny fraction of murder cases. However, murder is only part of the crime problem in the United States. In most cases, citizens are not afraid to walk the streets of our cities because they fear being murdered. Most killings occur between persons who are acquainted with each other. What makes citizens fearful for their safety are concerns related to muggings, rapes, and assaults. These are the offenses that occur with great frequency and that diminish the quality of life in many communities. During 1988, there were 542,970 robberies, 910,090 aggravated assaults, and 92,490 rapes reported to the police in the United States (Flanagan and Maguire, 1990:365). The death penalty is totally irrelevant in these cases. Not only would its imposition for these crimes violate the constitution, moral considerations make it unthinkable that the United States would execute citizens for such offenses when capital punishment has been banned even for murder in other Western industrial societies (Zimring and Hawkins, 1986:3).

Therefore, it must be concluded that the notion that the death penalty is a solution to the crime problem is a myth. Legally, it may only be imposed for certain types of murder; even under those circumstances, it is rarely used. It is totally irrelevant to the question of how to make our streets safe from the reported 1.5 million or so other violent felonies that occur each year. Perhaps the most unfortunate aspect of the debate regarding capital punishment is that it diverts attention away from legitimate solutions to the crime problem. It is far easier for a politician to flaunt his or her support for the death penalty (especially when opinion polls indicate that this is a popular position) than to offer meaningful proposals for reducing the level of street crime. As Robert Bohm has noted (1989:192) "capital punishment offers a simplistic and believable solution to a complex phenomenon of which the public is frightened and of which it is generally uninformed." Hopefully, a more educated public can serve as a catalyst to raise the level of discourse in this area.

Conclusion

This chapter has attempted to debunk a number of myths regarding the death penalty. The discussion began with a broad overview of the vast literature on the question of general deterrence. It was noted that despite a wide range of methodologies that have been employed to address this issue, there is no evidence that capital punishment is more effective as a deterrent to murder than incarceration. This was followed by a discussion of the costs that capital cases entail. Contrary to what many persons believe, it was noted that a system of justice which includes the death sentence is actually more expensive than one without this sanction.

Other myths were examined as well. Proponents of capital punishment often assert that executions are necessary to protect citizens from convicted killers who are likely to repeat their crimes. However, evidence was presented that suggests rather clearly that capital offenders do not present an inordinate risk to other inmates, correctional staff, or to persons in the general community. Finally, the discussion explored whether the death penalty is necessary to fight crime. It was concluded that capital punishment is largely irrelevant to the war on crime.

Having observed that the death penalty is not a more effective general deterrent to murder, that it is more costly than life imprisonment, that it is not necessary to protect society or to fight crime, the question remains: is there any rational basis for supporting retention of capital punishment? Clearly, this sanction can only be defended on grounds of retribution. However, proponents of this punishment should also consider other concerns not examined in the preceding discussion. Why have all other Western nations abandoned this practice (Zimring and Hawkins, 1986:3)? Are innocent persons occasionally executed (Bedau and Radelet, 1987)? Is the death penalty carried out in a racially discriminatory manner (Paternoster and Kazyaka, 1988)? Whether the public will remain supportive of capital punishment once executions again become routine events is uncertain (Wallace, 1989). Nonetheless, from a public policy perspective, whether or not we continue to employ this sanction is probably not as important as recognizing how little can be accomplished through its use.

Sources

Andenaes, J. (1974). *Punishment and Deterrence*. Ann Arbor: University of Michigan Press.

Bailey, W. C. (1991). The General Prevention Effect of Capital Punishment for Non-Capital Felonies. In *The Death Penalty in America: Current Research*, R. M. Bohm (ed.). Cincinnati, OH: Anderson Publishing Co. and Academy of Criminal Justice Sciences.

_____ (1982). Capital Punishment and Lethal Assaults Against Police. *Criminology*, 19:608-25.

Bailey, W. C. and Peterson, R. D. (1987). Police Killings and Capital Punishment: The Post-Furman Period. *Criminology*, 25(1):1-25.

Bedau, H. A. (ed.). (1982). *The Death Penalty in America, Third Edition*. Oxford: Oxford University Press.

Bedau, H. A. and Radelet, M. L. (1987). Miscarriages of Justice in Potentially Capital Cases. *Stanford Law Review*, 40:21-179.

Berns, W. (1979). *For Capital Punishment*. New York: Basic Books.

Bohm, R. M. (1989). Humanism and the Death Penalty, with Special Emphasis on the Post-*Furman* Experience. *Justice Quarterly*, 6:173-95.

Bowers, W. J. (1988). The Effect of Executions is Brutalization, Not Deterrence. In *Challenging Capital Punishment: Legal and Social Science*

Approaches, K. C. Haas and J. A. Inciardi (eds.). Newbury Park, CA: Sage Publications, Inc.

Bowers, W. J. and Pierce, G. L. (1975). The Illusion of Deterrence in Isaac Ehrlich's Research on Capital Punishment. *Yale Law Journal*, 85:187-208.

Bowers, W. J., Pierce, G. L. and McDevitt, J. F. (1984). *Legal Homicide: Death as Punishment in America, 1864-1982*. Boston: Northeastern University Press.

Bureau of Justice Statistics (1990). *Capital Punishment 1989*. Washington, DC: United States Department of Justice.

_____ (1987). *Sentencing Outcomes in Twenty-Eight Felony Courts 1985*. Washington, DC: United States Department of Justice.

Cardarelli, A. P. (1968). An Analysis of Police Killed in Criminal Action: 1961-1963. *Journal of Criminal Law, Criminology and Police Science*, 59:447-53.

Coker v. Georgia, 433 U.S. 584 (1977).

Dann, R. H. (1935). The Deterrent Effect of Capital Punishment. *Friends Social Service Series*, 29.

Ehrlich, I. (1975). The Deterrent Effect of Capital Punishment: A Question of Life and Death. *American Economic Review*, 65:397-417.

Ellsworth, P. C. (1988). Unpleasant Facts: The Supreme Court's Response to Empirical Research on Capital Punishment. In *Challenging Capital Punishment: Legal and Social Science Approaches*, K. C. Haas and J. A. Inciardi (eds.). Newbury Park, CA: Sage Publications, Inc.

Flanagan, T. J. and Maguire, K. (1990). *Sourcebook of Criminal Justice Statistics 1989*. Albany, NY: The Hindelang Criminal Justice Research Center.

Furman v. Georgia, 408 U.S. 238 (1972).

Graves, W. F. (1956). A Doctor Looks at Capital Punishment. *Medical Arts and Sciences, Journal of the Loma Linda University School of Medicine*, 10 (4):137-41.

Heckathorn, D. D. (1985). Why Punishment Does Not Deter. In *The Ambivalent Force: Perspectives on the Police, Third Edition*, A. S. Blumberg and E. Niederhoffer (eds.). New York: Holt, Rinehart and Winston.

Jamieson, K. M. and Flanagan, T. J. (1989). *Sourcebook of Criminal Justice Statistics 1988*. Albany, NY: The Hindelang Criminal Justice Research Center.

Klein, L. R., Forst B. E. and Filatov, V. (1978). The Deterrent Effect of Capital Punishment: An Assessment of the Estimates. In *Deterrence and Incapacitation: Estimating the Effects of Criminal Sanctions on Crime Rates*, A. Blumstein, J. Cohen and D. Nagin (eds.). Washington, DC: National Academy of Sciences.

Layson, S. (1985). Homicide and Deterrence: A Reexamination of the United States Time-Series Evidence. *Southern Economic Journal*, 52:68-89.

Lehtinen, M. (1977). The Voice of Life: An Argument for the Death Penalty. *Crime and Delinquency*, 23:237-52.

Marquart, J. W. and Sorensen, J. R. (1988). Institutional and Postrelease Behavior of *Furman*-Commuted Inmates in Texas. *Criminology*, 26:677-93.

Nakell, B. (1982). The Cost of the Death Penalty. In *The Death Penalty in America, Third Edition*, H. A. Bedau (ed.). Oxford: Oxford University Press.

New York State Defender Association, Inc. (1982). *Capital Losses: The Price of the Death Penalty for New York State*.

Passell, P. and Taylor, J. B. (1976). The Deterrent Controversy: A Reconsideration of the Time Series Evidence. In *Capital Punishment in the United States*, H. A. Bedau and C. M. Pierce (eds.). New York: AMS Press.

Paternoster, R. and Kazyaka, A. (1988). Racial Considerations in Capital Punishment: The Failure of Evenhanded Justice. In *Challenging Capital Punishment: Legal and Social Science Approaches*, K. C. Haas and J. A. Inciardi (eds.). Newbury Park, CA: Sage Publications, Inc.

Sellin, T. (1980). *The Penalty of Death*. Beverly Hills, CA: Sage Publications, Inc.

Shin, K. (1978). *Death Penalty and Crime*. Fairfax, VA: Center for Economic Analysis.

Spangeberg, R. L. and Walsh, E. R. (1989). Capital Punishment or Life Imprisonment?: Some Cost Considerations. *Loyola of Los Angeles Law Review*, 23:45-58.

Stack, S. (1987). Publicized Executions and Homicide, 1950-1980. *American Sociological Review*, 52:532-40.

Tabak, R. J. and Lane, J. M. (1989). The Execution of Injustice: A Cost and Lack-of-Benefit Analysis of the Death Penalty. *Loyola of Los Angeles Law Review*, 23:136.

van den Haag, E. (1978). In Defense of the Death Penalty: A Legal-Practical-Moral Analysis. *Criminal Law Bulletin*, 14:51-68.

Vito, G. F., Koester, P. and Wilson, D. G. (1991). Return of the Dead: An Update on the Status of Furman-Commuted Death Row Inmates. In *The Death Penalty in America: Current Research*, R. M. Bohm (ed.). Cincinnati, OH: Anderson Publishing Co. and Academy of Criminal Justice Sciences.

Wainwright v. Witt, 105 S. Ct. 844 (1985).

Wallace, D. H. (1989). Bloodbath and Brutalization: Public Opinion and the Death Penalty. *Journal of Crime and Justice*, 12:51-77.

Wilson, J. Q. (1983). *Thinking About Crime, Revised Edition*. New York: Basic Books, Inc.

Wolfson, W. P. (1982). The Deterrent Effect of the Death Penalty upon Prison Murder. In *The Death Penalty in America, Third Edition*, H. A. Bedau (ed.). Oxford: Oxford University Press.

Yunker, J. (1976). Is the Death Penalty a Deterrent to Homicide? Some Time Series Evidence. *Journal of Behavioral Economics*, 5:1-32.

Zeisel, H. (1977). The Deterrent Effect of the Death Penalty: Facts v. Faith. In *The Supreme Court Review 1976*, Philip B. Kurland (ed.). Chicago: University of Chicago Press.

Zimring, F. E. and Hawkins, G. (1986). *Capital Punishment and the American Agenda*. Cambridge: Cambridge University Press.

chapter 12

Merging Myths and Misconceptions of Crime and Justice

Eventually, public focus on a particular crime wanes allowing the mythical characteristics to settle into a form of accepted social reality. New social problems will then emerge or old myths will be dredged up to remind us of who the criminals are and how to go about solving crime problems. After the initial fear and panic surrounding a crime myth subsides, the conceptual residue becomes a frame of reference for determining our future views of social problems. Crime myths become mental filters through which social issues are sifted. Although crime myths fade, their effect on our conception of crime and justice linger. Once a myth becomes entrenched in thought, it takes only an occasional incident to fan the smoldering embers of the latent myth into another flame of public attention. This process of interpreting problems to fit our myth-based notions of crime and justice is enhanced if mythmakers construct new problems or events within the framework of previously constructed myths. Such characterizations and historical frames of reference insure that mythical conceptions of crime never truly die. One of the powers of crime myth is that past conceptions blend with present events to create future conceptions of crime.

It is too early to speculate on the lasting effects contemporary crime myths will have on our future conceptions of crime and justice, but it is not too early to heed the admonishment that our picture of violent crime in America results from a composition of panics promoted by the mythmakers of society. Moreover, these panics tend to fold into one another, supporting the idea that society is somehow under siege by crime (Jenkins and Katkin, 1988). As crime myths fold into one another, they begin a recycling process that can form a single, unified, and very popular conception of the reality of crime in America. Conceptual bits and pieces of the myths of stranger child abduction, serial murderers, and organized child abuse may merge to form an enveloping mythology of violent crime. Similarly, myths of the dangers of police work and misconceptions of punitive justice may fuse to create a single ideology of the proper social response to crime. Once a unified conception of crime and its control becomes a part of popular thought and governmental policy, the empirical reality of crime will mirror and even support our mythology.

Under our mythology of crime, the police role will be limited to vigorously tracking stereotyped criminals. Social service aspects of policing will be reduced to rhetoric, and crime fighting will truly become the police response to social problems. The role of the judiciary will be similar to an assembly line with judges moving through their dockets at great speed, unhindered by the niceties of due process. We will fill our newly built prisons with those who are "different" (the poor, minority members, organized criminals, and drug offenders), and we will continue to search for new technologies that enable the system to widen its net of social control. The empirical reality of crime (which results from the focus we choose) will be offered as evidence of our mythical conceptions—a neat tautology but dangerously unenlightening. We cannot look only at police records, court dockets, and the composition of prison populations to determine the characteristics of criminals or to determine if society is more dangerous today. Rather, we must examine all facets of the system to determine if our definitions and the processes we endorse are part of the problem.

Events of Today and Myths of Tomorrow

Is there support for a unified mythology of crime and criminal justice? Will mythmakers continue to promote current conceptions of crime and justice, or are these issues mere fads capturing the public's attention for a fleeting moment? In the sections that follow, we will consider several events that point to a continuation of existing myths of crime and hint at a unified picture of crime and its control in America.

Drugs, White Collar Crime and Criminal Organizations

The symbiotic relationship between organized crime, the government, and "legitimate" business is embodied in the activities of the Bank of Credit and Commerce International (BCCI). Yet, the media and public attention focused on these events pales when compared to the focus on traditional violent crime. The recent investigations of BCCI and its illegal activities around the world provide ample confirmation of the cozy relationship between drug traffickers, white collar criminals, the intelligence community, and leading politicians in the United States. BCCI was the seventh-largest privately owned financial institution in the world. It operated in seventy-three countries and had over four hundred branch offices (Schmaltz, 1985). According to Jack Blum, the former chief investigator of the Senate Subcommittee on Terrorism, Narcotics and International Operations, BCCI was, in the truest sense of the word, a "full-service bank."

> It offered full banking services to facilitate transactions that no one else would touch. It was the bank for drug dealers, arms dealers, money launderers—indeed whoever had an illegal project and money to hide . . . [BCCI was] a kind of Federal Express for illicit goods . . . ready to move currency, gold, weapons, drugs for anyone who wanted them moved (Meddis, 1991:9A).

BCCI's illegal activities have covered the full gamut of organized crime, white collar crime and political crime, including:

* laundering at least $14 million in narcotic profits for the Colombian cocaine cartels, shifting money to banks in the Bahamas, Britain, France, Uruguay, and Luxembourg to avoid detection (Schmaltz, 1988).

* playing a major role in the Iran-Contra scandal by acting as a conduit for weapons deals involving international arms merchant Adnan Khashoggi and drug deals (which funded the arms purchases) involving Panamanian president Manuel Noriega (Waldman et al., 1991). It is alleged that BCCI also served as a conduit for CIA funds destined for the Contras to support illegal arms deals and Contra-backed cocaine trafficking (Cauchon, 1991).

• helping Philippine president Ferdinand Marcos to transfer his personal fortune, accrued through corruption and graft, out of the Philippines before his ouster (Waldman, et al., 1991).

While the full extent of its criminal activities may never be known, BCCI was a major criminal enterprise operating within the corporate sector with cooperation from other "legitimate" financiers and businesses and with, at the very least, the acquiescence of those government agencies charged with ferreting out drug trafficking, terrorism, and business corruption. BCCI had powerful political allies including Clark Clifford (former Secretary of Defense and close adviser to presidents Truman, Kennedy, Johnson, and Carter), Edwin Meese (former Attorney General during the Reagan presidency) and Black, Manafort and Stone (the advertising consultants to the Republican Party). There were also political connections with Senator Alfonse D'Amato of New York; former president Jimmy Carter; and current president George Bush (Waldman et al., 1991).

The Justice Department is currently investigating allegations that BCCI directly bribed United States government officials. How thorough that investigation will be is open to considerable question. The Justice Department had complete information on BCCI's drug and arms operations and its illegal holdings in the United States for over three years before it even initiated an inquiry (Cauchon, 1991). Indications are, however, that this type of criminal conduct will not be treated with the same sense of panic or retribution as are other forms of crime. It is doubtful that the FBI or the Justice Department will establish international programs to analyze violent political crime and corporate criminals. There have been no public calls for enhanced funding to track, apprehend, and convict politically well-connected white collar criminals, nor are new prisons or the death penalty being proposed as the solutions to corporate and political crime networks.

The BCCI investigation leaves a vague sense of *deja vu*. Conspiracies involving banking institutions (i.e., the Nugan Hand Bank), the United States intelligence community, powerful politicians, arms merchants and drug lords have been commonplace since the Vietnam War. BCCI is just another example of how difficult it is to draw clear lines of distinction between white collar crime, organized crime, and political crime. It is also yet another example of how difficult it sometimes is to distinguish between the state, the mob and the corporate sector. Finally, it is an excellent illustration of how crime myths undermine our social response to crime and define our sense of who the criminals are.

The recent conviction of John Gotti on murder and racketeering charges has led to a rebirth of media attention focused on the activities of New York's fabled "five families." Federal prosecutors have been quick to capitalize on the Gotti conviction by calling him "the most powerful criminal in America" and predicting that his conviction will bring chaos to the well-structured world of the Cosa Nostra. A quick review of the facts of the Gotti case as revealed in testimony from the trials and the transcripts of wiretaps presented at those trials offers a very different picture.

No one will argue that John Gotti is an eclectic criminal. He has a "rap sheet" that includes hijacking, public intoxication, drug charges, assault, theft, burglary, gambling, and murder. Gotti is heard on the wiretaps alternately threatening, boasting, bragging and whining about the state of his criminal career. It is precisely this view of John Gotti, however, that is most troubling. For a man being touted as "the most powerful criminal in America," he has had a conspicuously troubled career, marked by a series of arrests and a string of unsuccessful criminal acts. John Gotti's career as an organized criminal has been somewhat limited. It is true that he runs a very large dice game in Manhattan. On the other hand, the wiretaps reveal that he was a notoriously bad gambler, frequently losing $60,000 to $70,000 a day. At one point on the tapes he complains that his luck was so bad he would "have to go on welfare." It is also true that Gotti provided leadership to a den of thieves operating out of the "Bergin Hunt and Fish Club." It is equally true that the members of his "crew" frequently complained about his inability to come up with targets for scores and his inability to create income-producing opportunities in other illicit ventures.

While in past trials prosecutors have alleged that Gotti had connections to several drug operations, most of the schemes hatched by his associates failed and resulted in the loss of money. While the wiretaps show Gotti to be a man who thought nothing of using intimidation or threats, they also clearly demonstrate that he was frequently out of control in this regard. He threatened to kill people with regularity — a very dangerous and costly action for a criminal entrepreneur to engage in repeatedly. He also pursued a series of personal, non-business-related vendettas, allegedly including the disappearance of a neighbor. His bail was once revoked because of an incident resulting from a fight over a parking space. While prosecutors have been successful in portraying Gotti as a dangerous sociopath, they have not been successful in portraying him as a major organized crime figure.

Simply put, John Gotti is no Meyer Lansky, no Sidney Korshak, no Alvin Malnik. It is simply inconceivable that someone in Lansky's position would have resorted to physical violence over a parking space. It is equally inconceivable that Lansky would be arrested with shocking regularity for nearly every venture he undertook. And, of course, it is inconceivable that Lansky would be tape recorded threatening to "whack" every other punk he came in contact with. The evidence presented against John Gotti portrays him as a hood and a criminal. A hoodlum with a long criminal record and frequent press notices does not qualify one as the head of organized crime. It does, however, make one a candidate for anointment by federal prosecutors as a target for a headhunting campaign. John Gotti is another in a long list of careless, boastful, somewhat unsuccessful pretenders who make easy targets for special investigatory treatment. The simple fact is that there are hundreds of John Gottis out there. Men like John Berkery of Philadelphia's K&A gang, Buster Riggins of Washington, D.C.'s sex rings, Jimmy Lambert of Kentucky's cocaine trade, and Jose Battle of the "Cuban Mafia" are every bit as formidable, powerful, and dangerous as Gotti. Every one of them, if we used John Gotti as a model, is a model candidate for "the most powerful criminal in America." To single Gotti out for a leadership role is to misunderstand organized crime and to confuse real power with notoriety.

The Gotti case has also obfuscated the true nature of organized crime itself. The thesis of the federal prosecutions has been that La Cosa Nostra (with its national commission, exclusive membership, and hierarchical corporate structure) remains the single license-granting authority in organized crime. The facts presented by the prosecutors belie the claim. The criminal enterprises described in the Gotti prosecution are not the result of careful planning by a corporate organized crime operation but rather a series of informal criminal relationships evolving out of social proximity and prior entrepreneurial connections. Gotti's alleged heroin operation, for example, was really headed by Mark Reiter and Angelo Ruggerio. They engaged in a series of opportunistic (and unsuccessful) drug deals involving amounts of drugs and money minute in comparison to the activities of dozen of other drug merchants. There is no indication of a monopoly or even dominance in the New York drug market by these actors; in fact, there is considerable evidence that they were fairly small operators. The "Bergin crew" was just that. It was not an offshoot of a powerful syndicate; it was an informal, social network of hoods. The "Members" came together to run a dice game, to do some "muscle work" for a loanshark, or to rob a drug dealer. They never formed a cohesive criminal organization. They were a group of individuals forming and reforming a series of criminal partnerships, some of which involved John Gotti. Even Gotti's most successful criminal venture, his crap game, involved a constantly changing series of participants from a number of crime networks. While the evidence may have been strong enough for federal prosecutors to allege a criminal organization for RICO purposes, it is not strong enough for students of organized crime to suggest anything beyond an informal, loosely structured, ephemeral criminal network.

Finally, the Gotti prosecutions raise serious questions about the whole process of investigating and trying organized crime cases, a process we have previously referred to as headhunting. Evidence presented in the case portrays a situation in which it seems that almost all of New York City was bugged by one agency or another. Literally thousands of hours of conversations were recorded, most of which were irrelevant to the carefully edited versions presented as evidence of a criminal conspiracy. Testimony in the Gotti case described in detail the careers of the informers the government used against Gotti, men like James Cardinale, "Willie Boy" Johnson, Matthew Traynor, and "Crazy Sally" Polisi. It is not a pretty picture.

The Gotti prosecution consisted of intense negotiations between criminals and the state, the issuance of crime-committing licenses for cooperative informers, duplicity and mendacity on both sides of the deal, and orchestration of both crimes and testimony by the state.

The Gotti trials raise serious questions about the process of "framing" organized crime cases by government prosecutors. All of the trials, including the four in which Gotti was acquitted, focused less on the guilt or innocence of the defendants than on the deals struck, the interactions between witnesses and prosecutors, and the details of personal relationships between investigators and the hoods they were investigating. Stories of drugs being supplied in prisons, sexual impropriety by informers and prosecutors, and outright deals allowing the continuation and furtherance of criminal activity by government witnesses were repeated in detail. The impression one is left with is that the government simply authorized some organized crime figures to continue dealing drugs, stealing and gambling to trap some other crime figures who were doing precisely the same thing.

Drugs, Cops and Capital Punishment

One of the most obvious effects of crime myths is political. Calls for stiffer penalties for the unpopular group and further protections of innocents are the two most prominent political actions requested. The emotional furor and fear generated by myth production can create an atmosphere conducive to political grandstanding. This grandstanding often takes the form of proposing new crimes and classes of criminals. It is common for political leaders to advocate the use of the most severe criminal sanctions, such as the death penalty, at the pinnacle of sensationalism over a particular issue. Although few of these calls are ever transformed into formal social control, they do promote current beliefs that existing solutions to crime are acceptable and viable options for reducing both crime and the related social problems.

Police and politicians pledge to eradicate mythical crime problems through more law and order. An inevitable part of fighting mythical crime is a call for more police power and harsher punishment for criminals. The mythmakers argue that if the police are unable to solve our crime problems it is only because they have been handcuffed by the courts, or because we have not allowed them to be aggressive enough in fighting crime, or because prisons are not punitive enough and we need to resort to the ultimate punishment—death.

As we have seen, the reality of crime fighting differs quite significantly from the myths of police and their work. There are, however, real consequences to promoting the myth of danger in police work and the growing dangerousness of criminals. Unfortunately, these myths recently merged to form federal legislation. In 1988, a New York police officer named Eddie Byrne was killed while investigating a drug-related crime. This incident, in part, led Congress to enact a federal death penalty clause that allows for the sentence of capital punishment to be imposed for "a defendant who kills or counsels to kill a law enforcement officer, while attempting to avoid apprehension, punishment, or sentencing for a drug violation . . ." (Williams, 1991:394). Williams' (1991) examination of the legislative history of the act indicated that "the murder of New York City police officer, Eddie Byrne, was one of the motivations for applying the death penalty section to those who kill law enforcement officers over drug-related offenses" (394). While the killing of any law enforcement officer is a tragedy that should not go unnoticed by society, it is a rare event. Law enforcement officers and their families, as well as the general public, may feel that this legislation is a necessary step taken to protect police officers. As noted earlier, however, the number of police officers killed in the line of duty has been declining for two decades. Very few officers are killed under circumstances that would allow for the use of the federal drug death penalty clause. It is ironic that the federal government created a federal death penalty law when the state in which the incident occurred did not deem such a law necessary. Another factor that makes the Congressional action noteworthy is that the government has helped to promote linkage between the myths of the dangers of police work, the evils of drug use, and the viability of the death penalty. Congress took no similar action against Miami police officers who killed drug traffickers in order to steal and later sell their drug cargo, and there are far more incidents of police drug corruption than there are cases of police officers killed by drug trafficking criminals. The drugs reach the same market whether sold by "criminals" or corrupt police officers. One question that remains unanswered is whether this statute would be applicable in a scenario where a corrupt police officer kills another police officer to avoid criminal apprehension for a drug violation.

Two explanations exist for the enactment of the federal death penalty clause. Either Congress was drawn into the myths of policing, drug crime and the death penalty, or the motivations were purely political. What better way for politicians to promote myths than to create a law that gives the impression of being tough on crime but which has little or no potential for use. Such a symbolic law does, however, reinforce myths of drug crime and police work while forging a symbolic link to the death penalty as the final solution to our crime problems.

There are very real consequences to supporting the hard-line law and order approach to crime control. One of these consequences is allowing the "troops" in the crime war to develop their own means for dealing with crime and criminals. In March of 1991, the public's focus on the victory in the Persian Gulf War was momentarily interrupted by a savage beating. An amateur video camera enthusiast captured footage of Los Angeles Police Department (LAPD) officers beating a young black man following a traffic stop. California Highway Patrol officers had detected Rodney King speeding in an automobile. Following a brief chase, the unarmed King exited his vehicle. Officers shocked him with a 50,000 volt stun-gun and savagely struck him at least fifty times as he lay upon the ground. Over fifteen police officers from several different departments stood watching or participated in the beating. King was stun-gunned repeatedly throughout the incident while other officers kicked, stomped and struck him repeatedly with nightsticks. The beating resulted in severe injuries that included a fractured skull, a broken cheek bone and ankle, various internal injuries, burns, and brain damage.

As disturbing as the beating was, the investigation of the incident by officials was even more shocking. Tests of vehicles similar to that driven by King found that even a newer version of his car could not travel at the speeds California Highway Patrol officers reported. "California Highway Patrol records confirm[ed] that during the car chase that preceded the beating, King was never going more than 65 mph, not 115 mph as police reported earlier" (Baker, 1991:19). Also, the LAPD officers' official arrest report claimed that King was under the influence of PCP—a strong hallucinogenic. According to blood tests, however, no PCP was detected.

LAPD officers have apparently learned that not only are they waging a war in society which calls for drastic and often brutal measures, but that characterizing suspects in terms of drug users and "enemies" insulates them from the consequences of misconduct. To characterize King as a PCP user might justify an aggressive police response, since the public knows that persons under the influence of drugs are violent. Would the incident have received any attention at all if there had not been a video tape detailing the severity of the beating? Would King have been characterized as a drug user and therefore just another casualty in the war against mythical crime? We should note that there were no calls for the death penalty for police officers who savagely torture motorists— only explanations: the police have a hard time fighting the war against crime; the LAPD is understaffed; police have to be aggressive; and remember—King had a criminal record.

Consider Otwin Marenin's (1991) reflections on the legacy of the law and order conservatism sweeping America:

> As rights were denounced, so were procedures which protect them. A false solution was created—if only some rights were stripped away we will succeed in fighting the scourge of lawlessness; if only the Police had a few more powers they might not have to beat on people who look as if they might insist on their rights; if only Judges were denied control of cases and evidence then guilty people could not avoid being found guilty; if prisoners could be housed four to a cell and deathrow inmates killed off speedily all criminals could be taken off the street. In practice, as all who work in the system know, these changes would be minor and have little systematic impact on crime or the effectiveness of criminal justice policies. For the public which knows how the system works from anecdotal cases and stereotyped cop-shows, such imagery hits the right note. Yet the promise made—crime will decrease and you will be safer— cannot be delivered . . . (17).

Serial Murderers and Missing Children

Recent media coverage has provided for the resurrection, reinforcement, and linkage necessary for a unified myth of violent predatory crime. In the summer of 1991, the nation was shocked at the discovery that a 31-year-old Milwaukee man, Jeffery Dahmer was responsible for the murder and mutilation of as many as seventeen people. The gruesome details of his crimes created such a sensation that virtually every major newspaper carried coverage of Dahmer's sadistic behavior. The reporting of his crimes was coupled with expanded coverage of other "related" sensational criminals and crimes of the past possibly setting the stage for a second serial murder panic and linking child abduction to serial murder.

In the July 31, 1991 edition of *USA Today*, Dahmer was the cover story. Coupled with this feature story was an article about "admiring females" that were said to have flocked to visit the "Night Stalker," Richard Ramirez, who was sentenced to death for several sex-related killings in southern California. The article reported that "dozens — possibly hundreds — of women" view Ramirez as a sex symbol. Satanic overtones of Ramirez's crimes embellished the article with discussion of pentagrams and pledges to Satan — sensationalized links forged in earlier reports of missing children and child abuse.

The same issue of *USA Today* also carried an article on the lesser-known convicted killer, John Joubert. Joubert was held responsible for the murder of three boys in 1983. The articles linked Joubert to Dahmer by suggesting that these two killers were of a single type or profile, child-cannibal-sexual killers, by reporting that Joubert's victims had bite marks on their bodies. The article quoted a former FBI agent as warning that this kind of crime is "escalating every decade." Recall that the serial murder panic of 1983-85 was also characterized as growing "immensely since the 1970s" and marked by savage acts and mutilation (Jenkins, 1988). Although the former FBI agent noted the difference between the reality of serial murder and the movie *Silence of the Lambs*, the article clearly created mental linkage by calling attention to the killers and the cinema portrayal of the fictional cannibal. The groupings of articles even dredged up the almost forgotten killer Ed Gein who, in the 1950s, became the basis for portrayal of the killer in the movie *Psycho* (Editorial Staff, 1991). Again, as with many other myths of crime, the reality of crime blends with popular fiction.

At the onset of the Dahmer investigation, major media sources reported possible links between Dahmer's criminal activities and the disappearance of Adam Walsh—a child abducted and murdered in the mid-1980s. Adam Walsh's abduction and the media attention given this child's horrible plight sent panic throughout the country and marked the beginnings of the child abduction scare of the 1980s. Such a link between this serial murderer and the possibility that his activities accounted for the disappearance of people across the nation prompted a police deputy inspector to tell journalists that "We've panicked half the Midwest . . . Everyone with a missing family member is calling" (Howlett, 1991:2A).

One should recall the similarities between the Dahmer case and that of Henry Lee Lucas. Lucas "began confessing numerous murders in the fall of 1983. By the end of the year, his 'kill' had exceeded three hundred, and he did much to shape the stereotype of the multiple murderer" (Jenkins, 1988:2). As Philip Jenkins points out, Lucas and his sidekick Otis Toole also claimed "responsibility for the killing of a vast number of children including Adam Walsh. Lucas led police on a wild goose chase around the country from site to site where missing bodies of his victims were supposedly located. After months of investigation, Lucas was convicted of thirteen killings but later claimed that the only person he really killed was his mother. This helped ensure publicity and linked the murder issue with other contemporary panics" like missing children and child abuse (Jenkins, 1988:2-3). With all the necessary characteristics of a crime myth in place and linkages forged between child abduction and serial murders, only a characterization of an epidemic remained to create another serial murderer panic. This too was to be achieved.

In the midst of the Dahmer investigation, the police paraded before the media a new serial murderer, perhaps responsible for even more killings than Dahmer. In August of 1991, the media and police called to our attention the existence of Donald Leroy Evans. Evans confessed to the rape and strangulation of a ten-year-old girl. Evans later led police to her body and was convicted of the kidnapping in October. Newspaper and television news reports labeled Evans as being the most prolific serial killer in history perhaps killing as many as sixty people, possibly even Adam Walsh. By early fall of 1991, the media had become silent on the Evans case except for an occasional video of Evans and the police in some desert searching for bodies. By late fall, there had been no reporting of uncovered bodies and all that remained was the media's created linkage between Evans, Dahmer, serial murder, child abduction and the movie *Silence of the Lambs* (Squitieri, 1991). The press was otherwise silent on the status of the Evans investigation except to raise the kill count to seventy (Leavitt, 1991).

No doubt incidents such as these will be used in the future to support claims for increased resources for the study of serial murders and child abduction. There will be calls for better law enforcement machinery to investigate these sadistic crimes. The two incidents below provide evidence that there should be public calls for help—but of a very different nature.

After the initial reporting of the Dahmer murders, it was learned that police officers had had prior contact with Dahmer. The police had received a report from neighbors of a naked, bleeding, intoxicated youth running in the street with Dahmer in pursuit. Officers responding to the call labeled it a homosexual lovers' spat and noted that Dahmer had evidence of the relationship when he showed them pictures of the two. Police tapes also indicated that the officers returned the juvenile to Dahmer's apartment; while inside, they failed to observe photos of other victims scattered about the apartment and even a dead body went unnoticed. Not only did the police fail to recognize this evidence, but if they had checked into the matter they would have learned that Dahmer was on parole after having been convicted of molesting the brother of the boy the officers returned to him. Dahmer later told police that after the officers left, he killed the youth (Howlett, 1991a).

The fall of 1991 also found that New York police officers failed to intervene in a child abuse case involving a young girl who had been chained to her bed by her parents. The youth apparently contacted the police about her treatment; when officers arrived at the home, they were instructed by her captor-parents that she had a drug problem and was prone to running away from home. The officers left the residence approving of the guardian's child rearing practices.

Incidents like these beg for increased expenditures for law enforcement—not for the development of national centers to track down serial criminals, mythical cults, or to monitor Satanic day care centers but to train law enforcement officers on the *realities* of social problems like murder, domestic violence and child abuse, as well as reasonable police responses. Through our growing panic and concern over serial murder and missing children, we have enhanced law enforcement resources, developed task forces, and implemented national programs and created vast bureaucracies to deal with crime myths. Once created, these machines are seldom dismantled even when their need is called into question. These machines take on a life of their own and have a vested interest in creating and continuing the very crime myths they were designed to eliminate. These crime control bureaucracies consume an ever expanding amount of social resources as they widen their sphere of influence and modify their missions to fit organizational and political goals. Such enforcement policies serve to burden an already overtaxed criminal justice system and mask other social problems.

Masking Social Problems with Myth

We have noted that fear develops based on the notion of victimization by strangers or persons different from ourselves. Children are abducted by strangers, and they are abused by day care providers. Organized crime is controlled and operated by foreign-born nationals having little allegiance to our way of life. Homosexuals and drug users carry with them the AIDS virus and threaten criminal justice personnel with infection. Serial murderers prowl looking for unsuspecting victims to slay, and police officers are under assault from criminals. Such characterizations of crime, criminals and the criminal justice system, as we have seen, have little basis in the reality of crime and justice in modern American society, but they are real to the public.

People fear walking the streets, avoid contact with strangers, and generally withdraw from society. Fear of victimization and social isolation begins a downward spiral that can produce more crime, more victimization, and more myth. As we remove ourselves from the street and isolate ourselves from the concerns of others in our communities, we abandon society and its real problems. We are no longer willing to become involved in our communities, much less in real crime prevention and the workings of the criminal justice system. We leave matters of justice to the mythmakers.

Government officials are free to spawn myths of crime and justice and to waste valuable resources on ineffective crime control practices that expand the crime control industry. When crime control policy is developed based on myth or misconception, it has the effect of diverting resources and attention from real social problems. To varying extents, each of the crime myths we have considered in this book blinds us to social problems of greater magnitude and consequence. When vast social resources are expended to hunt down mythical criminals, prevent stranger abductions of children or investigate foreign-born organized crime figures, resources are consumed that could be used to study and to control real social problems.

Crime myths divert attention. We are forced to overlook much broader, underlying social problems like teenage runaways, children abused at the hands of their relatives, and the crime "organized" in corporate board rooms and governmental offices across the country. We wage wars against inanimate objects such as drugs and pornography as if they have a life of their own — without considering the supply-and-demand equation and the spin-off crimes caused by waging crime wars and criminalizing behavior. Consider just a few of the questions and problems that are masked when we focus on mythical crime.

- Why do children run away from their parents?
- Why is law enforcement unable to deal with crime?
- What is the magnitude and cost of corporate crime?
- How many deaths are associated with drugs like alcohol and tobacco?
- What spin-off crimes are caused by the drug war?
- Can we reduce AIDS by implementing drug education programs?
- Are injuries caused by the government's drug crop eradication programs?
- How much corruption of governmental officials results from drug criminalization?
- What percentage of the public demands vice-related services and products?
- Is there a symbiotic relationship between government and corporate crime?
- Who pays the $231 billion dollar price tag of corporate and white collar crime?

Unfortunately, crime myths also serve to undermine the scientific study and treatment of crime. Crime myths change our perception and understanding of crime and criminal behavior by offering up simplistic solutions to complex problems. Crime myths are often "quests for evil." They sometimes use supernatural explanations for crime to the detriment of scientific understanding. This is especially the case in crimes that have been characterized as occult or Satanic. When crime is characterized as evil, rehabilitation is rejected in favor of harsh punishment including the death penalty. Less sensational, but equal in effect, is the characterization of criminal behavior as a product of freely chosen behavior. When the causal bases of crime are rejected, punishment becomes the logical social response. Legal prescriptions are used to treat the symptoms of social problems, and science is relegated to crime detection rather than understanding crime and its social causes. Offenders are stereotyped as pathological, homogeneous and violent, and their behavior is analyzed from a simplistic prey-predator paradigm. Challenges to the scientific study of crime often alter the empirical reality of crime. The restructured study of crime may then begin to mirror our mythical conceptions of crime by providing more "evidence" that is tainted by a detection, apprehension, and control paradigm of criminology.

Unfortunately, myths of crime and justice are not put to rest with the same vigor with which they are created. Debunking myths does not have the same attraction as does their construction. After clear definitions of criminal behavior have been developed and the actual frequency of the crime has been determined, there are few newspaper accounts, television documentaries, commercials, or calls by political leaders to demystify our images of crime. Often, all that exists in the aftermath of a crime myth are criminal law, harsher punishments, misplaced social resources, a feeling of moral superiority, and growing intolerance for human diversity.

We hope this text has challenged you to view crime myths with a critical eye — to think about the origin of issues and to watch for patterns of myth construction. Myths can only be challenged by critically processing information. Critical thinking must develop alternative filters through which to sift social myths — questions must be posed and stories must be challenged. We must begin to ask: Who is the mythmaker? What is the mythmaker's motivation? What group is being targeted by the myth? What behavior is being targeted for control and why? Most importantly we must ask: What are the consequences of waging war against mythical social problems?

Sources

Baker, J. N. (1991). Los Angeles Aftershocks. *Newsweek*, (April 1): 18-19.

Cauchon, D. (1991). Head of BCCI-linked Bank Quits. *USA Today*, (August 14):8A.

Editorial Staff (1991). Serial Killings. *USA Today*, (August 15):2A.

Edmonds, P. (1991). Profile: When the Fantasies turn Violent. *USA Today*, (July 31):2A.

Goodavage, M. (1991). Stalking the 'Night Stalker' Admiring Females Come Calling. *USA Today*, (July 31):2A.

Howlett, D. (1991). Suspect Admits Grisly Killings." *USA Today*, (July 28):2A.

_____ (1991a). Police Were in Dahmer's Room. *USA Today*, (August 15):1A, 3A.

Howlett, D. and Edmonds, P. (1991). A 13-year Tale of Horror: Investigations Trace Dahmer's Gruesome Trail. *USA Today*, (July 31):1A.

Jenkins, P. (1988). Myth and Murder: The Serial Killer Panic of 1983-5. *Criminal Justice Research Bulletin*, 3:1-7.

Jenkins, P. and Katkin, D. (1988). Protecting Victims of Child Sexual Abuse: A Case for Caution. *Prison Journal*, 58(2):25-35.

Leavitt, P. (1991). Mass Killer Case. *USA Today*, (October 2):A4.

Marenon. O. (1991). Making a Tough Job Tougher: The Legacy of Conservatism. *ACJS Today*, 10(2):1, 17, 19.

Meddis, S. V. (1991). U.S. Role in Bank Probe Criticized. *USA Today*, (July 30):9A.

Schmaltz, J. (1988). Banks Indicted by U.S. for Money Laundering Case. *New York Times*, (October 12).

Squitieri, T. (1991). Drifter; I Killed 60 People — Police Have Confirmed Just Three Victims. *USA Today*, (August 15):1A, 2A.

Waldman, S., Mabry, M., Bingham, C. and Levinson, M. (1991). The Unified Scandal Theory. *Newsweek*, (September 23).

Williams, C. J. (1991). The Federal Death Penalty for Drug-Related Killings. *Criminal Law Bulletin*, 27(5):387-415.

Index